YES, CHEF

RANDOM HOUSE TRADE PAPERBACKS NEW YORK

MARCUS SAMUELSSON
with Veronica Chambers

YES, CHEF
A MEMOIR

2013 Random House Trade Paperback Edition

Published in the United States by Random House Trade Paperbacks, an imprint of The Random House Publishing Group, a division of Random House, Inc., New York.

RANDOM HOUSE TRADE PAPERBACKS and colophon are trademarks of Random House, Inc.

Originally published in hardcover in the United States by Random House, an imprint of The Random House Publishing Group, a division of Random House, Inc., in 2012.

Library of Congress Cataloging-in-Publication Data
Samuelsson, Marcus.
Yes, chef / Marcus Samuelsson.
p. cm.
ISBN 978-0-385-34261-2 (paperback)—ISBN 978-0-440-33881-9 (eBook)
1. Samuelsson, Marcus. 2. Cooks—United States—Biography.
3. African American cooks—United States—Biography.
4. Swedish Americans—Biography. I. Title.
TX649.S226A3 2012
641.5092—dc23
[B]
2011042220

Printed in the United States of America

www.atrandom.com

1 2 3 4 5 6 7 8 9

Book design by Susan Turner

To my two mothers, Ahnu and Anne Marie

Chant another song of Harlem.
Not about the wrong of Harlem.
But the worthy throng of Harlem.
Proud that they belong to Harlem.
They, the overblamed in Harlem,
Need not be ashamed of Harlem.
All is not ill-famed in Harlem.
The devil, too, is tamed in Harlem.

—ANONYMOUS, circa 1925

PART ONE **BOY**

ONE **MY AFRICAN MOTHER**

I HAVE NEVER SEEN A PICTURE OF MY MOTHER.

I have traveled to her homeland, my homeland, dozens of times. I have met her brothers and sisters. I have found my birth father and eight half brothers and sisters I didn't know I had. I have met my mother's relatives in Ethiopia, but when I ask them to describe my mother, they throw out generalities. "She was nice," they tell me. "She was pretty." "She was smart." *Nice, pretty, smart.* The words seem meaningless, except the last is a clue because even today, in rural Ethiopia, girls are not encouraged to go to school. That my mother was intelligent rings true because I know she had to be shrewd to save the lives of myself and my sister, which is what she did, in the most mysterious and miraculous of ways.

My mother's family never owned a photograph of her, which tells you everything you need to know about where I'm from and what the world was like for the people who gave me life. In 1972, in the United States, Polaroid introduced its most popular instant camera. In 1972, the year my mother died, an Ethiopian woman could go her whole life without having her picture taken—especially if, as was the case with my mother, her life was not long.

I have never seen a picture of my mother, but I know how she cooked. For me, my mother is *berbere*, an Ethiopian spice mixture. You use it on everything, from lamb to chicken to roasted peanuts. It's our salt and pepper. I know she cooked with it because it's in the DNA of every Ethiopian mother. Right now, if I could, I would lead you to the red tin in my kitchen, one of dozens I keep by the stove in my apartment in Harlem, filled with my own blend and marked with blue electrical tape and my own illegible scrawl. I would reach into this tin and grab a handful of the red-orange powder, and hold it up to your nose so you could smell the garlic, the ginger, the sundried chili.

My mother didn't have a lot of money so she fed us *shiro*. It's a chickpea flour you boil, kind of like polenta. You pour it into hot water and add butter, onions, and *berbere*. You simmer it for about forty-five minutes, until it's the consistency of hummus, and then you eat it with injera, a sour, rich bread made from a grain called teff. I know this is what she fed us because this is what poor people eat in Ethiopia. My mother carried the chickpea powder in her pocket or bag. That way, all she needed to make dinner was water and fire. Injera is also portable, so it is never wasted. If you don't finish it, you leave it outside and let it dry in the sun. Then you eat it like chips.

In Meki, the small farming village where I'm from, there are no roads. We are actually from an even smaller village than Meki, called Abrugandana, that does not exist on most maps. You go to Meki, take a right in the middle of nowhere, walk about five miles, and that is where we are from.

I know my mother was not taller than five feet, two inches, but I also know she was not delicate. Those country women in Ethiopia are strong because they walk everywhere. I know her body because I know those women. When I go there now, I stare at the young mothers to the point of being impolite. I stare at those young women and their children and it's like watching a home movie that does not exist of my childhood. Each woman has a kid, who might well be me, on her back, and the fingers of her right hand are interlocked with another slightly older kid, and that kid is like my sister. The woman has her food and wares in her bag, which is slung across her chest and rests on her hip. The older kid is holding a bucket of water on her shoulders, a bucket that's almost as heavy as she is. That's how strong that child is.

Women like my mother don't wear shoes. They don't have shoes. My mother, sister, and I would walk the Sidama savannah for four hours a day, to and from her job selling crafts in the market. Before three p.m. it would be too hot to walk, so we would rest under a tree and gather our strength and wait for the sun to set. After eight p.m. it was dark and there were new threats—animals that would see a baby like me as supper and dangerous men who might see my mother as another kind of victim.

I have never seen a picture of my mother, but I know her features because I have seen them staring back at me in the mirror my entire life. I know she had a cross somewhere near her face. It was a henna tattoo of a cross, henna taking the place of the jewelry she could not afford or even dream of having. There was also an Orthodox cross somewhere on the upper part of my mother's body, maybe on her neck, maybe on her chest, near her heart. She had put it there to show that she was a woman of faith. She was an Orthodox Ethiopian Christian, which is very similar to being Catholic.

I don't remember my mother's voice, but I know she spoke two languages. In *The Souls of Black Folk*, W.E.B. DuBois spoke of the double consciousness that African Americans are born into, the need to be able to live in both the black world and the white world. But that double consciousness is not limited to African Americans. My mother was born into it, too. Her tribe was a minority in that section of Ethiopia and it was essential to her survival that she spoke both the language of her village, Amhara, and the language of the greater outside community, which is Oromo. She was cautious and when she left the Amharic village, she flipped that switch. She not only spoke Oromo, she spoke it with a native accent.

I don't know my mother's face, but I sometimes think I remember the sound of her breath. I was two when a tuberculosis epidemic hit Ethiopia. My mother was sick, I was sick, and my sister Fantaye was doing only slightly better than the two of us. We were all coughing up blood and my mother had seen enough in her young life to measure the ravages of that disease. She knew she had to do something. She put me on her back. It was all coming at her now: the fatigue and the fever; pieces of her lung splintering and mixing with her throw-up; the calcifications on her bones, where the disease had already spread. She and Fantaye walked more than seventy-five miles, my mother carrying me the whole way, under a hot sun, from our village to the hospital in Addis Ababa to get help. I don't know how many days they walked, or how sick my mother was by the time she got there. But I do know that when we arrived, there were thousands of people standing in the street, sick and dying, awaiting care. I do not know how my mother managed to get us through those lines and into that hospital. I do know that she never left that hospital and that perhaps it was only by the miracle of that henna cross that Fantaye and I got out alive.

TODAY, in the dead of night when I should be sleeping, I sometimes imagine the breath of the woman who not only gave me life, but delivered me from death. I sometimes reach into that tin by my stove and take a handful of *berbere*, sift it through my fingers, and toss it into the pan. I watch my wife cook and I imagine that I can see my mother's hands. I have taught myself the recipes of my mother's people because those foods are for me, as a chef, the easiest connection to the mysteries of who my mother was. Her identity remains stubbornly shrouded in the past, so I feed myself and the people I love the food that she made. But I cannot see her face.

TWO **MY SWEDISH MOTHER**

My father wanted a son. That is how I came to live in Sweden, of all places. My sister and I had been orphaned in Ethiopia in 1972, in the tuberculosis epidemic that cost my mother her life. And the Samuelssons of Göteborg, Lennart and Anne Marie, wanted a son.

They already had a daughter, an eight-year-old foster child named Anna, who had been born to a Swedish woman and a Jamaican man. While it would take decades for the United States to see a wave of international and transracial adoptions, this had been going on in Sweden since the 1950s and 1960s. In those days, it was nearly impossible to find a Swedish child to adopt. Single and pregnant Swedish women either had abortions, which were increasingly acceptable, or raised their children as single mothers, which was not frowned upon by the society at large. So in the mid-1960s, my parents were matched with fifteen-month-old Anna, who was not technically adopted but was doted on nonetheless by Lennart and Anne Marie, who were so thrilled to have their dream of becoming parents come true.

Before a family adopts a child, there's a journey they go on. For my parents, it was ten long, painful years of "We want to have a baby, but we can't." Today, if a couple is trying to get pregnant and it's not happening, doctors can do tests and, in most cases, offer up a relatively quick diagnosis and sometimes a measure of hope. Back then, there was just my mother sitting in the kitchen with *her* mother, wondering how she was going to become the woman she wanted to be without a child. She wanted to have a family. She was a very traditional person in that sense. When my parents adopted Anna, my mother hardly cared what race she was. Anne Marie Samuelsson, at age forty-five, was finally a mother. Anna wasn't black or white, she was joy.

In the Samuelsson family, the adoption chain goes back even further. Right after the Second World War, my mother's parents took a Jewish girl into their one-bedroom apartment. My mother was fifteen years old at the time and spoke fluent German. Sweden had remained neutral during the war and like many young people her age, my mother volunteered to go down to the port and work as a translator to help the thousands of Jews who were traveling from Denmark to Sweden, seeking refuge. On the docks, she met a sixteen-year-old girl named Frieda. Frieda was Czechoslovakian and had been in a concentration camp. She was all alone. My mom and Frieda became friendly and one day she said to my grandfather, "Can't we just take her? Can't we save one person?" My grandparents didn't have any money, but they did it, they took her in. And the happiness that Frieda brought to my mother's life led to the happiness that Anna brought to my parents' life, which paved the way for us.

My father wanted a son. He didn't care what color the boy was; he just wanted a boy he could teach to hike and fish. He filled out adoption forms in triplicate and considered offers from any part of the globe where orphaned baby boys were seeking homes: Greece, Vietnam, Korea, Russia, the continent of Africa. Anyplace that had been touched by famine or war, anyplace poor enough to part with a fatherless boy.

I'd been hospitalized in Addis Ababa for six months, but was on the mend when Anne Marie and Lennart got the call saying I might soon be up for adoption. It wasn't just me, though: I had my four-year-old sister, who had also been hospitalized, and our Ethiopian social worker didn't want to separate us. We had already lost our mother to disease, she told the Samuelssons; it would be best if we didn't lose each other now.

Yes, Anne Marie and Lennart said almost instantly. Yes, why not two?

It would take nearly a year for my sister and me to make the journey from Addis Ababa to Göteborg, a blue-collar city on Sweden's southwest coast.

ON TUESDAY, MAY 1, my father's mother, Lissie, died in Smögen, a small island off the west coast of Sweden where my father and his siblings had been raised. The next morning, the old priest stood in the pulpit of the brick Lutheran church with its whitewashed walls and dark wood pews. He said the Church of Sweden liturgy and each mourner placed a flower on Lissie's casket, which was then ferried over to the mainland to be buried in a graveyard next to her husband and four generations of Samuelssons. On Thursday, the family gathered for *gravöl*, "grave beer," and the toasts and reminiscing went on for hours.

On Friday, my parents received a phone call in the Smögen house. It was my mother's parents. The Swedish adoption agency, unable to reach them directly, had called with news: My sister and I were on our way from Ethiopia. My parents raced back to Göteborg, stopping along the way to purchase a bunk bed and linens, and then booked round trip tickets to Stockholm—three going and five returning—for the next day. As our parents would always say, with both grief and gratitude, never before had they seen so clearly how when one life ends, another begins.

My mother never gave birth, but as any adoptive mother knows, the journey to meet the child you hope to call your own is its own kind of labor. When Mom, Dad, and Anna arrived at the customs area, they learned that our flight had been delayed for several hours. My father, a scientist, and Anna, his shadow, sat quietly reading, while my nervous mother proceeded to unpack a picnic in the airport waiting area. A large thermos of coffee for her and Dad, a small thermos of *saft*, a sweet red-currant drink, for Anna. Then came two types of sandwiches, both on heavily margarined multigrain bread. One was made of *västerbottensost*, a hard, parmesan-like cow's-milk cheese from the north of Sweden, and a few thin slices of green pepper. The other was stuffed with slabs of a rough, country-style liver pâté. My mother's mother, Helga, had not only made the pâté, but topped it with slivers of homemade pickles and a smear of grainy mustard. For dessert, there was apple cake, which, my mother explained to anyone who would listen, would have been so much better with the traditional vanilla sauce topping, but since they had been in a rush, and had traveled by plane, compromises had to be made.

A dozen times a week, easily, I am stopped on the street in New York City by someone, most often a woman, who tells me that she is the mother of an adopted child. More and more over the past few years, these women have adopted their children from Ethiopia and have read about me or seen me on TV and know my story. What they want to tell me is about the moment when they met their child in person for the first time. I try to be polite, but the hard thing is that after hearing so many of their stories, each a little different, it becomes difficult for me to distinguish their story from my own. What's real and what's imagined? Was it my adoptive mother who cried when she first picked me up, or was it that woman I met a few weeks ago outside my restaurant? Was I the one who was handed an apple and spat it out because it was the very first time I'd eaten a piece of fruit, or was that my sister? Was I the one who smiled shyly and sweetly, or did I hide? The stories of the adoptive parents I've met stay with me long after we've crossed paths, so for accuracy, I must depend as I always have, on my sister Linda. She was five and I was three and she remembers the moment when we met our adoptive parents with far more clarity than I ever could. Here's how she describes it:

When our plane finally landed, our escort, Seney, got off first. She was tall, thin, with medium brown skin. Very pretty Habesha, meaning someone like us, Amhara heritage. She held you on one hip and held me tightly by the hand. I didn't want to be there. A porter pushed a cart with our "luggage," a suitcase for Seney and a small cloth satchel for us. Seney handed you to Anne Marie, then opened her suitcase to present our new parents with gifts, Ethiopian handmade crafts that Mom still proudly displays in her living room. Seney had no money of her own; she must have budgeted carefully the cost of getting us to the airport, and the plane tickets, making sure to have enough so that we could be fed in the airport if the Samuelssons were late. But it would not have been our people's way to just hand these two foreigners these motherless kids. It would have been important to Seney that we come bearing more than the pale skin on our open palms.

On their flight from Göteborg to Stockholm, my parents had chosen our Swedish names. I was born Kassahun but would be called Marcus. My sister Fantaye would become Linda. They began to call us by these names right away. My father bent down to say hello to Linda, who vanished behind the folds of Seney's skirt.

Linda was five, old enough to have remembered everything: our village outside of Addis, our mother, the hospital where she died, and the wards where we'd competed for food, attention, and survival. Linda was silent all the way home from the airport. The only thing that gave her comfort was holding on to a small square of tattered fabric she'd brought from Ethiopia. She didn't cry, she remembers, because tears and the vulnerability they symbolized were too rich a gift to give to Anne Marie and Lennart, the man and woman she now viewed as potential enemies. So she sat next to Anna in the backseat of our parents' car while I sat in the front, sleeping in our new mother's lap.

In his application, my father promised to raise his adopted children in a good family, one with a dog and a cat, "both very friendly toward children." He described their neighborhood, Puketorp, as having about three hundred families with a surrounding forest where "we hike in the summer and ski and saucer in the winter." He promised small lakes with crystal clear waters, perfect for skating and swimming, and a modest house with a flat lawn and an outdoor playhouse, tailor-made for "jumping and playing with balls."

The house, neighborhood, and surroundings were all as he described, but it would take more than the comparative opulence of Göteborg to win Linda over. She trusted no one except her new sister, Anna. Linda was my protector. If our new mom reached down to pick me up without securing Linda's permission first, Linda would pry me out of her arms and scold my mother in Amharic. When my mother tried to put me into the bathtub, a frightful contraption with a mad gush of water, the likes of which we'd never seen before, Linda would cling to me so tightly that my father would have to lift the two of us, stuck together like conjoined twins, and drop us into the tub together.

My mother learned to ask Linda's permission each and every time she wanted to make contact with me. Mom spoke to Linda in Swedish, enunciating each word carefully and raising the volume a notch or two, as if that might help. With a mime's gift for hand gestures and facial expressions, each day my new mother made herself more easily understood, and after many months, Linda loosened her grip.

THERE IS AN ETHIOPIAN FAIRY TALE called "The Lion's Whiskers." It's the story of a woman who is in an unhappy marriage. Her husband comes home late from work every day, and some nights he does not come home at all. Distraught, the wife goes to see the village elder. He assures her that he can fix this trouble. "I will prepare a medicine that will make your husband love you with an unbounded devotion," he says.

The woman can barely contain her excitement. "*Abba,*" she begs, using the word for a man who is father to the entire village, "make the potion right away."

The elder shakes his head. "I need one essential ingredient and it is not an easy one to get," he explains. "You must provide me with a whisker plucked from a living lion."

The woman is in love and unafraid. She says, "I will get it for you."

It was not the elder's wish to cause the woman any harm. On the contrary, he had lived a long time and he believed that in asking her for an ingredient that was as fantastical as fairy dust, he was letting her down easy. Some things were the way they were and always had been. Husbands got bored and sometimes came home late or not at all. Time had taught the elder that his most important job was not to mix potions but to listen. For a woman who is anxious and lonely, the reassuring counsel of an elder was its own kind of balm.

But that was not the case with this woman, for when she loved, she loved fiercely.

The next day, she took a slab of raw meat down to the river where she had, on many occasions, watched a lion take his morning drink. She was afraid, but found the courage to walk up close and throw the meat to the lion. Each morning, she returned and fed the beast, getting closer and closer to him until, one day, she was able to sit by his side and, with no danger to herself at all, pluck the whisker from the lion's cheek. When she returned to the village elder, he was shocked that she had completed the seemingly impossible task.

"How did you do it?" he asked.

The woman explained and at the end of her story, the village elder spoke to her with deference and respect. "You have the courage, patience, and grace to befriend a lion," he said. "You need no potion to fix your marriage."

This is a fairy tale that all children in Ethiopia learn, but for me, it is also the story of my early days in Sweden and how my sister and I became Samuelssons. The brave woman was my mother, Anne Marie, and Linda was the lion.

THREE **SWEDISH FISH**

MY LOVE FOR FOOD DID NOT COME FROM MY MOTHER.

For my mom, putting dinner on the table was just another thing to get done in the course of a long, busy day. Cooking competed with ferrying her three kids back and forth to soccer, ice skating lessons, horseback riding, doctors' and dentists' appointments. Once I became old enough to test my daredevil skills (Dad wanted a boy!) on my skateboard and bike, there were regular visits to the emergency room as well.

It's not that my mother was a *bad* cook, she simply didn't have the time. In the late 1970s, she subscribed to a magazine that had "try it at home" recipes for the busy homemaker, slightly exotic concoctions that featured canned, frozen, and boxed ingredients. This was her go-to source of inspiration. She made pasta as not even a prisoner would tolerate it, with tinny tomato sauce and mushy frozen peas. She served roast pork from imaginary Polynesian shores, with canned pineapple rings and homemade curry whipped cream. She experimented with something called soy sauce. She wanted us to eat well, to experience other cultures, but she also didn't want to be tied to the stove the way her mother had been. Her mother, Helga, had worked as a maid since the age of eleven, and now, even in retirement, was unable to break the habit of cooking and serving, cooking and serving. My mother saw that and ran the other way.

What she valued in a meal was convenience. It's funny that the one dish of hers I adored was the one that could not be rushed: cabbage rolls. I loved sitting on the counter and watching as she blanched the cabbage leaves, seasoned the ground pork with salt and pepper, then scooped the pork into the leaves, wrapping them like cigars and placing them carefully on a platter. My mother's cabbage rolls were special because the very preparation of the dish forced her to slow down so I could enjoy her presence as much as her cooking. The literal translation for *dim sum* is "little bits of heart." My mother's cabbage rolls were my dim sum.

My mother organized our dinners the way she organized the household—efficiency and routine ruled the day. No more than ten dishes made it into her regular rotation. On Mondays, we had meatballs with mashed potatoes, lingonberries, and gravy. On Tuesdays, herring. On Wednesdays, a roast. On Thursdays, we ate split pea soup and on Friday, fish casserole. Once in a while, we veered from the routine. But not often.

Tuesdays I loved most of all. That was the day the fishmonger drove his beat-up Volvo panel truck into our neighborhood's modest shopping area, which consisted of a tailor we never used, a grocery store owned by the Blomkvists, and the newsstand guy from whom I could occasionally cadge a peppermint and where my father bought canisters of loose tobacco and cigarette papers.

My father, the son of a fisherman, was no fan of the fishmonger. "His fish is not fresh," he said disapprovingly.

"Day-old is better than frozen," was my mother's ever-practical reply. "And his prices are better than good."

My mother always took me with her to the fishmonger on Tuesdays, but not before raking a comb through my hair, yanking so hard that for the next hour, I could feel the aftershocks on my scalp. My laces had to be tied, my freshly ironed shirt tucked in. My mother dressed up, too: lipstick, a leather purse, and a sharp red felt cap that she felt gave her a more sophisticated air.

We would both watch as the fish man, Mr. Ljungqvist, parked his truck at the curb in front of the Blomkvists' market and unfurled his blue-and-white-striped awning. Mr. Ljungqvist was shaped like a bowling ball, with thick white hair curling out from under his black fisherman's cap. He wore a sweater under his smock and a red apron on top. No matter how cold it was, his pink hands were bare, chafed and scraped from handling so much ice, sharp belly scales, and spiny fins.

I liked to hoist myself on the bottom lip of the service window and see what was waiting on Mr. Ljungqvist's icy deathbed. It never turned out to be anything too exciting—some cod, some perch, some *sill*, which is what we called herring—but I always hoped he'd procured something more surprising and exotic from the bottom of the sea, like an eel or turbot or squid. But there were no surprises as to what my mother would buy or how my mother might cook it. The big, oafy-looking cod would be ground into fish balls. Perch would be broiled and served with butter and lemon. And the herring? The herring was our hamburger.

Herring is the classic Swedish fish. It was on almost every table at every meal, figured into almost every course but dessert, and showed up at every holiday. It was even woven into the language. You could be deaf as a herring or dumb as a herring. Tram conductors who carried trolleys full of commuters were called herring packers. If you were exhausted, you were a dead herring. Smelly shoes were called herring barrels.

Ljungqvist's customers bought lots and lots of herring—to poach, pickle, bake, and layer into cheesy, creamy casseroles with leeks and tomatoes. On the nights my mother would fry the herring, she bypassed the ten-inch-long Atlantic herring in favor of the smaller, silver-skinned *strömming* that came from the Baltic and fit better in her cast-iron pan. As a Swedish woman who came of age in the 1950s, she may have happily served mushy peas from the tin, but she scaled, gutted, and filleted the herring herself. For her, that wasn't a kitchen skill. Knowing how to clean a fish was as innate as knowing how to open a door.

I helped my mother pick out our fish. What you wanted to avoid at all costs were cloudy eyes and blood spots on their gills, telltale signs that the fish was not fresh. My father, who had grown up in a family of fishermen, did not trust my mother to pick the fish. It was *my* job, he told me secretly, to make sure she made the right choices. When we found the acceptable choice for that night's supper, Mom nodded to me, I nodded to Mr. Ljungqvist, and he picked the fish out of the ice, added it to the others he had laid into the crook of one arm, and wrapped them in newspaper.

Next, my mom would pick out the anchovies for our Friday night dinner, Jansson's Temptation, a traditional Swedish casserole of potato, anchovy, onion, and cream. Mr. Ljungqvist dug into a shallow pail of anchovies with his red scoop, and then shook out the extras until he had exactly the right amount. They glimmered, metallic and shiny, against the ice. Put that one back, my mother would say. No, no, I want *that* one.

There was a kind of "who'll blink first" thing going on between my mother and Mr. Ljungqvist, each respectfully trying to gain the upper hand. To this day, I could not declare a winner in their silent battle of wills, except to say that learning how to pick the freshest fish, for the best value, helped lay the groundwork for my work as a chef. And as my sisters did not accompany us on these fish-buying expeditions, they would never know that, occasionally, despite her virulent anti-sweets policy, our mother could be swayed. Every once in a while, after we'd made our purchases from Mr. Ljungqvist, I would talk her into walking over to the newsstand and buying a little candy. Salted licorice for her. Colored sour balls for me.

FOUR **HELGA**

AFTER MY PARENTS ADOPTED ANNA, MY MOTHER'S PARENTS, WANTING to be nearby and to help in any way they could, moved to Göteborg from the southern province of Skåne. They bought a small one-bedroom house just a few minutes away by bike, close enough that we crossed paths several times a day. We called Helga and Edvin Jonsson *mormor* and *morfar*—terms of respect that translate to "mother's mother" and "mother's father"—and loved them like the adoring set of bonus parents that they were.

At *Mormor*'s, the smell of food was omnipresent: The yeasty aroma of freshly baked bread or the tang of drying rose hips hit you as soon as you walked in. Something was always going on in her kitchen, and usually several things at once. My grandmother would start chopping vegetables for dinner while sterilizing jars for canning, while stirring a pot of chicken stock or grinding pork for a month's worth of sausages. If I had to try to pinpoint my earliest food memory it would not be a single taste, but a smell—my grandmother's house.

Before moving to Göteborg, my grandmother lived where she had grown up, in the province of Skåne. To say a person comes from Skåne carries a lot of meaning for a Swede. At the southernmost tip of the country, Skåne is to Sweden, in many ways, what Provence is to France. With the mildest climate and the most fertile soil in Sweden, it is the country's chief agricultural region. Not surprisingly, Skåne has always been known for its rich culinary landscape, a landscape that gave birth to a generation of instinctively inventive cooks. My grandmother was no exception. She spent so much of her time at the stove that when I close my eyes and try to remember her, it's that image of her back that I see first. She would toss smiles and warm welcomes over her shoulder, never fully taking her eyes off the pots she was tending.

Mormor had the unique experience of being surrounded by luxury despite living in poverty her entire life. Her work as a maid for upper-class Swedish families had kept food on the table for her family through the lean years surrounding the rationing of two World Wars. From the families she worked for, she learned how to make restaurant-worthy meals. This kind of training, coupled with her own thriftiness, meant that she made almost everything we ate from scratch and wasted almost nothing; her larder was so well stocked that I barely remember her shopping. Maybe she'd send me out to get sugar or she'd go to the fishmonger herself, but otherwise, everything she needed seemed to appear, as if by magic, from her pantry or emerge from the garden that she tended with the same careful devotion that she used to prepare our family's big Saturday suppers.

Mormor's one indulgence was wallpaper. The walls of her house were covered in exuberant flowers, exploding colors, and bold vertical stripes. But other than that, her house was simple and quiet, much quieter than ours. You could open the door and know that no children lived there: There was just the low murmur of my grandfather listening to the news on the radio and my grandmother clanking away in the kitchen. She did all of her prep work by hand and preferred mortar and pestle to the electric mixers and blenders my mother bought her in the hopes of making her life easier. She was suspicious of newfangled inventions. Having cooked most of her adult life on a woodburning stove, she never entirely warmed to the electric oven in her modern kitchen.

Mormor treated her house like it was her own little food factory. She made everything herself: jams, pickles, and breads. She bought large cuts of meat or whole chickens and game animals from the butcher and then broke them down into chops and roasts at home. It's so funny to me how, today, we celebrate braising as some refined, elegant approach, when it's the same slow cooking method *Mormor* used. Her menus followed a simple logic:

You have bread today because it's fresh.

You have toast tomorrow because the bread has gone stale.

You make croutons the next day, and whatever bread is left after that gets ground into crumbs that you'll use to batter fish.

I don't think I saw a rib-eye steak until my late teens when I started working in restaurants. At home, we ate mostly ground meat that was rolled into balls and stretched even further by ample additions of breadcrumbs. We ate our own Swedish version of a hamburger: pan beef, a patty topped with caramelized onions. Sometimes we ate beef Lindstrom: a hamburger patty mixed with onions, capers, and pickled beets before being seared in butter. That's comfort food where I come from, and it's damn good.

In the United States, the best-known Swedish dish is meatballs, but pickles and jams connect the dots of Swedish cuisine and make an appearance in almost every meal and dish. At breakfast, we'd pour buttermilk over granola and sweeten it with black-currant jam. A favorite summer dessert was ice cream topped with gooseberry preserves, and a late-night TV snack would be toast with cheese and jams. Seared herring would be served with lingonberry jam, and liver pâté sandwiches were topped with pickled cucumbers.

Swedes traditionally prefer a pickle that is salty, sour, and quite sweet. To achieve that blend of flavors, we use a solution called 1-2-3: one part vinegar, two parts sugar, three parts water. But for the pickle to be truly Swedish, the vinegar has to be *ättika*, a beechwood-based product that has a sinus-clearing, eye-tearing bite to it, twice as acidic as American vinegars. *Mormor* spent an enormous amount of time pickling and preserving, using the 1-2-3 solution to pickle cauliflowers and cucumbers, herrings and beets, which she stuffed into jars and stored in her pantry.

Pantry is almost too fancy a word for where *Mormor* stored her food. Hers was a closet at the foot of the basement stairs. A pull-chain light hung from the ceiling and the single bulb revealed a space so small that by the time I was ten years old, it was no longer a viable option for me in our games of hide-and-seek. The closet doubled as a root cellar with burlap sacks of potatoes lining the floor along one wall. Above them were shelves of savory foods—pickled onions, cucumbers, beets, and different types of herring: *strömming*, *sill*, and the store-bought *matjes* herring, prized for its delicate, less fishy flavor. The far wall held the sweet preserves, which were placed in rows that went back three jars deep. Each was covered with a handwritten label:

Röda vinbär, augusti 1980 (Red currant, August 1980)
Saltgurka, oktober 1981 (Pickled cucumber, October 1981)

Mormor made jams from the berries she grew in her front yard as well as from what she found in the woods near our house, like lingonberries, the quintessential Swedish fruit, which have a texture and tang similar to cranberries. She preserved cloudberries, black currants, raspberries, and gooseberries; and made jam from apples, pears, and plums, all of which came from her own trees. That dark little closet was my grandmother's version of a jewelry case, and the bright jellies and jams were her gemstones.

I LOVED SATURDAYS as a kid. Saturdays meant soccer practice for me, ice-skating and riding lessons for my sisters, and almost without exception, Saturdays meant the best meal we would have all week because dinner was almost always at my grandparents' house. As soon as I got home from soccer, I would jump on my bike and speed over to *Mormor*'s house. It took me exactly seven minutes to cut across the nature preserve that abutted our property, speed down the road on the other side, and make it up the long driveway to my grandparents' house. I dumped the bike at the foot of their steps, took the stairs two at a time, and walked as fast as I could to *Mormor*'s kitchen. There was *no* running in my grandmother's house. She'd look at me standing there out of breath and say, "Ah, there you are. Come. I have a job for you." She would pull out a stool and set me to string rhubarb or shell peas or pluck a chicken. I'm not sure why my sisters never joined us in our Saturday afternoon cooking sessions; and, at the time, I didn't care. I was only too happy to have *Mormor* to myself.

Her signature dish was roast chicken, which meant chicken soup the next day. In kid words, it was yummy, the perfect food, warm like the kind of hug only a grandmother can give. Looking back, my grandmother's food was my introduction to rustic cooking. It had more levels of flavor than a twelve-year-old boy could understand. She didn't know how to build textures the way chefs build texture, but she got it. In her *body*, she knew how to create those levels.

Growing up in Skåne, my grandmother had learned to kill a chicken old-school style. Grab the bird, knife to the neck. Like, "Come here, boom." You learn to respect food in a different way when you have to kill it yourself, she would say. I never forgot that lesson, even though when I was a kid we didn't kill the chickens we ate for dinner. But the fresh birds my grandmother purchased still looked like birds—they had feet and feathers and we had to handle them and pluck them ourselves. It was something I got good at, too, the kind of tedious work that needs to be done carefully and quickly, that would one day prepare me for the lower levels of professional kitchens.

After we plucked the chicken, my grandmother would salt it generously. Right there, she created a level of flavor. But why did she salt it? Because even though she had a refrigerator, she wasn't *raised* with a refrigerator. In her mind, she couldn't be sure how many days the chicken would last. And what happens when you salt something? The skin gets firmer. You've preserved it and the meat gets more tender. Right there, she was creating texture.

After she salted it, she would put the chicken in the basement and leave it there for a couple of hours, because that's where it was cold and dry. As a chef, you would leave the chicken by the air conditioner so the skin gets dry, which helps you when you roast it. Same basic principle. She had these intuitive moves that we teach in chef school.

When she was ready to cook the chicken, she showed me how to add spices—cardamom, ginger, coriander seeds—that we'd grind and rub all over the skin. Then she would put carrots in the roasting dish, making a little bed for the chicken to sit on. She stuffed the bird with ingredients that came from her own yard: rosemary, apples, onions, maybe a little garlic. She'd sew the chicken up and put it in the oven. While it was roasting, she'd get going on the stock. Everything that was left over—the extra skin, the neck, the giblets—went into the soup pot for stock. Then she'd put any vegetable scraps into the pot, too, and let it simmer.

Mormor had this bad Chinese soy sauce, which was the best she could get in Sweden in the 1970s. She'd say, "I don't like white sauce. Gravy has to have color." *Mormor* thought like a chef. She wanted the food to be not only tasty, but visually appealing. She'd take a pan, the drippings, flour, soy sauce, and make gravy. She wasn't raised with butter because she couldn't afford it, so she cooked with grease fat. That's the flavor she put into a lot of her gravies and sauces. Then she'd take a few tablespoons of the stock she'd just made and use that to thin out the gravy. She'd hand me a slotted spoon and say, "OK, Marcus, get the lumps out."

Later that night, she'd serve the meal we'd created, always giving credit to "my little helper." No matter how many times we prepared the same dish the same way, I was always excited to see the meal I'd helped to make, presented formally on a silver serving tray: chicken roasted with rosemary, accompanied by carrots glazed with a little bit of honey, ginger, and sugar.

The next day my mother, my father, my sisters, and I would often come back for chicken soup. She'd have taken all the meat that was left over from the Saturday night supper and added it to the stock along with a boiled pot of rice or potatoes. And that was the meal. It was so full of flavor because of her upbringing, the poverty that she came from. The preserving technique that made everything taste richer, deeper. The fresh chicken that she had hand-picked. Drying the bird, which gives you the perfect skin. The salting because she never trusted refrigerators, the two or three days' worth of meals that she would create from one chicken because being poor makes you inventive.

The roast chicken I make today is a homage to hers. I have luxuries that she didn't. I use perfectly fed chickens, ones that weigh exactly three pounds. My grandmother bought whole chickens from the market, some fat and some skinny. I use real butter instead of grease fat. But the layering of flavor and the techniques? They're all hers.

FIVE **WITH RESPECT TO THE SEA**

EVERY SPRING WHEN I WAS GROWING UP, MY FATHER WOULD TAKE A TRIP to Smögen, the island off the west coast of Sweden where he'd been born and raised and where our family spent most of its vacations. Every Easter break, he drove there alone to prepare the summer house and the family's fishing boats. I was twelve, just about to start middle school, when he invited me along for the first time.

"This is not a holiday," he warned. "We are going to get the boats ready. You can't come along unless you're willing to help."

During the summer, Smögen was flooded with tourists who came to see Sweden's longest boardwalk and eat prawn sandwiches from brightly colored wooden huts which, from afar, looked like they were made of Popsicle sticks. But this was not summer and we were not tourists. In March in Smögen, the salt air coated your skin and its gritty texture made you feel tougher, both inside and out. "Just us two men," my father said, my father who had so longed for a son that he had flown paper planes—adoption forms in triplicate—all the way to Africa to make his dream come true.

The road from Göteborg to Smögen was a patchy two-lane that veered between rugged shoreline, thick forests of pines and spruce, and meadows full of yarrow and twinflower. Sometimes there was no vegetation at all and the road cut through vast rock formations, endless fields of dark gray granite that looked, from the car window, like elephant hide. It took almost three hours to get there, and I measured our progress by the blue road signs showing how many kilometers were left to go: Smögen 13, Smögen 6, Smögen 2. We skirted the edge of Kungshamn, the last mainland town at the tip of the thumb-shaped peninsula, and crossed the Uddevalla Bridge. We were close, I knew, when I saw the first cluster of red-roofed houses, the docks, the bobbing boats, the small beach, and the steely water of the fjord that would eventually spill into the sea. And then I saw it, the first sign that we had arrived: a white two-story house with a red roof, set back from the road, with no other houses around. This was the house of my great-uncle Torsten, my father's uncle and the closest thing I had to a paternal grandfather, since my father's father had died more than twenty years earlier. Torsten's house sat at the foot of the new bridge, one that hadn't existed when my father had been a boy. To get to school each day, he'd had to row himself and his three siblings forty minutes each way across this inlet of the Baltic. I wondered what sort of prayers he must have said on stormy days when his boat seemed so small and the fjord seemed so wide.

Our family's house was a three-story wood-frame Victorian built in the 1800s. The house could sleep forty; back when my grandmother was alive, she ran it as a boardinghouse for fishermen, feeding them and doing their laundry. During the summer, my family stayed on the third floor, my uncle Leif and his wife and their two children stayed on the first, and the second was rented out to vacationing families from Stockholm, the logic being that Leif's family had the benefit of having no one underfoot and easy access to the yard and street. Our family had the benefit of being on top—the best views and no noisy neighbors overhead. And the renters, sandwiched in the middle, didn't have many benefits at all. They paid the expenses necessary to keep the house going.

"We'll stay down here this time," my father said, taking our bags into Uncle Leif and Aunt Barbro's room. His entire academic career had been designed to escape this hard fisherman's life, but I could tell from the way he inspected the rooms, cranked up the radiators, cast his gaze toward the sea, and breathed deep in the cold salt air that my father had missed Smögen. That, in fact, he'd been counting the days until he could get back.

I woke up at 5:30 the next morning to the sound of a radio news program and the smell of hot chocolate. Groggy, I walked into the dark kitchen just as my father's best friend, Stellan, burst through the back door. In Hasselösund, which was the tiny community where my father was from in Smögen, no one bothered to knock or call before coming over.

Stellan had been a *yrkesfiskare*, a professional fisherman, for twenty-five years. The punishing sixteen-hour days out in the boats were like too many rounds in a boxing ring: They made his body sore in ways that sleep and ointments could never fix. He now held the less demanding role of handyman for the Smögen elementary school. As soon as my dad started speaking to Stellan, he lost his city accent. He no longer sounded so intellectual, choosing instead to speak in a local dialect so thick I could barely follow along. I sat at the table and ate the breakfast my mother had packed—orange marmalade and sliced *hushållsost*, a mild farmer's cheese, on a triangle of rye crispbread—and I listened, picking up a word here and there. My dad and Stellan drank coffee and talked about how well the fish were biting, what mackerel was going for at the local fish auction, and what we were about to do with the boats. They talked about the sea, always with great deference to its power. My father's father had died at age fifty, on a boat, and it scared him, I think. It made him want to go to university, to make a living with his head, not his hands. He wasn't afraid of hard work and he wanted to work outside, but he didn't want a fisherman's life. Geology was a way out.

It was a three-minute walk to our boathouse. Like every other boathouse in Hasselösund, ours was painted a carnelian red with an even darker red pitched roof and white trim around the eaves, doors, and windows. The houses were small, not much bigger than the average American two-car garage, and arrayed in a perfect line up and down the pebbly beach. Inside was our boat and a mishmash of tackle: nets, traps, rods and buckets, buoys and oars and fish knives. When I got a little older, my father promised, we would also store water skis there.

The day before our arrival, Stellan had drowned the boats, pulling each one out about four feet from shore and filling it with rocks until the hull filled with water. The boats had been out of the water all winter, so the aim was to make the wood swell, which in turn would make it easier to shave off the old paint in preparation for a fresh coat.

My great-uncle Ludvig met us at the boathouse and he, Stellan, and Dad waded into the water, wearing rubber boots that came up to their thighs. They surrounded each boat and, on the count of three, pushed and pulled it up to the shore as cold, brackish water sloshed out. They tilted it to one side, dumping out the rocks and the last of the water, then inverted it over two thick boards they'd laid out on the beach.

I grabbed my own scraper and joined the men as we took the paint off each boat until it revealed its shell of plain wood. Every once in a while, Ludvig might correct my grip or Stellan would remind me to go along the grain of the wood instead of across it. We kept going until each boat was as brown and smooth as a walnut shell. In the hours that I worked my father said nothing, but I basked in his smile—so much more relaxed and easy than it ever was at home.

UNCLE TORSTEN WAS A TALL MAN, easily clearing six feet, and he kept his wiry salt-and-pepper hair tamed and slicked back with plentiful amounts of grease and the comb he holstered in his pocket. For more than fifty years he had supported his family by wrestling his living from the sea, and it showed in the deep lines and dark tan of his face. He had hard, rough hands, a ready laugh, and an easy grin, and he smelled, alternately, of tobacco and alcohol, musky and sweet. He was, to my mind, a Swedish version of the Marlboro Man.

Torsten was a strong old man. Freaky strong. Farmer strong. Even after he'd retired from fishing, he could lift an *eka*, a stout wooden rowboat, and flip it onto its blocks, by himself, as easily as a mother turns a baby over to change its diaper. By this time—he must have been in his late sixties then—Torsten earned his living as a handyman for summering Norwegian tourists and the island's fish processing plant, Hållöfisk. He wore paint-splattered overalls, and balanced a ladder on his bicycle as he rode from job to job. He also loved a stiff drink. He had this thermos of black coffee spiked with homemade vodka, and he carried it with him everywhere. When friends visited him from the city, they brought him Jack Daniel's, a rare and luxurious treat. But Torsten, deep down, was a man of simple tastes and comforts: He liked his vodka moonshine better than anything you could buy in a store.

Later, I'd think of men like Torsten and Stellan often as I made my way up the punishing ladder of the world's finest kitchens. Those Smögen men, and I count my father among them, were unafraid of hard work. They were their own doctors, therapists, and career counselors. I constantly reminded myself that they would never quit a job just because of the name-calling and plate-throwing and brutal hours that are common in a professional kitchen. I made it my business to be tough in the ways that they were tough—on the inside, where it counted.

The best memories of that first trip alone to Smögen with my father were when Torsten invited me to his smokehouse. My time spent in the kitchen with *Mormor*, combined with my own growing passion for food, had me intrigued by the process of culinary transformation: How did you take one thing and end up with something so different? Uncle Torsten's smokehouse—the mysterious, rectangular wooden building at the back of his yard—was as important as any course I would take in culinary school. Here, I could watch that transformation occur.

There was a loop of rope where the door handle should have been and when I pulled it open, a surge of smoke practically sucked all the air out of my lungs. The fire pit was a smoldering oil drum in the center of the room. Torsten tugged on a pipe while he smoked the fish: tobacco smoke mixing with the pungent smell of the curing solution mixing with the driftwood smoke to create the kind of odor that would penetrate deep into your skin and cling to your clothes through several washings. I remember, as I stood there, thanking God my father and I had come on this trip to Smögen alone. My mother, as friendly as she was with Torsten, would have had a fit. More than once during our visits to Smögen, we'd seen or heard of a family's smokehouse blowing up like a meth lab. The men were careful, but the buildings were old and makeshift. Without official regulations or inspections, they were also unsafe.

The floor was littered with spare rods, old fish skin, and the odd pieces of stone that Torsten occasionally dropped into the drum with a clank and a hiss. Six or seven metal rods hooked into the side walls and spanned the width of the room; each rod could hold up to forty fish. Depending on the day's catch, Torsten cured eel, herring, or mackerel. Eel was a rarity and therefore highly prized, but my favorite was the mackerel, which the smoking process magically transformed from a stripy gray and green to a shimmering gold and black.

Hanging with Torsten in his smokehouse was more than a way to spend the afternoon. It was an initiation of sorts, into manhood. Chest puffed up, I stoked the fire, yanked fish off rods, and piled up stones. Torsten talked the whole time, loud and clear, always telling me what he was doing, asking me if I understood the process, what came next, why we did what we did.

"Low heat, close the door, leave it overnight."

"I've done this before, Uncle Torsten."

"Come back every other hour," he ordered. "Check the wood."

He handed me a pan of cured fish. "Has your father caught any mackerel lately?"

"We brought in twenty-five this morning," I told him.

Torsten raised an eyebrow. "Well," he said, smiling. "Your father's been down in Göteborg a long time. No one can hold such a modest number against him."

My great-aunt Nini, Torsten's wife, screamed from the back door of the house, "Are we ever going to get any fish? Time for lunch already!"

"Finally, she appears," Torsten said, as he handed me two smoked mackerel.

In the kitchen, Nini had laid out four open-faced sandwiches: sliced boiled eggs, roe paste, mayonnaise, and a sprinkling of chives on a piece of brown bread. With a knife, she quickly filleted the mackerel, dressed it with black pepper and garlic, and topped each piece of bread with the warm, flavorful fish.

I carried Torsten's plate over to the table, placing it in front of him. He took a bite, and I could see in his face the pleasure he took in the rich simplicity of the meal: the flaky chunks of fish, the velvety texture of the egg, the saltiness of the roe. Then he closed his eyes. "That's a good life," he said.

Torsten and Nini had a louder, more brash style than my parents, and I loved to watch the way they mirrored each other. Their shouts and seemingly exasperated murmurs were the words of two old people who had stood, united, against the harshness of the cold blue sea for sixty years and made a life together. I looked at the two of them and the simple but hugely satisfying meals they shared, and I thought, Torsten is right. That *is* a good life.

AT 5:00 ON OUR LAST NIGHT IN SMÖGEN, my father and I walked down the hill to visit Ludvig. He had been widowed young and lived by himself on the top floor of a large house that had tenants on the first floor and nothing going on, as far as I could tell, on the floor in between. Stellan had dropped off some mackerel earlier in the day and Ludvig was halfway through cleaning it when we walked in. He'd gutted the fish and cut off their heads; then my father took over, sharpening a thin, curved knife on a block of stone and deftly slicing the flesh off the bone.

"Marcus, if you don't cook, we don't eat," my father joked.

It was a joke, of course, because my father knew I needed no prompting to cook, which is probably why he let me take over the meal. This was my first time cooking on my own, as opposed to helping my grandmother or mother. Just as I had with the boats, I was eager to show I was a big man, that I didn't need anyone's help. I quickly washed some potatoes, then boiled them in a pot of salted water with dill, just like *Mormor* did. My father had brought our frying pan from home and I set it on the stove, put the flame on high, then added a large knob of butter, which slowly melted at the center. While I waited for the pan to heat up, and for the butter to bubble and turn golden, I dipped each fillet in a mix of flour, breadcrumbs, salt, and pepper. I waited until the butter was good and hot, and I tested it the way I'd seen Helga do many times, by scraping into the pan a tiny bit of flour that had caked on my finger. When the flour sizzled and popped, I laid in the strips of fish, side-by-side. I knew then, maybe for the first time, that I wasn't just my grandmother's little helper. I had absorbed some of her gift for the movements and the timing, but the sense of how to make the meal taste *just* right— more salt, less pepper—came naturally to me, even without *Mormor* there to supervise me.

My father and Uncle Ludvig drank beers and spoke in their dialect while I cooked and they didn't seem to notice that I had put the dill in with the fish too soon, so it was a crispy black by the time I retrieved it from the pan. The meal was more than the thrown-together ingredients that we'd eaten the entire week; it was a reward for a week of hard work: quick, delicious food for hungry, hardworking men.

We ate the potatoes and the fish and I was proud to have not only helped my father do his work but to have prepared the workingman's simple meal. The next day, as I helped my father give the boats a light sanding and a final coat of paint, I thought of what Uncle Torsten had said about our mackerel lunch and how much he might have enjoyed the supper I had prepared. Although I was still a kid and years away from any thought of becoming a chef, I was learning the beauty of food within a context: how important it is to let the dishes be reflective of your surroundings. Hot smoked-mackerel sandwiches on dark brown bread in the smokehouse with Torsten. Panfried fish and potatoes with my father at the end of a long, hard day. If the ingredients are fresh and prepared with love, they are bound to be satisfying.

"Marcus," my father called out after me when the last boat was done. *"Väl gjort, lille yrkesfiskare."* Well done, little fisherman.

SIX **MATS**

It wasn't until I'd started grade school that the question of race became real for me and my sister Linda, in large part because Anna had integrated the Samuelsson household years before we'd arrived. For Anna, biracial and fair-skinned with an Afro that could have rivaled Angela Davis's, the arrival of two dark-skinned siblings was a revelation. At nine years of age, she had never known children who were browner than she was. In those first few days, she would stroke my cheek and run her hands through my woolly hair, curiosity overriding her Swedish reserve. We may have been a novelty to my oldest sister, but because of Anna, Linda and I were never the "black kids" in the family. We were two *more* black kids in the family. All the skin touching and hair pulling and curious questions came to Anna first and by the time we arrived, it went without saying that this was a mixed-race family. As a black girl in Sweden, Anna always stood out. But she handled it all in her own elegant way, in part because my mother and her parents never made race an issue. We were Samuelssons now and that was all they felt they, or anybody else, needed to know.

Once we got to school, there were comments, at first more curious than cruel. And as I got older, as a boy, there were more than my fair share of taunts and playground fights. Still, it's important that you know that growing up black in Sweden is different than growing up black in America. I have no big race wounds. And I owe that to Anne Marie Samuelsson.

We had arrived in the early 1970s, in what was then a small, working-class Scandinavian city, but my mother wanted to do more than make us Samuelssons: She wanted to embrace black culture however she could. Because Anna's birth father had been Jamaican, my mother spent what little pocket money she had on Bob Marley records. I can still picture her singing along to Bob as she stirred her spaghetti and peas. When Linda and I showed up, Anne Marie added Miriam Makeba to the mix. Makeba was not exactly Ethiopian—not Ethiopian at all—but African and beautiful all the same. Even now, I can't hear a song like "Three Little Birds" without thinking of my mother blasting her music, like she blasted her love, out loud.

I might have looked on my childhood differently if I hadn't met Mats Carestam. He's my oldest friend. We met when I was five years old and I realized there was only one kid in the neighborhood who was as good as me at soccer. That was Mats, and I knew, even then, that we were going to either hate each other or become the best of friends.

We became the best of friends.

From the beginning, my battles were his battles. Which was great because Mats was a guy who took no shit. It's not so much that he had a quick temper. It's more that he was always this big kid who was never afraid to get down in it. No matter how nicely his mother had dressed him before he left the house, within minutes the knees of his pants would be muddy and grass-stained, and he'd be a mess. His shins were always a collage of bruises. Whenever I think of Mats, even today, I picture him wiping the back of his hand across his face and all over his clothes like a kid in a laundry detergent commercial.

I ate at Mats's house as often as I ate at my own, and I lived for his mother's creamy macaroni and cheese. A dish like that was way too modern for my mother. Mats's mother served store-bought meatballs, which my mother would *never* do. My mother didn't love to cook, but certain things she would never cut corners on. There was also a generational gap between our families. Mats's parents were much younger, more on the go, much more contemporary.

Everything Mats ate, he covered in ketchup. Which was fine with his parents, but always left me slightly bewildered. How could you taste the cheese or the meat or the potatoes when they were drowning in cold red tomato sauce? And Mats would eat fast. He'd make himself a giant plate of mac and cheese, meatballs, pickles, lingonberries, cover the whole thing with ketchup, and wash it down with a pint of milk in about two minutes. Mats didn't care what you put in front of him as long as there was plenty of it. He was a big kid and he ate not out of greed but because his body was this *machine* that demanded it.

It helped that my best friend was built like a tank when we started junior high school. I'd long healed from the tuberculosis and the distended belly of poverty was gone, but I was still built like an Ethiopian runner—lean and wiry. In my mind, I was as cool and powerful as any of the American black men we saw on TV, but in the land of Vikings, I stood out as a scrawny little kid.

ONE DAY AFTER SCHOOL, Mats and I were headed to his house for an afternoon of listening to music, reading soccer magazines, and chowing down on the kind of packaged pastries and soda my mother never had in our house. We'd made it halfway across the school playground when a basketball hit me in the back so hard that I stumbled forward.

"Hey, Marcus, why don't you teach us how to play *negerboll*," a kid named Boje called out.

It was always a little hard to tell if Boje was honestly mean-spirited or if he'd been drafted to play the part because he was a big, muscular kid, even in the sixth grade, like a nightclub bouncer. In either case, he was the closest we had to a bully at our school and I'd been lucky enough to escape his attention. Until now.

Negerboll. The word hung in the air as the boys around us, all kids in our class, froze. There couldn't have been more than twenty boys in the group, but I felt like there were a hundred eyes on me. Boje had thrown the ball hard, but the word hit me harder. Mats picked the ball up and stood protectively in front of me, but the words kept bouncing up and down against the pavement:

Neger
Boll.
Neger
Boll.
Neger
Boll.

Although it sounded like *nigger* and Boje spewed it with that level of venom, *neger* was the Swedish word for *Negro*. There was even a Swedish cookie called *negerboll* or, in English, *Negro ball*: It was made from cocoa powder, sugar, and oats. But Boje was not calling me a cookie. And he had thrown a basketball at me, which I took as its own kind of loaded symbol. It was the early 1980s, the dawn of the Michael Jordan era, and most Swedes associated that orange ball with dark-skinned men.

Boje wasn't done with me yet. "What, does the *neger* not know how to play *negerboll*?"

Mats looked like he might shove the basketball down the tall, blond boy's throat.

"Leave him alone," Mats growled.

Later, back at Mats's house, all my clever, cutting retorts would come at me in a kind of beautiful wave, like the way genius mathematicians scrawl numbers and letters on chalkboards in movies. But in the moment, the very first time in my life someone called me out as *neger*, I had said nothing. I had spent years growing in the quiet confidence of being Anne Marie and Lennart's son. I knew that they did not look like me and that I had come from a faraway place called Africa, but it was no more mysterious for me than it was for kids who still believed they had arrived on their parents' doorstep by stork. When Boje called me a *neger*, when he threw an American basketball at me and tried to hurt me, physically and emotionally, I had to ask myself for the very first time—*was* I different? How was I different? And in the same way that five-year-old Linda had kept vigilant for months on end, the question occurred to me for the very first time—where was home? Was this place it?

In his *Letters to a Young Poet*, Rainer Maria Rilke wrote that the young poet should "live the questions now. Perhaps you will then gradually, without noticing it, live along some distant day into the answer." I was an eleven-year-old kid in Göteborg and not particularly bookish. I'd never read Rilke at that point, but somehow I came to the same conclusion that I would have to live the questions.

That night, when I described the incident to my family at the dinner table, my father seemed concerned, but my mother jumped right in with what she thought was a viable solution: *"Kalla honom vit kaka,"* she said. Call him a white cookie.

I moaned and tried to explain that it would not have the same effect. But my mother, like the mother of bullied children everywhere, could not understand that in middle school there was no such thing as a fair fight.

For the next three years, Boje hardly let up. Anything spherical could be lobbed at me and turned into a taunt. A little Sambo had long been used to advertise *negerboll* cookies in Sweden and I felt a sense of dread anytime I saw a boy open a package of them at lunch because I knew that the wrapper would soon be coming my way. Mats never hesitated to stand up for me. He wasn't just defending me as a friend, he was standing up for what was right.

I later learned that Mats's parents had anticipated the racial taunts way before my own parents had and had instructed their son not to tolerate anyone picking on me. I wondered then about the boys who stood up for me and the ones who shied away from the fight. How had Team Marcus and Team Boje been formed? Was it boys who were raised right and boys who were not? Was it boys who were scared and boys who were not? The lines were split and it wasn't about friendship. Inside the *negerboll* coliseum we were all gladiators. Outside of it, almost all of us were friends. It was puzzling. But I had gleaned— even without reading him—the lesson of Rilke. I learned to live the questions.

SPORTS, IN MY CHILDHOOD, was the great equalizer, the safe space. When skateboards came onto the scene, Mats and I practiced kick-turns for hours, wiping out, racing down our driveways. We'd race everything, including bikes, although on those we preferred to pedal full speed at each other just to see what a head-on collision would feel like. (Not so great.) We hiked around the woods in our backyards, playing hours of elaborate hide-and-seek games or pretending to be mountain men or survivors from a plane wreck, desperate enough to turn to cannibalism. When we were with other kids, we dared them to skateboard down hills with no padding or shoes; we ran tennis tournaments that blocked the street, using string for a net and chalked court lines; we never stopped.

The sport we most loved was soccer. Mats and I were equally obsessed with it, but like every other Swedish boy my age, he was taller and heavier than I was. By Swedish standards, he was an average height and somewhat thickly built, with powerful legs that he put to good use on the soccer field. I might have had speed and natural ability, but Mats had that, size, *and* a superstar dad. Rune Carestam was a much better player than the other dads. In scrimmages, he could take on any of us kids and outrun us, outscore us, outthink us. We'd lunge at him and before we landed, he'd be past us, setting up a teammate with the perfect pass. My father was strong on defense, and in a neighborhood game he could hold his own, but he was also a good ten years older than Rune. Not to mention ten years slower.

When we'd play all-kid pickup games in the neighborhood or kick balls around during school recess, the only real competition Mats and I faced was each other. Instead of that making us jealous, it made us closer. Soccer was our bond. The first non-school book I ever read was one Mats lent to me, which he'd taken out from the local library.

"Du skulle gilla den här," he said as he chucked it in my direction. You might like this.

It was the autobiography of Edson Arantes do Nascimento, better known as Pelé, better known as the greatest soccer player in the world. I sat rock still as I read of Pelé coming to Göteborg (Göteborg!) at seventeen to play in the 1958 World Cup finals. Pelé described walking onto the field of Nya Ulleví Stadium, a few miles from my house, wearing his number 10 jersey: He knew the crowd was focused on him, wondering who "this skinny little black boy" was. Pelé was my first hero and my first black role model, and that book meant the world to me.

When Mats and I weren't playing soccer, we were listening to music, to whatever new singles fell into the rotation on Göteborg's pop radio station. One day, he called me over to his house to hear a new album that an older cousin had passed along, by a band called Kiss. We stared at the album cover, stunned by the men in outrageous makeup, kicking up their legs, sheathed in skin-tight silver and black leather costumes. Mats held the album up to his face and pouted, just like the guys in the band.

We ran into his parents' bathroom and ransacked his mother's makeup bag. Shouldering each other aside for the best spot in front of the mirror, Mats took the eyeliner and drew on the black star-shaped eye patch of lead singer Paul "Starchild" Stanley while I penciled in black flames around each eye to turn myself into bassist Gene "Demon" Simmons.

For a few months, playing Kiss was definitely among our favorite pastimes. Mats was taking a woodworking class at the time, and while the other kids made toolboxes and desk caddies, he built a wooden microphone and stand, complete with a leather "electric cord" that we could incorporate into our performances. When we wanted to perform as the whole band, we brought in other kids, but more often than not, it was just the two of us in Mats's room, listening to each of the album's nine songs in order, following along with the lyrics printed on the album sleeve. Sometimes we'd just replay our favorite, "Detroit Rock City," again and again and again. We played a lot of air guitar—Mats on lead and me on bass—and we thought Göteborg had never seen anything as fierce as us when we screamed out, "First I drink, then I smoke!" We were good Swedish boys, but we meant, when the time was right, to get into some serious trouble.

Eventually, our tastes matured, and by seventh grade, we had progressed to . . . I hate to say it . . . Sweden's own ABBA. Now, instead of wanting to strike poses, we wanted to dance. We held disco nights: We'd gather up all the candy we could find and invite a dozen neighborhood girls to dance with us in Mats's basement to ABBA's latest release. No other boys; just the girls and us. And Mats's mom as DJ.

For the fourteen years that we lived in Skattkärr, until I left Sweden for good, Mats and I spoke to or saw each other ninety-nine out of any hundred days. In our minds, we ruled the neighborhood; and since we were in the same class and went to the same school, we ruled there, too.

IN SWEDEN, if you're serious about a sport, you don't waste your time with a school team: You join a club. The club teams in Sweden operate like a farm system for the pro leagues, and going pro was all Mats and I ever thought about. By the time we were eleven, we had outgrown the small neighborhood team we played for. We both tried out and were both accepted into GAIS, short for Göteborg Athletic and

Sports Association, our city's premier football team. GAIS was Sweden's answer to Leeds United, and its fans, including Mats's dad, were legendary in their devotion. To be accepted into their youth program was a huge deal. It meant you had a shot at going pro.

For the next four years, Mats and I lugged our bags to the practice field every day after school and every weekend, making the five-mile trek by bus, by tram, with our moms or in the backseat of my dad's rattly old Volkswagen Beetle. And when we took the tram, we never waited for it to pull up to our stop. We always jumped out early and ran the four blocks to the stadium where our teammates were waiting.

Until I joined GAIS, I was used to being the only outsider in any given room. At school, diversity took the form of one Finnish kid and one Indian girl who, like me, had been adopted young and spoke Swedish without an accent. But in GAIS, only six of the twenty-two team members were Swedish and almost all of them were from working-class homes. All of a sudden, I had friends from Yugoslavia, Turkey, Latvia, and Finland, friends who were not named Gunnar and Sven, but Mario and Tibor, friends with darker skin and darker hair. From my new teammates, I learned to speak a patois that blended foreign words with abbreviated Swedish sayings. Instead of saying *"Vad händer annars?"*—What's going on?—we'd say *"Annars?"* To get someone's attention, we would say *"Yalla,"* which meant "faster" in Arabic. And if we made a mistake, we used the English word *sorry*. It was, by our parents' standards, a lazy and improper way of speaking. To us, it was the epitome of cool.

My new teammates—even the white Swedes—all called themselves *blatte*, a historically derogatory term for immigrants that my generation claimed with pride. *Blatte* meant someone who was "dark" but, more, someone who was an outsider. It wasn't quite as charged as the term *nigga* that was favored among hip-hop-loving black people, but it was a term that made liberal-minded Swedes deeply uncomfortable. I liked that *blatte* covered everyone from displaced Ugandan Indians to former Yugoslavians to someone like me.

Unlike some of my team members, I'd been adopted as a toddler. Culturally and linguistically, I was Swedish. But as I got older, the more I could feel people respond to me as a young black man, instead of a cute little black kid. The subtle shift in the body language of strangers was something I never discussed with my parents, my sisters, or even Mats. But it was lucky for me that this deepening racial awareness happened at the same time I joined GAIS. While I was beginning to sense the ways that I didn't fully belong to Swedish society as a whole, I had found a place and a group of people with whom I felt very much at home.

AFTER PRACTICE, my teammates and I usually walked over to McDonald's, which was still relatively new in our city, and gorged on junk food. We were fascinated by how American it all seemed. Some of my school friends had gotten part-time jobs working the grill and fryers, and by the time I was in eighth grade, I decided I wanted to work at McDonald's, too. Why not get paid to be where I was hanging out every day anyway?

One day before practice, I went in and asked for an application. When I had finished it, the kid behind the counter pointed me in the direction of his manager, who couldn't have been older than twenty-one. I handed over my form, smiling and standing up straight the way my mother had taught me.

The manager held my application like something he'd picked up off the floor, touching it with only his thumb and his index finger.

"I'll let you know," he said.

I knew then and there I was not going to get a call. He hadn't actually said anything racist, but I ricocheted, as I so often did in those teenage years, between trusting my gut and being afraid that I'd misread the entire situation. I walked out of the restaurant, not sure whether I wanted to cry or hit someone.

At practice the next day, when I told my teammates what had happened, they laughed. They thought the very notion of me, a black kid, applying to work at a place like McDonald's was hysterical.

"You applied *where*?" my teammates asked, incredulous.

"Of course you didn't get a job!" they said. "Have you ever seen a *blatte* behind a McDonald's counter?"

At home, when I told my mother about the way the manager treated me, she did what mothers do: She offered to fight my battles for me. "I'll call him right now," she said. "He can't get away with that kind of treatment."

"No, no, please," I insisted. "I'll work somewhere else. I'll work somewhere better."

"*Bry dig inte om honom*," my father said. Ignore them.

Soccer, then, became not only a beloved sport, but GAIS, with its *blatte* crew, became a reprieve from what felt like an increasingly white world. Everything about GAIS was a perfect fit for me, from the sense of identity it gave to the green-and-black-striped jersey that earned us the nickname "the Mackerels." I wore that jersey, and that nickname, with an unbelievable amount of pride. I like to tell people that my hometown, Göteborg or Gburg, is like Pittsburgh by the sea. For me, wearing that jersey was like being on the kid's version of the Steelers: It said I belonged in Gburg, even if my skin said I didn't.

Shortly after Mats and I joined, the adult GAIS division signed its first black player, a Tunisian midfielder named Samir Bakaou. Bakaou was not olive-skinned, like so many North Africans; he was as black as I was and he made a point, whenever our paths would cross, of acknowledging me. He was a cool dude, never stressed on the field, always in control. The only other black males I ever saw were on TV—Carl Lewis, Michael Jackson, Desmond Tutu. They were all so far away. But Samir Bakaou trained where we trained. We didn't speak the same languages—I spoke Swedish and English, he spoke Arabic and French—but he always nodded his head or winked at me, gestures that assured me that we were connected. Along with Pelé, Bakaou immediately joined the pantheon of my black male role models.

The Mackerels were good, better than good. We traveled all over Northern Europe during the seven-month season: up to Stockholm and over to Denmark, Holland, England, and Yugoslavia. We practiced two hours a day: dribbling, passing, jumping, shooting, and running wind sprints, blasting at top speed across our half of the practice field, touching the center line then an end line and back again as many times as we could in five-minute intervals. When the coach's whistle finally blew, we fell down onto the ground wherever we were, sucking wind. Lying there with that feeling of having gone full out, staring up at the sky, blood and adrenaline pulsing through my body: I lived for that sensation.

In terms of philosophy, our coach Lars was influenced by the Brazilians—masters of the passing game. While many of the youth teams played one strategy—pass to the fastest guy and hope he can score—our coach wanted us to play with a mix of precision and poetry. Lars was just as proud of a fifty-yard sideline pass or of a perfectly executed cross as he was of any goals we scored. What he wanted to see on the field—the skills he taught us that are with me to this day—were the control and finesse that makes soccer both a joy to play and a joy to watch.

"I'd rather you lose than win ugly," Lars said.

We weren't the top team in the league, but we won more than we lost. Mats played center defender and I was center midfield, which made me the link between offense and defense. Lars typically put us both in his starting lineup, although we were on the young side. In our first year on GAIS, we were playing against boys who were three or four years older—which only added to the thrill whenever we were lucky enough to win.

By our second year on the team, scouts had begun to appear on the sideline, looking for talent they might siphon off for their semipro adult divisions or the all-out pro teams. When a sixteen-year-old Finnish boy we often played against got scooped up for his club's pro team and became his team's high scorer, we all dreamed of following his lead. I practiced harder than ever, and for the first time I felt a pull between wanting to do the best for the team and wanting to stand out enough to be noticed.

I knew I was good, and with each winning match it became easier to envision a life in soccer, with GAIS as a launching pad to a pro career. I practiced every hour that I wasn't doing homework or chores. I honed every move, not just my own. I borrowed the latest soccer magazines from Mats (my father believed in only newspapers and proper books) and, alone in my room, I devoured them.

In those days, there were three posters on my bedroom wall: Michael Jackson, the king and queen of Sweden (thanks, Mom), and Pelé, the man who had changed the game. I spent hours imagining myself on the field as a little Pelé, dribbling down fields in Barcelona and London, outmaneuvering world-class players as I drove to the goal, winning the World Cup with a header that would be played and replayed in slow motion on sports channels for years to come. Soccer was going to be more than my career. It would be the thing that got me out of Gburg. With soccer, I would get to see the world.

BY THE TIME I TURNED SIXTEEN, I had been on GAIS for four years. My life had taken on a steady, comforting routine: seven months of soccer, three months of school in which I would spend the majority of my time thinking about soccer, and two summer months in Smögen, fishing with my dad and my uncles, practicing my moves, seeing the green and black GAIS jersey in the scales of every beautiful fish.

At the start of our fifth season, Mats and I went to see the new team roster posted on the wall outside of the coach's office. We wanted to suss out the competition: Who were the new kids; who might be competing for our spots in the starting lineup? We were also looking to see whom the coach had axed: We wished nothing but the worst for the lazy bums who were finally getting their comeuppance for skipping one too many practices.

We looked at the list. There was Carestam, up toward the top of the alphabetized page. But when we got to the S's, there was no Samuelsson. I looked again. Not there. My brain refused to process what was clearly visible in front of me. For a few moments, I just kept looking at the list, reciting the alphabet in my head. Q, R, S, T. *Where was I?* My name wasn't there, no matter how many times I looked. It sounds melodramatic to say it, but I simply couldn't imagine that there was no place for me on this team, with my friends, in the game that was my world.

I slammed my fist into the bulletin board, as Mats stood by, toeing the ground with a tip of one sneaker, averting his eyes.

"*Javla skit!*" I screamed. "*Skit! Skit! Skit!*" Holy shit. Shit. Shit. Shit.

The office door opened and Coach Lars stuck his head out to see what was up.

"Come inside, Samuelsson," he said. "Carestam, wait here."

I followed Lars into his office and he shut the door behind us. I sank into the chair across from his desk, which was scattered with the playbooks and lineups and photocopied schedules that represented all that had been taken away from me. I took deep breaths and tried to keep my hands from trembling.

"Marcus," he said. "I know this is disappointing. You're a great player, but you're too small. The other sixteen-year-olds outweigh you by forty or fifty pounds, some of them more. You should keep playing, but it can't be with us. Sorry."

It was the first time in my life that I had ever been fired, and I didn't even see it coming. I worked hard, I didn't flaunt the rules, I was diligent, I was disciplined, I was *good.* I was also out. Cut from the team. The only career path I'd ever considered for myself was now closed.

Although I would continue to play soccer in a smaller, lesser league, even working with a special coach to bridge that size and strength gap, eventually I had to let the dream go. And when I did, food entered my life fully.

Maybe one of the reasons that I come on so hard in the food game is that I've been cut once before. I know what it's like to see your name on the list year after year, and I know the heartbreak that comes the day you look up and your name is no longer on that list. Even now, all these years after GAIS let me go, I sometimes think of myself more as a failed soccer player than as an accomplished chef.

With a soccer career off the table, I decided to apply to a vocational high school. Sweden's school system was compulsory only until ninth grade, at which point many kids went on to two or three more years of gymnasium, specialized high schools meant to equip you for either a job or university.

As I considered my options, I began to play around with the idea of being a chef. Cooking was something I loved and was good at. At fifteen, I applied for and was accepted into Ester Mosesson, a school where creative types from all over Gburg studied subjects like cooking, fashion, and graphic design. It was like a *Saturday Night Live* sketch of a European high school of the performing arts: Instead of bursting into song or dancing on the cafeteria tables, students at Mosesson sketched intensely and learned to make flawless soufflés.

I had never excelled in academics the way my father had, so here was a curriculum that I could finally get excited about. My only formal classes were in Swedish and English—I loved languages, so that was always fun. There was a mandatory PE program, which consisted mostly of easy soccer scrimmages—again, fun. The rest of the day was spent cooking. By this point, I'd been around food and cooking for so long that I couldn't remember *not* knowing my way around a kitchen. I walked into the class feeling more than confident. On the third day, one of our instructors was running through basic knife skills for prepping vegetables. "Soon enough," he promised, "you'll dream about chopping onions."

The teacher's pattern was to demonstrate—from julienne to chiffonade—then have a student take his place at the cutting board and attempt to imitate. I held back at first, curious to see how much experience my new classmates had. Even under close supervision, blood was drawn. The kitchen, we quickly learned, was no place for the clumsy or distracted.

After a brief demonstration of how to cut a classic batonnet—a squared-off oversize matchstick—a kid named Martin got a turn at the chopping board. The teacher handed over his knife, and Martin said nothing. He just took the knife and, in one fluid motion, topped and tailed the potato, cutting off the rounded ends and edges so that he had a rectangular block. He sliced the block into quarter-inch-thick slabs, then stacked the slabs in piles of three and sliced them again, lengthwise.

The group fell silent, admiring the perfectly uniform pile of potato sticks. Martin took a towel from a peg below the counter and wiped down the knife blade.

"Did everybody see that?" our teacher asked.

My grandmother had been such a thorough and patient teacher that I came into school with basic techniques, far beyond most of the kids in my class. I knew how to hold a knife. I knew how to fillet a fish.

I knew how to sauté meat in a cast iron pan over high heat to produce a nice crust. But I could see in that mound of potatoes that Martin knew everything I knew, and more. Cooking was incorporated into his body like pure muscle memory, the same way I dribbled a soccer ball, the way the rest of us walked and breathed. From that day on, as I saw it, there were only two students in the entire school—me and Martin. He was the one to beat and I was the one to do it.

One of our instructors was a young Brit named John Morris. His job was to teach us how to grill, fry, sauté, and poach, all using French techniques and terminology, of course. Unlike most of our other teachers, he insisted we call him Chef John, as if we were in a professional kitchen. Chef John spoke in Swenglish, starting each class in polite Swedish and gradually slipping, as the day ground on, into a string of English curse words. He'd started off in his hometown pub, cleaning chickens and cooking liver. Then he moved to London and worked in the kitchen of the opulent Dorchester hotel, where he was promoted to *chef de partie* and cooked for the likes of Queen Elizabeth and Jimmy Carter. If he hadn't met a Swedish girl in a bar, he said, he'd still be there. But that girl had become his wife, and love had led him to Gburg.

Chef John did not have an easy task. Try demonstrating the difference between simmering and poaching on an old government-issue stove whose gas line delivered its fuel in uneven hiccups. In a professional kitchen, if a pot burns one too many times, you throw it away. At Mosesson, if teachers had discarded every utensil that had been burned one too many times, we'd have had nothing left.

Chef John's biggest obstacles, however, were his students.

"How do you know if the oil is the right temperature?" a kid named Niklas asked, interrupting Chef John's lesson on deep-frying. It was a straightforward question, but Niklas was the type of entitled kid who thought he was funnier than he actually was. I could tell by the smirk on his face that he was up to something.

Chef John answered him straight. "There are three ways to tell.

One, drop in a couple of test fries. If they float up to the surface and start to bubble, and if you can hear a sizzle, then the oil's hot."

"I don't want to lose a fry," Niklas moaned dramatically. "I looooove my fries."

A few scattered snickers rippled through the room.

"The second way is to simply watch the time," Chef John continued. "If you give it fifteen minutes and then use a thermometer, it should read 360 degrees Fahrenheit."

Then he turned to Nik, who stood on the other side of the vat of the hot oil. "Of course, you can always put your bloody finger in the fryer."

Nik, being more moron than comedian, chose this method. His finger wasn't in the fryer for more than a second before he began screaming, a shocked look on his face as if he hadn't actually expected it to hurt. Chef John was screaming, too. "You stupid fucking bastard!" he said. "Why the hell did you put your fucking finger in there? Have you lost your mind?"

Niklas quit the program a couple of months later, but I learned an invaluable lesson from his stupidity. The kitchen is a dangerous place and if you want to stay safe, you've got to not only watch your own back, you've got to keep your eye on all the weak links.

In any professional kitchen, the lower-ranked staff responds to any request from above with military-like respect. "Yes, chef" is what I was taught to say whether he or she asks for a side of beef or your head on a platter. Yes, chef. Yes, chef. Yes, chef. I had failed at soccer and the failure made me humble and determined. At Mosesson, I was determined to be the best. Soon I was serving up not only classic three-course Swedish smorgasbords but damn good renditions of coq au vin, steak au poivre, and bouillabaisse.

Halfway through the first term, my class started working in the restaurant school, cooking for customers. Most of the time, our lunch menu was pure Sweden: plates of gravlax with boiled potatoes and herring in all manner of sauces—mustard and dill, cream, curry, and 1-2-3 with slivered onions. We also prepared contemporary classics like toast Skagen: a sautéed round of bread topped with shrimp salad, finished with a spoonful of whitefish roe. Dinner, on the other hand, was typically French, which was considered an elegant cut above homey Swedish fare: sole meunière or duck a l'orange.

We worked in rotating shifts, so I might be a waiter for three weeks, then a dishwasher, then a line cook. I was a decent waiter and I knew it was useful to see how customers behaved in the front of the house, how they ordered, and how they regarded their meal once it was served, but I never felt at home in the front like I did in the back. The back of the house was where the real action, the real creativity, was. Even with only forty seats in the restaurant, and even if only half of them were filled, the kitchen was guaranteed to be humming at a pitch that bordered on chaos. And it was that organized chaos that I loved. I still do.

At restaurant school, the kitchen hierarchy was structured like most professional kitchens—using the classic French *brigade de cuisine*. Each *chef de partie* was assigned a distinct task—meat, fish, salads—and one person was designated the expediter, who organized and dispensed orders as they came in from the dining room.

Although teamwork systems had been around in professional kitchens since the Middle Ages, it was the now legendary French chef Georges Auguste Escoffier who codified it and put it all down on paper at the beginning of the twentieth century in his classic book, *Le Guide Culinaire*. The success of the *brigade* depended on employees understanding and embracing two tenets: one being the hierarchy system, and two being the *chef de partie* division of labor, which compartmentalized the tasks of the kitchen into *parties* or parts, each with its own managing chef. Whatever your status, from *garçon* and *commis* at the bottom to *chef de cuisine* at the top, you had to learn where you were in the pecking order. When anyone above you asked for something, you said yes and double-timed it to meet his demands. In turn, you had the right to order around whoever fell below your rank.

In restaurant terms, an expediter is only as good as her or his ability to "order fire." This means that as the orders come in, the expediter must order the dishes so that everything will be ready to serve at once. A table of four might be having a broiled chicken, a medium steak, a rare steak, and a poached turbot fillet: Each entrée would be cooked for a different amount of time and by different *chefs de partie*. The expediter calculates when to start each dish, using backward-counting math and accounting for any extra steps, like pan deglazing or meat resting. The ability to impose order on so much fire is the difference between a great restaurant and one that is merely good; the difference between a flawless service and one that has customers complaining and skimping on tips.

The meals we cooked had been copied straight out of our cooking bibles: *Larousse Gastronomique* and *The Escoffier Cookbook*. Appetizers led sensibly into main courses and side dishes counterpointed or complemented entrées, but nothing about them seemed exciting or surprising or fresh. Every day I would look at the menu and wonder, What if we paired the duck a l'orange with curried fried rice instead of serving it with the traditional potatoes dauphinoise? If thyme and mustard added such wonderful flavors to the roasted lamb, couldn't we do a similar variation with roasted goat instead? It was in me already, the desire to mix cultures and foods. But this wasn't just about my desire to introduce international flavors into traditional cuisine. I could also see that at the school, we prized French food above our own national culinary treasures. It was the 1980s and the locavore movement may have been in full swing in northern California, but it sure as hell hadn't yet come to Scandinavia. I learned more about the foods of the Alsace than I did about Västerbotten, the Swedish county that produced the country's best cheese. Soon, that would begin to change.

EIGHT **EARNING MY KNIVES**

PEOPLE WENT OUT ALL THE TIME IN GÖTEBORG, BUT NOT TO EAT. THEY might meet for a beer after work or to watch soccer together at a bar, but food was never the center of socializing, the way it is in cities like Barcelona or Paris, where people live their lives in restaurants. Gburg's blue-collar roots fed into this eat-at-home lifestyle. Factory workers had neither the time nor the disposable income to waste an evening over a leisurely meal. In truth, it wasn't just about time or money: As a whole, Sweden was way behind the curve on fine dining. It wasn't until the mid-1980s, when I was starting at culinary school, that the first Swedish restaurants, Eriks and L'Escargot in Stockholm, received major recognition outside Sweden.

Despite the training ground of the forty-seat restaurant, Mosesson really groomed its students for institutional placements such as hospital and school cafeterias. Practically speaking, there was no local restaurant scene to provide jobs for the graduates, even if they wanted to. The result was an environment that didn't foster much creativity or competition among those of us who had chosen to cook for a living. There were no customers to build a relationship with; the only people willing to pay for haute cuisine were foreigners and corporate diners with expense accounts, neither of whom offered the steady, loyal patronage that restaurants count on to survive. Without a fine-dining culture, it's difficult to develop a palate that extends beyond whatever it is your family serves you.

My own family ate out two or three times a year, tops. We'd go out to celebrate the big events, like Anna getting into a selective school, Dad getting his PhD, or Linda landing a job at a record company. For the fanciest occasions, we would go to a classic Swedish place, where we'd order grilled pike with dill butter and boiled potatoes. For more casual celebrations, we went to La Piazza, a local pizza place where Linda and I would argue over toppings. I liked the exotically named Capricciosa: mushroom, artichoke, ham, and olive. Linda preferred the royally named Vesuvio, which was just a plain cheese pizza. Eventually, my father decided that we'd eat only foreign food when we went out because my mother would find any Swedish meal we were served in a restaurant lacking and, thus, would have a hard time enjoying herself. "Helga could do this better," she would sniff disappointedly. And, probably because of its familiarity, Swedish food was never worth the price. "Look at what this costs!" she'd say, pushing the menu away.

The ultimate luxury for most of the people we knew was peel-and-eat shrimp. Most of the shellfish in the area had been caught in my father's hometown, Smögen, where it was boiled right on the boat, trucked down to Göteborg, and served with white toast, mayonnaise, and lemon. Peel-and-eat shrimp was popular because of the method of eating it. Proper table manners in Swedish homes required the use of a fork and knife for everything, from fruit to sandwiches, but peel-and-eat was a vacation from all that buttoned-up propriety. The shrimp came out on a big platter, pink and plump, with the heads still on, and each person took a handful to his or her plate. From there, you would peel about ten at a time, then dip your hands in a bowl of water to clean them off. Next, you smeared a piece of toast with the mayo, arranged your peeled shrimp on top, and finished it with a sprinkle of chopped dill and a squeeze of lemon. Once you finished, you'd start the routine all over again. It was that tasty.

Everyone in Gburg grew up on peel-and-eat, but my family had it more often than most because of my father's Smögen heritage. Dad taught my sisters and me how to eat shrimp properly, sucking the meat out of the head, much the same way that people from New Orleans eat their mudbugs at a crawfish boil. My mother, Skånskan that she was, had a hard time adopting my father's approach. She stuck to the tail meat instead.

Decades later, when I met one of my most treasured mentors, the legendary New Orleans chef Leah Chase, I know that the way I attacked her crawfish was one of the reasons that she took a liking to me. I wasn't just a European-raised/African-born chef with a big profile and a big head full of highfalutin ideas. No, ma'am. Leah Chase saw me eat and knew that I was a brown-skinned boy who loved good food and also knew better than to waste any of it.

BY THE TIME MY SECOND YEAR at Mosesson rolled around, my ambition for food was such that the curriculum seemed not only limited, but a waste of time. I didn't know where I would end up or what I would cook, but I had a vague sense there was a world of amazing restaurants outside of Göteborg. Without classmates or professors to push me or encourage my dreaming, I feared I would become complacent. We continued to focus on the basic skills, everything from butchering to food-handling safety, and to split our time between lectures and hands-on practice. I enjoyed learning the classic preparations of herring and appreciated the pride and confidence our older teachers took in teaching us how to lay out a proper smorgasbord, but most of my classmates had no real ambition and their attitude was distracting. They actually threw rotten tomatoes at each other when the teachers turned their backs. It was as if we were in junior high, not culinary school.

To keep myself sharp, I turned each exercise into a little contest. Could I fill the pastry shells faster than any of my classmates? Could I wash and chop that dill faster than the teacher? Could I finish each squirt of whipped cream with the exact same curl?

A few weeks into my second year, it was clear that I'd outgrown what the school had to offer. But if I left before the program was over, my father's disappointment would be too much to bear. I'd already decided not to go to university, a big blow for a man with a doctorate and a deep belief in higher education. If I dropped out of culinary school, even if I dropped out because I wanted something more challenging, my father would see me as a quitter and see any future success as accidental, instead of being the result of the two things he valued most: focus and discipline. The only way out, as I saw it, was an off-site internship in a real restaurant. They came up frequently and were listed on a board at my school. For the next few months, every time I saw a new listing, I applied. Every time, I got no further than I had when I submitted my application to work at McDonald's.

One afternoon early in the fall term, I took the bus to the opposite side of town, walked three blocks from the bus stop, and found myself standing in front of Tidbloms, which had posted a notice on the board. Tidbloms was housed in a stately brick Victorian that dated back to 1897, when it had served as a dormitory for Scottish craftsmen who came to work at a nearby lumber mill. Over the years, it had gone through tough times, operating as a warehouse, then a flophouse, then a deli. When I came along, it had just been renovated into a charming inn, and the restaurant had been made over accordingly.

I walked through the dining room and into the kitchen, where a shaggy-haired young guy, probably in his midtwenties, was picking through a tub of oysters, smelling some, knocking on some others with his knuckle, and cocking his head to listen for something.

"These are good," he said to the guy standing next to him. "You can accept the delivery."

The guy said nothing, but turned and hustled toward the kitchen's back door. I introduced myself. "I'm looking for the chef," I said.

"I'm the chef," he said. "I'm Jorgen. How can I help you?"

Every bit of buzz I'd heard about Tidbloms centered around what Jorgen had done in its kitchen. How he'd assembled a strong team of cooks, and how consistently he turned out high-quality food, a blend of Swedish ingredients with the sauces and attitudes of French cuisine. At lunch you could get the standard *husmanskost* fare—a plate of meatballs, cream gravy, and mashed potatoes for forty-five kroner, about two dollars—but for three times that price, Tidbloms offered an *affärslunch*, a business lunch, like a roast leg of lamb with mustard sauce and a potato gratin. Still meat and potatoes, but fancy meat and potatoes.

Dinner, I was told, was when the best ingredients came out: the morels, the cherry tomatoes, the fresh basil and tarragon. I wanted to be around this higher class of food, but I also sensed a seriousness about the work that would be an antidote to what I was getting at school. Even though late afternoon was the slow prep period, with no customers in the front of the house, no one seemed to be slacking off. Even the porter who brought in the oysters did his job as if a fire were lit under him.

"I'll work hard," I promised Jorgen, after detailing my Mosesson studies and summer jobs. He agreed to give me a four-week internship.

WHAT A RELIEF IT WAS to work in a real kitchen, serving real food made by real cooks to real paying customers. I was assigned the most basic of tasks, just above dishwasher, but from my first shift, working side by side with a professional restaurant staff, I felt the camaraderie and effort I knew on the soccer field. I turned the plate warmer on precisely at 11:00 each morning. I stocked the walk-in refrigerator as soon as the chef cleared each delivery. I set up the station for the *saucier*, replenishing his *mise en place*, which meant chopping, shredding, and slicing every herb, condiment, and flavoring ingredient the chef would need during his shift, and putting each one into small plastic containers that lined the perimeter of his counter work space. I did more than peel potatoes by the hundreds; I washed them, peeled them, and tournéed them, cutting them into identical shapes, two inches long with seven equally wide sides. For this task, one of the cooks would lend me his own tourné knife—real cooks owned their own sets of knives, which they carried in long, soft cases, and the tourné had a curved blade that looked like a bird beak, the name often used to describe it. I was always careful to wipe down the blade and handle before giving it back, another sign of care and respect. There may have been clear lines of status in the hierarchy of the kitchen, but we had a common goal, and everyone understood that his contributions mattered.

Bengt, one of Tidbloms' cooks, lived near my parents in Säve-dalen and gave me a ride home whenever we worked the same shifts. He was only a couple of years older than me, but he drove his ten-year-old Volvo like a fogey, slow and cautious, both hands on the wheel. As we puttered along the E20 highway, we talked about our plans to conquer the cooking world.

"My next step," he announced one night, "will be to work for Leif and Crister." Leif Mannerström and Crister Svantesson often worked as a team and were currently helming La Scala, Göteborg's most upscale eatery. Leif had an eye for opportunities: He was well connected to politicians and businessmen, and typically served in more of a management role. Crister was a creative type, with a reckless flair in everything he did, but no one would dispute that a talent for cooking was in his DNA. Despite the name, the menu at La Scala was French, with the finest wine list in town, and its location near the city's concert hall ensured a steady flow of well-heeled guests.

I had a little trouble swallowing Bengt's confident pronouncement and let him know. He was competent, but I didn't think he was that much better than me. I really believed I could get there.

"Listen," he said, ignoring my lack of enthusiasm, "if you do well at Tidbloms, if you impress them, I'll see what I can do about getting you into La Scala down the line, too." He didn't even have his own job yet, but he was promising to bring *me* along? I would soon learn that this was the way among chefs and their tribes: You follow a great chef anywhere he might go.

I learned something with every shift. My first week, I learned how a proper fish stock was made. Where my grandmother threw a mishmash of bones into a pot with water and chopped red onions, mixing salmon and haddock and letting it cook at a furious boil, Tidbloms used only finer, more delicate fish, like turbot and sole. They added fresh thyme and parsley, peppercorns, white wine, and the white part of the leek, cooking it slowly, barely simmering, coaxing out flavors rather than bludgeoning them. I learned how to fillet fish faster and without wasting any flesh. I learned how to slice just under the tough, pearly silver skin when cleaning a tenderloin of beef so that I could pull it away from the bone more easily, and how much simpler it was to fillet a tenderloin than a rack of lamb. Most of all, I learned what it meant to never gear down, to work with a constant sense of purpose. In school, we'd do only one thing at a time: Today, we're going to make whipped cream. Today, we're going to make veal stock. At Tidbloms, everyone had five things on his plate, and all of them needed to be done right then.

After four weeks, when my time with Tidbloms was just about up, I couldn't bear the thought of going back to Mosesson full-time. I went to see Jorgen between lunch and dinner services. He had no office, so any clean stretch of counter could become his desk. That day, I found him at the salad station, writing out a menu for the next week. I waited for him to notice me, but his head remained bent over his task. I cleared my throat, and he looked up.

"Hey, Marcus. What's going on?" Jorgen asked.

I was so afraid of him saying no that the plan I'd hatched came tumbling out in one nonstop flood: "Chef, I can't go back to that rinky-dink school restaurant when I could be here working with you. I have to do a certain number of hands-on cooking hours for school, and if I did all my cooking hours for free here at Tidbloms, do you think you'd be able to sign for them so I can get school credit? You'd have to let my cooking teacher know it's OK with you and then sign off on my hours at the end of each reporting period. I can give you the guy's number and if there are any forms, I'll get them from the school. You don't have to do anything extra besides letting me stay." I took a breath. "What do you think?"

Jorgen smiled. "Why didn't you ask sooner?" he said.

With the placement figured out, I took the idea back to my cooking teacher.

"Why should we make an exception for you?" he asked. "This is not standard policy."

I responded with the confidence of a cocky teenager. Or the desperate. "You know I'm going to become a real cook when I leave here," I said. "Unlike most of the kids here, I'm serious about it. And if I don't get more real-world experience, I'll fall behind in my chances of getting a good job after I graduate. Please?"

"OK, Samuelsson, we'll give it a try," he said. "But you can't miss any of your other classes. Remember: You're still in school."

WHEN I ARRIVED IN SWEDEN, I was assigned a birthday of November 11. Each year, on that day, my mother or grandmother baked a cake, and at the end of supper, I opened a handful of presents. My grandmother gave me sweaters she'd knitted herself; my father gave me books; and my mother gave me clothes she thought I needed, usually more stylish than I would have picked out on my own. I could count on Linda and Anna to go in together on something cool. The year before, they'd cooked up the perfect Afro-Swedish gift: a Public Enemy album and a pair of turquoise Converse high-tops.

That year—my seventeenth birthday—as my mother cleared the cake plates from the kitchen table, Anna leaned over to Linda and whispered something in her ear. Linda sprang up from her chair and ran downstairs to Anna's room. She was back a minute later with a long rectangular box wrapped in paper I recognized from the previous Christmas.

"Open it," Anna said.

I took my time peeling the tape off. The box seemed awfully similar to the ones we gave to my father on his birthday, the ones that held ties he promptly wore to the office for the next week straight and then buried in the sock drawer of his closet. With the paper off, I could see it was a box from Holmens Herr, the classiest—and least cool—menswear store in town. I tried to mask my disappointment and lifted off the lid, psyching myself up to show them only happiness.

It was not a tie. It was a brand-new cook's knife with an eight-inch-long carbon steel blade. This was the multipurpose knife every chef needs, with a blade thin enough to chop herbs, but a wide flat surface for crushing or picking up food. Better still, it was the Rolls-Royce of knives, brand-wise, made by the French company Sabatier.

"I don't know what to say," I said, and when I hugged them, I meant it.

I worked at Tidbloms every day for the rest of the year, which made school bearable. My father might have known next to nothing about fine dining, but he had ingrained in me a flawless work ethic: I knew to show up on time, to listen to instructions, and never to talk back to my bosses. And the hard work paid off. I may have lost my place on the soccer team because I wasn't as big as the rest of the guys, but in the kitchen, my size didn't matter. All that mattered was the work.

The cooks thanked me by letting me do more than simple prep work; I began to make *à la minute* sauces—those we cooked to order. For sole meunière, I'd step in after the fish had been cooked in butter, then add a few more tablespoons to the pan and watch until it turned a golden brown. At that point, I stirred in some minced parsley and poured in lemon juice, then took a half-teaspoon taste of it to see if it needed salt. Once I got it right, I handed the pan back to the cook, who checked my flavoring and drizzled the sauce over the plated fish.

At Tidbloms, I learned the danger of complacency. Dialing it in is one of a chef's worst habits. No matter how tired you are, no matter how stressed, you can't take shortcuts. One day, we were serving a broiled cod special. I was helping out at the fish station and doing some of the final seasoning adjustments with salt and pepper. After half a dozen orders went out onto the floor, I had my seasoning down pat. The next day, I helped out at the fish station again, and I performed the same final role of seasoning the daily special. All seemed to be going well until Jorgen passed by and saw me shaking salt onto the plate.

He came over and took a taste of what I'd been working on.

He spit it into a napkin. "What the hell is this?" he asked. Turns out I'd been salting gravlax, a salt-cured fish.

He was furious—wasting good food was a no-no—and I thought I'd be fired. I felt sick. But he didn't fire me. My mistake was one of judgment, not of laziness, and to him, the difference between those mattered.

I redeemed myself by working harder and faster than I ever had before. That was the pace of Tidbloms all the time—guys cooking six things at once with a constant sense of urgency but never panic. If we had an unusually busy lunch service, Jorgen would ask me to stay on beyond my scheduled shift, and I always said yes. "Yes, chef" is such a common parlance in a professional kitchen. You don't even have to think about it for your mouth to form the words. You get asked to do something and you say yes. "Yes, chef" were the first words out of my mouth each morning and the last words I uttered as I left the restaurant each night. "Good night, Marcus," Jorgen would call out. I wouldn't say, "Have a good night, too." I'd say, "Yes, chef." I didn't want to miss any chance I got to see the world that was opening up before me.

No matter how much I learned at Tidbloms, I never caught up with my classmate Martin back at Mosesson. The day we graduated, he won the school's top honors. Martin was too nice a guy to resent, but there was another difference between us that kept me from feeling a twinge of envy. Since the age of twelve, Martin had worked in his family's catering business. While we were at Mosesson, he continued to work for his dad in his off-school hours, and when a big job came in, he'd miss out on a few days of school. I envied Martin's proficiency and talent, but I did not envy that his fate was sealed. He would eventually step into his father's shoes, take over the family business, and never leave Göteborg. Maybe he could live with that, but the mere thought made me feel like the walls around me were closing in.

I graduated second in our class and walked away with a handshake from the principal, a diploma, and my first full set of knives, carbon steel blades and riveted wood handles, the blade's weight counterbalanced by the tang, a strip of metal that continued through to the end of the handle. I would cherish those knives for years. They were the one constant in my luggage, along with my journals, as I made my way from country to country, continent to continent.

NINE **BELLE AVENUE**

IN THE WINTER OF 1989, WHEN I WALKED THROUGH BELLE AVENUE'S doors as its newest *köksnisse*, or kitchen boy, it was probably one of the top five restaurants in Sweden. In the front of the house, three layers of white linen covered each of the room's fifty tables. Leather banquettes ringed the room. Knowledgeable, seasoned waiters were never more than a few steps away. A sommelier with a sterling silver tastevin around his neck stood by the bar, ready to guide guests through the extensive French wine list. The room operated at a muffled murmur as if both servers and patrons had agreed to treat the chef, and the meals he created, with the same deference one might show a great opera singer.

Attached to the main dining room was a kitchen that served more than just the restaurant. It fed all of the Park Avenue Hotel, including its bar and grill, a dinner theater with singing waiters, room service, and three banquet halls on the mezzanine floor. From sunrise to midnight, there was hardly a minute of downtime for the staff, fifty men and also a few women scattered in the traditional female kitchen roles of salad-making and pastry. I came in at the level of *köksnissen;* the only ones who ranked below me were the *garçons*, or interns, young guys who worked in the basement doing thankless prep work and cleanup. On my first day, I was issued my first chef's jacket and houndstooth kitchen pants and told to report immediately to the fish department.

Gordon was my boss. He was a fortysomething former rugby player from Australia who seemed to have a perpetual sunburn, even in winter. He was the *boucher*, the butcher, and his job was to process all the meat and fish when it came into the kitchen. Gordon was physically powerful, with a personality to match. He was quick to laugh at a joke, but he didn't hesitate to shut you down if you were wasting time. He taught me everything I know about cleaning fish. Not just cleaning the fish, but what you could do with the bones, how you stored each piece, and what the different fish were for. I understood the difference between herring and mackerel, but now I was looking at exotic stuff like turbot and sole, learning in a tactile way about the different qualities of each species, which types could hold up under poaching versus grilling, and whether a fish's flavor stood up to a flavoring of lemon or a particular herb.

My main tasks were to unload fish orders and keep the refrigerator clean. The box, as we called the walk-in refrigerator, was lined with shelves and had four tall rolling trolleys in its center. Keeping it clean was the most physically difficult job I've ever had in a kitchen, not just because the fish came packed tight in large, cumbersome crates, but also because I had to haul hundreds of pounds of ice each shift to keep it from spoiling. You knew you'd done the job right if you didn't smell anything when you walked into the box; even fish that had been in-house for two or three days shouldn't give off the slightest odor.

I started every morning at six a.m. I emptied out each shelf and trolley, transferring the fish temporarily to the produce refrigerator. I poured hot water over each shelf to melt any stray ice, then wiped it down with a diluted bleach solution. I scrubbed the floor with a steel scrubber, and refilled the à la carte trolley with the fish that had been butchered for that day, so cooks could come and grab what they needed as soon as it had been ordered. Deep plastic bins filled the shelves along the wall. They, too, needed to be wiped out and re-iced, and they held some of the longer-storage items, like the caviars and roes; the crabs, lobsters, and shrimp; the gravlax and smoked salmon. By ten a.m., my time in the box was done.

Between lunch and dinner I restocked the fish station's *mise en place*, so that the chef could fill any order during meal service without having to hunt down an ingredient and chop it. In Sweden, dill was a principal seasoning, but chives, fennel, and other spices were also important.

In the beginning, I couldn't see past my mountain of tasks to absorb the approach and creativity of the lead chefs, but I tasted the food and saved the menus, and noticed when the maître d' and servers seemed especially excited about a particular dish. I saw decanters for the first time and asked my *commis* buddy Peter why they poured wine from one bottle to another before drinking it. Peter didn't know, so I went to Herved Antlow, the older chef who was in charge of banquets and didn't make fun of my naive questions. He was old enough to be my father; maybe he saw me as a son rather than a competitor. When I was working with him on an event, he always saved a small piece of meat or a taste of a sauce for me.

"Marcus," he would say, "this is quail."

"This is the rouget fish from France—see how sweet and nutty it is?"

"This is how you taste wine," he would say, swirling the glass and then putting his nose at its rim to catch the aromas he'd released.

"Mmm, can you taste the oak? Can you taste the oak cask it was aged in?"

I would nod in agreement, even though at that point, I couldn't have told the difference between a fully mature Bordeaux and red wine vinegar. I'm pretty sure Herved could see right through me, but he just kept showing me more. He told me good cooking was something that engaged all of your senses. "You're not a shoemaker," he said. Which meant you had to know that a truffle opens up its flavors in heat, so you added your truffles to a sauce at the very end so you didn't cook them out. You checked a sauce not by looking at it, but by dipping a spoon into it and then watching how the sauce stuck to the metal. If it slid right off, the sauce was too thin; if it coated the spoon, it was ready. I tasted and learned, and I knew he was showing me purely out of generosity. I promised myself that when I became a chef, I would do that, too.

On Saturday nights, when I wasn't working, I would go to *Mormor*'s and help prepare the big family supper. She loved to ask me questions about the kitchen at Belle Avenue as we stood at her counter, mixing cod with breadcrumbs to make fish balls. "Mackelille, what do you cook at Belle Avenue?" she asked, cracking open an egg and adding it to the fish mixture.

"I don't actually cook yet," I explained. "Mostly I chop and mop."

Ever faithful, she assured me that my time would come. "Don't worry," she'd say. "Soon they'll have you cooking and they'll be sorry they waited so long."

THE FIRST DAY I WORKED AT BELLE AVENUE, I didn't finish with the fish station until two in the morning. But I got faster and more efficient as time went by, and by three months in, I was done by one in the afternoon. I fell into a rhythm and learned certain tricks, like not even attempting to skin a sole unless it had been thoroughly chilled— otherwise you'd pull off as much of the costly flesh as you would the skin. Speed was valued, but it was also risky. There were certain jobs where you just couldn't go faster or cut corners. Usually, you learned this the hard way.

One morning, another *nisse* named Jakob and I were in charge of breaking down fresh hunks of turbot for the day's lunch service. They would be used in one of my favorite dishes: braised turbot on the bone. Jakob and I were not yet cooking the dish, but we were charged with cutting eleven-pound hunks of turbot into steaks. Even with our carefully honed fillet knives, the task promised to be slow; cutting through bone was tough.

"Let's use the band saw!" Jakob said. We had seen Gordon use it to butcher dense cuts of beef and frozen fish, but never with wet, fresh fish. No matter: The first fish went through perfectly, and we thought we were in business. We did another, then another, no problem. But when Jakob got to the fourth fish, it slipped out of his grasp. The blade went through his finger instead of the fish, fully severing its tip. Blood spurted everywhere.

Jakob writhed on the floor, screaming in pain and holding his hand. I started shouting something along the lines of "Holy shit! Holy shit!"

All the commotion brought over the executive chef, who looked down at Jakob and chimed in at the top of his lungs.

"What have you idiots done?" he screamed.

Someone, definitely not me, kept his wits about him, picked up Jakob's fingertip, dropped it into a bag of ice, and rushed him to the hospital. A few hours later, it was successfully reattached. But Jakob would never come back. At staff meal later that day, there would be no mention of what had happened. The older crew knew it was stupid rookie work; the younger ones realized it could have been any one of them.

At Belle Avenue, I learned what it was like to serve a meal to guests who were in no rush at all. When people booked dinner at our restaurant, they came to spend the evening. This gave the kitchen more time to work on each dish, to replace speed as a priority with attention to detail. I started to appreciate the implications of this careful work, how differently garlic cooked depending on whether it was sliced, chopped, or crushed, how differently it released its flavor into the pan. Up until this point, fine dining had been an abstraction, a distant summit to ascend. Now that I saw how much strategy and how many levels cooking could operate on, it was clear to me: What we did in the restaurant was not all that different from the work the museum curators did across the street. We were both, in our way, trying to engage our customers' senses, take them out of their day-to-day lives, and every once in a while, when they fell in love with a really well-executed Rydberg (pan-seared beef and potatoes in a red wine sauce) or ended their meal with a sweet botrytis Sémillon, they looked at the world in a slightly new way.

In jazz, a musician who is striving for a new kind of perfect is said to have gone "deep in the shed." That's what happened to me at Belle Avenue. It went from being a gig—a highly coveted one, but a gig all the same—to being my laboratory, my studio, my church. I never left. I worked my shift as quickly as I could, but it was never about getting done so I could get out, it was so I could learn something else. I started in the fish-cleaning department and then I went into the meat-cleaning department, then I got bumped up to junior cook on the fish station, then *commis* on the meat station. I did a turn in pastry and in *garde manger*, where we handled cold hors d'oeuvres, salads, and charcuterie. There were fifteen separate service stations in that kitchen, and I was determined to go through each one.

ON MY RARE NIGHTS OFF, I met up with my friends at one of the local cafés. One night there was a group of girls at the next table, and one in particular caught my eye. She was speaking Swedish, but she didn't look Swedish; she had dark, shiny hair and almond-shaped eyes. I was never shy with girls—I have my sisters to thank for that—so I went over and introduced myself.

Christina was cute and smart and she was, like me, Swedish but not Swedish. Her father was a Swede, but her mother was Japanese.

We started dating, and quickly became a couple. I ignored the fact that she smoked cigarettes, something I'd never done and which, as I developed into a chef, seemed like the ultimate palate killer. I also came from a family of women who wore only simple makeup, if any, and Christina seemed to spend hours putting on layer after layer of the stuff.

"She's such a pretty girl," my mother said after meeting her. "Why does she need all that paint?"

Christina's family lived in a rooftop apartment in the center of town, and while most teenage boys would be happier to be alone with their girlfriends, I was secretly pleased whenever her parents were around. They represented a world outside of Gburg, and for me that glimpse of the larger world was everything. I loved Sweden, but I didn't want to stay there. I took my job at Belle Avenue so seriously because I hoped that it would lead to bigger things—in France, because all great chefs had to do a stint in France, but also London and New York. I was interested in anybody and anything that represented the places I hadn't been, but wanted to see.

Christina's father, Jens, was an architect in the city planning department, and he would talk to me about the way a city's environment can influence people's lives. Like my father, he was the first white collar professional to come out of his family. Her mother, Aiko, had a little shop in the city center, where she sold Japanese imports and foreign novelties, everything from Hello Kitty to Snoopy. Sometimes, when I'd go over to Christina's house to hang out, her mother would make us Japanese snacks. The flavors blew my mind: This food seemed to be based on an entirely different calculation of flavor, texture, and balance. The first dish I remember her offering me was a plate of cucumber spears drizzled with white miso and topped with bonito flakes. Crisp, cold vegetables, earthy fermented sauce, and delicate slivers of fish that practically melted at the touch. Could that even be called a dish?

Yes, it could be called a dish. A great dish.

From that point on, I tried to look hungry whenever Aiko was at home. When she wasn't, Christina and I would cook together and argue about which Japanese condiments I could or couldn't use. I couldn't read the labels, of course, and even the translated ones meant nothing to me, so I was ready to taste and try everything.

A YEAR LATER, I had fully settled in at Belle Avenue. Hard work there was rewarded a number of ways. You could get a raise, you could get moved up in the *brigade*, or you could be sent away. To be sent away was the highest honor: It meant that you would be sent off to spend a week, a month, or a season doing a *stage*, which was an unpaid apprenticeship. Typically, your boss would find the placement for you, and then he'd send you as his representative, with encouragements and threats to do well by him. The idea was that you'd either come back, bringing those new techniques and skills you'd picked up with you, or that your boss's kindness would come back to him someday, in some form. Tony Bowman, the chef in charge of all hotel dining other than Belle Avenue, knew I wanted to see the world.

"Marcus," he said after we'd finished breaking down a banquet buffet one afternoon, "I'm going to send you to *stage* in Amsterdam."

I held off from calling my mother and telling her immediately so I could break the news to her and Dad at the same time, in person, over dinner.

"Amsterdam?" my father said. "I don't think that's such a good idea. I've traveled there for work and I don't think they have much in the way of food. And besides, it's a very druggy society. You could fall in with the wrong element."

I appealed to my mother. "Mom," I said, "I'm not messing up. I'm not out there drinking like a lot of the guys. I work and come home and that's it. Besides, you don't have to leave Göteborg to do drugs."

Mom agreed, but Dad held firm. "If they are willing to give you Holland now, something else will come in time. France is where you've always wanted to go. I think you should hold out for something better."

In one day, my whole world had come together and then, a few hours later, completely fallen apart. I didn't know enough about Amsterdam to argue with my father, and while I had never been reluctant to debate him, I felt I had to respect his wishes. After all, I still lived under his roof.

The next day, I looked at my shoes while I told Tony I couldn't go. He looked at me intensely, as if he were trying to bring my face into focus.

"I thought you were in charge of your life," he said. "You're eighteen now, Marcus, how come you're not in charge?"

PART TWO **CHEF**

TEN **SWITZERLAND**

THE JOURNEY TO INTERLAKEN TOOK THIRTY HOURS. IT BEGAN WITH A late-morning ferry from Göteborg to Denmark, during which the normally quiet boat was overtaken by boozy Danish college kids who started pounding overpriced beers from the snack counter even before the cranes of Göteborg harbor disappeared from sight. Passenger traffic was light that day, so I took my duffel to the far end of the cabin, away from the commotion, where I could stretch out on a bench with my bag for a pillow. As loud as the Danes were, I fell into a dead sleep. I'd had none the night before. Mats and I had been out all night, leaving me just enough time to pack my bag before dawn. I woke up to a staticky voice on the PA system announcing our arrival in the port town of Frederikshavn and to the gentle bump of the boat as it kissed the side of the pier.

Using the duffel's handles as straps, I slung the bag over my shoulders and headed out for the fifteen-minute walk to the train station. Because I'd made this same transfer traveling with my soccer teams many times before, and because I was still in a Scandinavian country, I felt more at home than abroad, a feeling that stayed with me all the way down through the peninsula of Jutland, until the train crossed over the border from Denmark to Germany.

I was going to Switzerland, to be a *commis* for six months at a famous resort hotel in Interlaken called Victoria Jungfrau.

My father had greeted the news of this job as he did anything that had to do with the physical world—through the lens of geography. "Ahh, you'll be right at the foot of the Jungfrau," he said, pulling an atlas from the shelf. "That's in the Bernese Alps." As he ran his index finger down the book's index, he squinted, scanning his memory for the details of Switzerland that mattered. He spread the open book across the kitchen table. "It is a landlocked country," he said, lips pursing in disapproval. His Smögen-born bias toward living near the ocean was immense. "But at least you'll be between two lakes. That's how the town got its name, of course. *Inter. Laken.*" He tapped at the three-mile-wide strip of land that bridged the Thun and Brienz lakes. "There you are. And you have the Aare River running through." Once again, he narrowed his eyes, then talked about how significant water was for the Swiss: how it had been harnessed for centuries as a source of manufacturing power; how two of Europe's most significant rivers, the Rhône and the Rhine, started there; and, of course, how important it was when it came in the form of snow, to support the ski tourism that held up a large portion of the economy.

My mother passed through the room just as he finished his assessment. She looked over his shoulder at the map.

"Is it cold there?" she asked. "Will he need to bring extra sweaters?"

First and foremost, I had packed my knives—my most treasured possessions—which I'd wrapped in the leather roll my grandmother had made for me.

"Don't buy that," she'd said when she saw how much the rolls cost. She went and studied them in a store downtown, then came home and fashioned one herself, sturdier and more handsome than the cheap nylon ones she'd seen.

I wrapped the roll, my French pepper mill, and a Japanese sharpening stone Christina had given me inside the two chef's jackets that my Belle Avenue coworkers had presented to me as a going-away gift. On my last day of work the hotel chef, Tony, had handed them to me, which seemed fitting since he was the one who had arranged the gig for me at Victoria in the first place. He'd been a *commis* there himself, ten years before.

"Don't fuck this up," he told me. "I'll hear about it if you do."

My other essentials included jeans, running shoes and the turquoise blue Converse sneakers I wore for work, my Walkman, and a pile of fresh notepads and pens so I could write down everything I saw, learned, and tasted.

Back in Göteborg, I'd left some ends tied up more cleanly than others. Belle Avenue was easy: Tony was part of the establishment and he was the one sending me away, so everyone treated me as a graduate rather than a traitor. My girlfriend, Christina, on the other hand, didn't want to let go. When Tony made me the offer, I thought the timing was perfect. Christina had gotten an offer to model in Japan, a place she had wanted to know better and where her half-Swedish looks would definitely give her a competitive edge. We would both move on to the rest of our lives, I figured. It was time.

Christina saw it differently.

"I'll wait for you, then," she said when I told her about Switzerland.

"No, no," I said. "You should go to Tokyo and live with your aunt."

"No. I'll wait for you right here."

I didn't want her to wait. I didn't want to have any ties to Sweden beyond my family. I was moving on.

"I don't know when I'll be back," I said.

"That's OK," she said. "I'll wait."

After a point, I stopped trying to talk to her. We were breaking up, as far as I was concerned. Cooking was the only thing I had room for. Cooking was the only thing I wanted to make room for.

There was nothing clean about my last loose end, which was the question of what I was going to do about the army. Sweden may not have taken part in a war for the last hundred years—not officially, at least—but it maintained an army, and service was mandatory. In my father's generation, this duty was something you never questioned. In mine, and especially among my *blatte* friends who felt only marginally welcome in the country much of the time, the army seemed obsolete, a waste of time.

But once I had turned eighteen, my father started to bring up the topic every now and then. "Which station do you hope to go to?" he'd ask out of the blue. "You definitely don't want to end up in Lapland."

"Don't worry about it," I'd say. "I'm not going."

This was a position my father simply couldn't understand. To him, the only reason you should be excused from military service was if you were mentally ill, physically incapacitated, or, consistent with his generation's ideas of maleness and gender, gay. I was none of those, so I should go. I suspect, too, that he felt I was a little too close to my mother, too protected by her. Maybe my cooking even baffled him. The army would make a man out of me.

"You can do something that has nothing to do with guns," my mother suggested, trying to broker a compromise. But it wasn't the guns; it was that nothing about the army fit into my dream of becoming a chef.

POLITICAL BOUNDARIES between one country and another are artificial divisions, of course, and in Europe, they have shifted more times than anyone can count. But almost the moment the train crossed from the small town of Padborg, Denmark, into the slightly larger town of Harrislee, Germany, something broke open inside of me. I felt like I was at the beginning of a new path, one I'd forged by myself. This was a job I'd gotten, that I'd earned, and for the first time in my life, I recognized the weight of adult responsibility and welcomed it. By the time I changed trains in the Hamburg station, the comforts of Scandinavia seemed fully behind me.

When I finally felt hungry enough to get food, I walked to the café car and came back with a large, buttery soft pretzel and a fat pink wurst on a bun, swimming in sauerkraut and sweet brown mustard. I conducted the transaction in German, but it wasn't pretty: Every time I opened my mouth I wished I'd practiced more, instead of goofing off with Mats during the three years of German I'd had in school. German was the language of business at Victoria Jungfrau, Tony had told me, and in order to keep up, I'd need to get fluent fast.

Our route took a fairly direct path south, and every couple of hours, we'd stop in a town big enough that I recognized the name: Hannover, then Göttingen, then Darmstadt. The closer we got to Munich, the more languages I heard, and I recognized many of the tongues of my *blatte* GAIS teammates. Poles and Slavs boarded, and when I switched trains again, this time in Munich, my seatmates were a Greek family who had brought a multicourse picnic with them. They spread paper napkins across their laps and ate olives and pita bread they dipped in garlicky eggplant spread or covered with slices of feta they cut from a block with a pocketknife. I tried not to stare, but the mother must have seen me sneaking glances. She put two dark dolma rolls on a napkin and handed them to me, smiling and nodding as she pressed them into my palm.

"*Efkharistó,*" I said, using the one Greek word I'd learned from hanging out at my friend Tomas's apartment. Thank you.

The mother laughed. I'd probably butchered the word, but she seemed pleased that I would even try. I bit into the soft, fat finger of the stuffed grape leaf. I had tasted these once or twice before at a café in Gburg, but they'd always seemed too dense to me, the rice packed too tight and with little flavor beyond the tang of the leaf. These dolmas, though, were different. They were lighter. They had currants and pine nuts mixed in with the rice, a hint of fresh tomato sauce and lemon juice. They were also warm, as if they had been made that very morning. I closed my eyes and smiled to show how much I liked what I was eating, and from that point on she fed me as if I were another one of her children.

Beyond Munich, it wasn't only the passengers who were different. The landscape had grown progressively greener—June in central Germany was certainly further along than June in Denmark, but now we were heading southwest and into the Alps. As soon as we crossed into Switzerland, the train started to climb and the mountains exploded all around us. My mother would love this, I thought. They looked just like the ones in *The Sound of Music*, one of her favorite films.

My last transfer was in Bern, where I moved from a sleek, modern train to its older, clunkier cousin, its smaller cars better equipped to make the tight turns and bends of the last twenty-five miles we had to cover in order to reach Interlaken. Once again, a new crop of people boarded the train with me. These people spoke only German, and they seemed more reserved; they were quieter and more formal in their interactions with each other, even when they were obviously family. There were still picnics here and there, but now it was wine, cured meats, and hard cheeses. People spoke quietly. No one offered food to strangers.

I tried to nap, to catch as much rest as I could, not knowing what the situation would be when I arrived, whether I would be expected to work the dinner shift on the day of my arrival. But sleep was impossible. I was so close now that I felt like everything I saw through the window belonged to my new life—each chalet, each cow, each distant peak. I would see these again, I thought. Soon I would know these places. I would learn them as I was starting to learn each new world I entered. Through food.

EVERYTHING ABOUT Victoria Jungfrau signaled grandeur. The sprawling rectangular building, long and white, had a massive central tower with a slate-roofed dome. Wrought-iron balconies covered its facade and overlooked a perfectly trimmed green at the center of town. A man wearing a white jumpsuit clipped away at the hedges in front of the hotel.

In my broken German, I asked for the staff entrance, and the man pointed his clippers toward the back.

The rear of the building had been updated to make it into a modern, highly functioning point of entry, with cement loading docks and corrugated steel ramps for all the food trolleys that came and went. In the office inside, a young woman in a dark suit rose from her desk and put out her hand.

"Hello, Herrn Samuelsson," she said. "I am Simone. *Wie gehts es Ihnen?*" How are you?

She gathered up a handful of the other new guys who'd been waiting in the conference room and led us on a tour of Victoria at breakneck speed, mixing German and English the entire time. She took us to the staff dormitory, a separate building, so that we could drop our bags in our rooms. Mine was small and immaculate, and outfitted with a single bed, a clothes cupboard, and a sink. A single window cast a ray of afternoon light onto a cracked mirror above the dresser, and the walls showed the scuffmarks of interns who'd come before me. I loved it.

We reconvened in the hall and walked back to the main building. More than two hundred guest rooms and suites spread across three stories and, below them, a lobby floor that was nothing short of palatial. I took note of the stained-glass windows, gold-framed mirrors, fountains, atriums, and elaborately carved moldings I wasn't likely to see again. Finally, we passed a dining room far more opulent than Belle Avenue's, with upholstered chairs and coffered ceilings, sparkling chandeliers, and columns carved from marble. Suddenly, I saw

Belle Avenue for what it was, a hotel restaurant wedged in off to the side of a lobby, rather than a grand space intended for its purpose from the start.

"You'll see the kitchen soon enough," Simone said, "but now we go to the staff cafeteria, where you can wait until Chef Stocker is ready for you. It will be twenty-five minutes." Simone left us with a brisk good-bye and good luck. *"Auf Wiedersehen. Viel Glück."*

The staff cafeteria was called the Chatterbox and its food line reminded me of elementary school, with trays at the start and a shelf to push them along as you picked out your meal. A mix of round and rectangular tables, eight-tops and six-tops, filled the dining area. Picture windows and French doors led to an outdoor terrace with additional seating.

The other newcomers walked around the Chatterbox, then drifted out onto the terrace to smoke. I bought an apple and ate it while scanning the bulletin board. One corner was dedicated to staff-to-staff messages, people looking to sell cars and skis or to find roommates for apartments in town. But most of the notices came from management. Praise for beating the forecasted number of room reservations that week. Warning that breakage was up. Employee of the month. Polaroids from the latest hotel team soccer match. Articles about the World Cup surrounded by flags from the countries of staff members whose teams had made it to the finals.

When I'd covered every inch of the board, I walked over to the tables, where one guy was sitting by himself, kicking back with a magazine.

"Can I sit here?" I asked in English.

"Of course," he said with a wide, welcoming smile.

I liked Mannfred right away. He was from a town just on the other side of Lake Thun, where his father had a small restaurant that served traditional Swiss food. While Mannfred was tall and blond and just as polite as every Swiss person I had met, he had a warmth that made him stand out from the rest. He was happy to speak to me in English, thanks to having spent a year as an exchange student in Australia, and we chatted easily. To me, Mannfred was a veteran—he'd been at the hotel a full month already, and he was willing to explain everything I needed to know, from where the bathroom was to which chefs had the biggest tempers. We all got the *Zimmer stunde*, the room hour, he explained, and the one chance each day to fit in all of your life—laundry, letter writing, and, if you'd been out the night before, sleep—between shifts. By the end of that first conversation, he'd invited me to go mountain biking with him. I'm going to like it here, I thought, even as I turned him down.

"I don't have a bike," I said.

"We can always get you a bike to borrow," he said. That was Mannfred; he was a problem solver.

After precisely twenty-five minutes, Simone returned to round up the newbies. She led us to the kitchen, which was bigger than any I'd ever seen and gleaming with sleek, pristine equipment. Tony at Belle Avenue had given me a heads-up about the Swiss and their machines before I left. "Just look at their watches," he had said. "They're like that about everything. Perfectly engineered and machined. Nothing's ever more than a couple of years old. You'll see."

I saw. We were there in the lull between lunch and dinner service, so everything had just been wiped down, but even when it got busy later, you weren't going to find anyone smoking over the pasta pot, the way they did at La Toscana, a family-style Italian joint in Gburg I had worked in while I was still a student. More striking still was that I couldn't smell anything except for the faintest odor of detergent and bleach. Nothing. How could they possibly have produced hundreds of meals a couple of hours earlier with not one hint of garlic or lemon or butter lingering in the air?

We stood in a cluster filling the central aisle of the kitchen. A door opened, and in walked a man trailed by a half-dozen cooks. Never mind that underneath the skyscraper-high chef's hat, he was shorter and older than the others, slightly stooped and walking with a trace of a limp: He was in charge. You could tell from his bearing, the way he set the pace and the others fell in behind him, the way he stopped short knowing that they were keyed to his every move. He wore a spotless white apron, its strings crossed and brought around to the front, where they were tied in a bow above his thick midsection. His chef's coat and knife-creased black pants were perfectly clean and pressed, and he wore a pair of black Doc Martens boots. His name was embroidered on the left side of his jacket, Herrn Stocker, and sticking out from the breast pocket was the bowl of a small gold spoon.

Simone spoke. "This is Herrn Stocker, everyone. Chef?"

Herrn Stocker gave Simone a nod—gratitude and dismissal combined in one quick tuck of the chin—and silently looked over the lot of us. Once he got to the end of our line, he gave a second nod of dismissal. Somehow, all of us knew not to move. Instead, we waited as Stocker made a quarter turn and continued down the main aisle of the kitchen and back out the door, his pack of chefs silently falling in behind.

I SLEPT FITFULLY IN MY NEW QUARTERS, relieved when the alarm clock began ringing at six the next morning and my day could finally begin. At the end of my hall, two *commis* were lined up ahead of me, waiting for the shower. Each was in and out in less than five minutes. I followed their lead and was dressed and ready in no time. The formality of my new home had started to sink in, and as I crossed the back courtyard between the dorm and the cafeteria, I looked down and gave silent thanks to my mother for her obsession with ironing. My chef's coat and pants barely showed the wear of the thirty-hour road trip they'd just been through. On the other hand, the turquoise Converse sneakers, one of two pairs I'd brought along, looked a lot less cool than they had in the Belle Avenue kitchen.

Thirty minutes before my shift began, I walked into the Chatterbox for breakfast. Unlike my first visit, the cafeteria was jammed with people and the tables had self-selected into tribes. The dining-room waiters, decked out in black suits and ties, sat with their backs straight and their cutlery properly lined up next to their plates. The

Portuguese dishwashers and cleaners sat together, their language an easy singsong compared to the harsh, guttural staccato of German that surrounded them. Busboys sat with busboys. Cooks sat with cooks, never more than a couple of stations above or below their own.

The only free agents in the room were the so-called international students, in from Mumbai and Tokyo and Buenos Aires. These were either hospitality junior execs sent by their companies to learn from Switzerland's renowned hospitality industry, or rich kids whose parents were indulging a whim or desperately investing in something to keep Junior occupied. Members of this group didn't observe the hierarchy; they sat wherever they wanted.

The food in the cafeteria line looked good—not the sloppy-seconds kitchen staff often got—but I could already feel my stomach tensing so I grabbed a coffee. I took my cup to a table where a guy wearing a cook's uniform was sitting. He looked to be only a few years older, so he couldn't be too high up on the food chain.

"*Grüezi,*" he said, offering up the Swiss-German version of "good day." His greeting was formal, not the *hoi* I had already heard buddies our age calling to each other, but he was welcoming when I asked if I could join him. Jan came from the town of Thun, thirty minutes to the northwest, at the opposite end of the lake of the same name, and he'd been at Victoria for about eight weeks. I asked what the kitchen here was like, and his bottom line was a warning.

"If you work hard and stay out of trouble, he'll leave you alone."

"Who?"

"The boss," he said. "Mr. Stocker."

"Mr. Stocker?"

"Shhh," he whispered. "Not so loud. Don't say his name." Jan looked over at the wall clocks hanging above the newspaper rack. Four identical clocks were mounted beside each other, each displaying a different time. Each had an engraved plaque below it. *Paris. Moscow. New York. Interlaken.* The last clock read 6:45.

"We've got to go," he said, stacking his plate, glass, and coffee cup onto his tray.

I followed Jan at a pace most people would consider a jog. When we got to the kitchen, it was already in full action mode—chefs running around this way and that. Then I heard the loudest scream I had ever heard in my life.

"*Scheisse!*" Shit!

"Mr. Blom," Jan whispered. "The *sous-chef.*"

Blom was yelling at one of the cooks for messing up an order of eggs, then, with an exasperated look, threw up his hands and turned. In our direction.

"Look busy," Jan instructed, so I ducked into the nearest walk-in and began to order the vegetables. After a few minutes, I peeked out. Even more people were in the kitchen now, and they'd started to gather under a large bulletin board that had a schedule grid at its center. All conversations came to an abrupt halt when the door to the executive chef's office opened. Herrn Stocker entered the room, stopped just under the schedule, and addressed us.

"The new *commis* group, please."

We lined up and one by one stepped forward, said our names, got our assignments, and dropped back into formation. So much for avoiding the army, I thought, as the guys before me took their turns.

Blom, the *sous-chef,* announced our stations as Stocker stood and watched.

The kid before me, Johannes, got posted with the *saucier,* more or less the most desirable station in any kitchen, the one with the most prestige, the one that gets credited with taking any dish from competent to transcendent.

When my turn came, I stepped forward.

"Marcus Samuelsson," I said, somehow getting the words out without choking.

Blom consulted the clipboard in his right hand. "*Kräutergarten,*" he announced.

Herb garden? I might as well have been sent to Siberia. I said nothing and stepped back into the line.

Victoria's garden was a plot about three times the size of a large home garden, and at least a third of it was dedicated to herbs. The rows were neatly divided by wood-chipped paths, and at the end of each row, a metal marker bore the name of what was planted. My chef's whites stood out against the bright morning sun, but also against the green coveralls of the four permanent gardeners I worked alongside. I saw the other gardeners weeding, so I bent down and pulled up weeds, too, until the head gardener, Herrn Banholzer, appeared. Banholzer, a wiry man in his late fifties whose sun-soaked, leathery skin reminded me of Uncle Torsten and other men I knew who lived more outside than inside, gathered us around a row of empty service trolleys.

"Here is what we'll need today," he began, reading from a pocket-size notepad. Each gardener had to fill a trolley or two and each trolley had a specific destination: for room service; for the main kitchen; for the smaller kitchens of the cocktail lounge and the spa; and for any special off-site events.

In less than a minute, I was literally and figuratively in the weeds. It wasn't that Banholzer's accent was hard to understand, but he spoke quickly and with a flatness that made it hard to build a context in cases where I didn't know the word.

"Samuelsson, you will prepare the trolley for the *entremetier*," he said. "*Kartoffeln*. Two boxes . . ."

Not a problem to understand that *kartoffeln* was potatoes, thanks to my grandmother's tendency to sprinkle German words into her speech. Nor was *rhabarber* a problem, since it sounded so much like the Swedish word for rhubarb, *rabarber*. But *erdbeeren*? What the hell was that?

I pulled a scrap of paper out of my back pocket, the stub of a train ticket, and started to take notes. This new word I wrote out phonetically and circled it. By the time Banholzer finished with me and walked off, I had about ten words circled. I could have asked him to translate as he went along, but that went against the universal rule of kitchen work: Stay invisible unless you're going to shine. This was not a shining moment.

Fritz, the youngest of the gardeners, patiently helped me decipher the mystery words. When we got to *erdbeeren*, he laughed.

"Look down," he said, and there was a patch of strawberries at my feet.

"Erdbeeren," he said.

The garden wasn't where I wanted to be—in fact, I would have died if the guys at Belle Avenue knew I was out picking fruit instead of cooking—but that didn't keep me from enjoying the work. I snapped off the outer rhubarb stalks from their plants, dug up the potatoes and carrots, and snipped off the freshest, leafiest stems of the herbs: sage, thyme, rosemary, mint. To pick the fava beans, I reached through the gray green leaves on the plants' bushy stalks to snap off the pods. The weather was beautiful and everything smelled good, including the dirt.

After harvesting, I washed off the loot in one of three outdoor sinks and arranged it all carefully on the top tray of my trolley. Following Fritz's lead, I wheeled my full trolley to the door of Banholzer's office, a little room next to the toolshed, with big windows and a door that looked out over the beds. Banholzer had a pair of half glasses that he wore on a chain around his neck. To inspect my trolley, he balanced the glasses on the end of his long nose and went box by box, shelf by shelf.

"One more box of potatoes," he instructed, when he'd finished giving my work the once-over. "And then take it inside."

During that afternoon's break, I sat in the Chatterbox with Fritz and had a coffee. I told him I'd messed up by not picking enough potatoes.

"No way Banholzer could have let you go without criticizing something," Fritz said. "But he didn't *reject* anything you'd picked? He didn't throw anything out? That's unheard of." I beamed. I may have been relegated to being a garden gnome, but I was going to be the best damn garden gnome that they'd ever seen.

I must have been doing well enough, because after one week, Blom announced at our morning huddle that I would switch to Herrn

Thoner, the *entremetier*. The *entremetier* station prepared cooked vegetables, soups, eggs, and nonmeat entrées.

I was finally back on the front lines.

ONE OF MY GOOD FRIENDS in the Jungfrau kitchen turned out to be an Irishman named Gary Hallinan. Like so many of the Irish men and women I would meet in restaurant kitchens over my career, he was friendly and generous and easy to get along with. Gary—who had jet-black hair, pale skin, and a smile that cut deep dimples into his cheeks—never let the stress get to him. In fact, just exchanging a few words with him had the invaluable effect of bringing my blood pressure down. He was from a hotel family, had earned a degree in hotel management, had already worked at Dublin's posh Shelbourne Hotel, and would eventually go on to a very successful career in San Francisco, but the truth was that he wasn't much of a cook. At Victoria, his time in the kitchen was just a part of learning the ropes, and he approached it sportingly. One day, while trying to sharpen his knife against a long steel, Gary slipped and cut his arm pretty deeply.

The first-aid station was right outside Stocker's office, so Gary walked over and sat down on the floor in front of the office door as he waited for treatment.

Eventually Mr. Stocker came along, and as he came up to this injured man, blood everywhere, Gary looked up at him, and in the middle of what was probably true shock, still managed to keep the hierarchy front and foremost.

"I'm sorry, Mr. Stocker," he said. And then he passed out.

Stocker stepped over Gary, saying nothing, and went into his office, shutting the door behind him.

Which is not to say that Stocker wouldn't get vocal when he saw a screw-up in process. In another kitchen disaster, not long after Gary, a kid named Otto was put in charge of grinding meat for the day's meat loaves. Otto was German, so he had no problem understanding instructions, but he was distracted by the pressure, and in what would turn out to be his last day, he took a shortcut: He piled cubes of raw meat into the feeder tray that sat on top of the grinder. Normally, you would use a wooden dowel-like pusher to force the meat down the neck of the machine, where it would make contact with a spiraling auger that caught and cut the meat, forcing it out a side tube. Otto didn't have a pusher within reach, so he picked up the nearest substitute, a metal ladle. At first it worked well enough, but on one pass, he pushed the ladle too far down into the neck and the auger blade caught it. Otto didn't let go fast enough, and his arm was stuck in the machine, twisting his hand downward toward the pulverizing auger. The second that Otto realized he couldn't retract his arm, he let out a howl. Out of nowhere, it seemed, Stocker showed up and slammed off the power, two seconds before Otto's hand was ground into mincemeat. Stocker and a couple of others untwisted Otto's arm from the machine, and the whole while, Stocker never once asked if Otto was OK, he just berated him.

"Why the hell are you using the wrong tool?" he screamed. "What were you *thinking*? You were *this close* to losing your arm! Are you trying to get our department in trouble? Trying to get me fired?" While Stocker yelled, the few women who worked in the kitchen sobbed in the background. I simply turned my back and got to stirring a veal stock, wondering how Stocker could get onto the scene so fast. I came to learn that a great chef kept an extra eye on the lightweights, the lazy, and the nervous.

They were all dangerous, to themselves and to others, and Stocker couldn't afford to let them screw up. You don't lose your arm in a typical office job. And because of that, his *sous-chefs* were given the power to fire anyone they found wanting. Often, this was the druggies, the guys who spent all their time off up in Zurich—the best place to get drugs—and who showed up for the morning shift in sunglasses. No hard evidence was required, but the *sous-chefs* must have had some eyes and ears in the dorms, because in all my time there, when they picked someone to dismiss, they were never wrong. And when people got fired, they were erased. No one reminisced about them openly. No one even said their names.

Another way of weeding out the weak links was through on-the-spot tests. You might be going along in your shift, and suddenly Stocker would stop at your station and instruct you to perform a task.

"Chiffonade of basil," he'd bark, arms crossed. "*Sauce beurre blanc.*"

If you didn't respond fast enough or well enough, you were put on notice. If your game didn't shape up immediately, you were gone.

I took away lifelong lessons about staff management from Stocker, but I also learned about fairness. Stocker rewarded the hardworking crew in ways that mattered. If you did your job well, he made sure that your days off would be scheduled consecutively, so you could take advantage of Interlaken's central locale and take the night train to Paris or make the two-hour trip to Milan. If you didn't, he made sure you never got advance notice of your free days, which never came more than one by one.

The key, I realized, was to do the work and keep your mouth shut. This was easy for me on both fronts. I loved the work and I could barely speak the language.

I WASN'T A BOY SCOUT. Like everyone else at Victoria, I went out at night once the dinner shift ended, and definitely had my share of fun. Because I spoke English well, I had an edge with the backpacking Yankee girls who were passing through as part of their summer adventure between college terms and who liked European guys who would buy them beer. But no matter how late I'd been out, I showed up at work the next morning an hour early.

The kitchen at dawn reminded me of a soccer field before a big match. The grass is perfectly mowed; the field is empty of people but full of anticipation. It was the calm before the day's storm, and I used that time to get a jump on my tasks but also to study the menus and notices posted outside of Stocker's office. The menus were in French, Italian, and German, so I brought along my pocket dictionaries and my journal and I copied each one down, from appetizers to desserts, looking up whatever I didn't understand. I didn't want Stocker to see me, not that there was anything wrong with what I was doing. It was just that the less you put yourself in his line of vision, the better.

Just as I had stayed late working at Belle Avenue, I put in extra hours before and after my shifts, doing advance prep work in the mornings and meticulous cleanup at night. All I had to offer was my labor and my attention, and I was willing to give both. The only time I skipped out was for what had become, since my arrival, a daily ritual: throwing up. Every morning, I came into work and felt the familiar knot tie itself in my stomach. The knot would soon be followed by bile filling the back of my throat, and it was only a matter of time before I'd have to bolt to the bathroom. I'd experienced the problem now and then at my Göteborg jobs when the stress got too high, but now that I was completely without that hometown comfort zone, the frequency of the nausea ratcheted up to coincide with the increased pressures of the job.

For the most part, I was able to keep my nerves under wraps, doing my business quietly and then going right back to work. Until they installed a new key card entry system, and on the day the system went into effect, my card for the kitchen's exit door demagnetized at the least opportune time. I panicked, and then I spewed. As the spilled contents of my stomach dripped down the face of the door, three *sauciers* came along, deftly stepping past while nodding at me and saying only, "*Guten tag. Wie gehts*, Mr. Samuelsson." Take it easy.

As soon as I felt the first wave of queasiness each day, I looked for an opportunity to leave my station. I didn't want to be noticed, which meant I couldn't be away for more than five or six minutes. Health codes dictated that we leave our aprons in the kitchen so that we wouldn't get any bacteria on them in the bathroom. But if I put mine on a peg, it was like a red flag showing I was gone. So I wore it to the bathroom and left it outside the door.

Which bathroom to choose? When you spend enough time with your head in a toilet bowl, you become a connoisseur, and what you want is the cleanest and least used facility, which meant bypassing the toilets adjacent to the kitchen and instead taking an extra ninety seconds to go down a long hallway that led to the bathroom by the administrative offices and loading dock. Running through the halls would get you written up, so you had to walk as fast as possible without breaking the rules.

I took off my chef's coat and hung it on the peg inside the stall, making sure not to touch it again until I had thoroughly washed off. If no one else was in the bathroom, I could proceed undisturbed, but if other stalls were occupied, I would flush as I puked in order to cover the sound. Having food in my stomach made the process go faster, but I threw up even when I hadn't eaten, and the dry heaves took longer and were more physically taxing as my body cramped harder to expel what wasn't there. I carried mints in my pockets just for this daily episode, but I was careful not to pop in so many that I froze out my palate.

Wash off, pop a mint, coat back on, apron on, speed-walk back through the hall, and back to the station as if I'd never been away.

ELEVEN **STOCKER**

Every Sunday morning at eleven, the staff on duty convened in the kitchen for a fifteen-minute meeting known as *assemblé*. Stocker's *sous-chefs* would lay out a platter of good cold cuts and open a bottle of wine. It was a get-together for the kitchen only, not the front of the house, and Stocker used the time to announce who was getting promoted, how he felt last week's special events had gone, and what was on the schedule for the week.

Sunday mornings were always busy, and as we stopped our work to attend this meeting, we all tried to act calm and relaxed when we were anything but. We were all dying for the meeting to be over quickly so we could get back to our stations and the relentless work of covering our asses, but at the same time, *assemblé* was that rare moment when we, especially the lowly staffers like me, felt like we were part of the bigger picture: actual members of the team.

When you have a *brigade* of sixty people working for you, you need a consistent method of letting them know what's going on. The wall postings and daily *sous-chef* meetings got some of that job done, but for interns like me, *assemblé* was a rare chance to hear directly from the general's mouth—and in a setting where he was not yelling at you for some mistake you'd made. This was no holding-hands moment, of course. The hierarchy of the kitchen was zealously maintained, even in meetings: Line cooks and *commis* stood in the back of the room and said nothing.

My favorite part of *assemblé* was when Stocker talked about upcoming events. Because he had traveled so widely, he took a real interest in the international travelers who made up more than 80 percent of the hotel's guests, and he would tweak the menu accordingly. On a week when we had several Arab parties coming in, he would tone down the pork entrées and amp up the vegetables and fish. When a group of wealthy Japanese people came in for a week of skiing, lots of sticky rice and exotic mushrooms suddenly appeared on the menu. He was very clear that our guest population was not homogenous, and we did our job well not only when they were happy with what they had ordered, but when, before they had arrived, we had the experience and ingenuity to figure out what the guests might want, before they knew they wanted it. When Stocker sensed how many customers were making special requests that had more to do with health than palate, he developed a spa-cuisine submenu and hired a full-time dietician.

The presence of Margrit, the dietician, a beautiful young woman with dark hair and blue eyes, completely threw the rest of us. She was not only the rare female in the kitchen, she was a female with privileges: She worked out of Stocker's office, was the only non-chef to sit in on our meetings, and, most alarming of all, was treated by Stocker with a respect that bordered on deference. She helped Stocker tweak

the menu and together they composed new dishes that would be at-
tractive to guests with diabetes, heart conditions, and various food
allergies. Heart-healthy symbols on menus are commonplace now,
but in the early nineties, it was practically unheard of even in finer
hotels. I was a cocky nineteen-year-old at the time, and back then, I
dismissed the guests who asked for special menus as finicky or unad-
venturous, not real eaters. But Stocker's example nurtured my respect
for guests with unique dietary needs, and for chefs as smart businessmen. More important, watching my boss interact with Margrit taught
me an invaluable lesson for an up-and-coming chef: He didn't live to
torture us, he lived to give the guests the best service possible.

Stocker was a master at many things, but when it came to banquets and large formal affairs that numbered up to 1,500 attendees, he
was a genius. Everybody's been to a rubber-chicken banquet where
the food was a cold, bland disaster, where one table or more sat without their dinners while everyone else was finishing dessert. This never
happened at Victoria. Stocker could get a thousand meals out of the
kitchen in a flash, all of it hot and all of it cooked to perfection.

He did this mainly by making great use of all that insane Swiss
machinery. He had purchased powerful freezers to chill-shock vegetables blanched the day before the event. We plunged the vegetables
into hot water, then scooped them out and immediately arranged
them beautifully onto plates, covered the plates with foil, and put
them onto trolleys that we rolled into the freezer. By chilling them so
quickly we arrested the cooking: Peppers stayed red and spinach
stayed green. Like I said, genius.

Stocker also used his armada of carefully calibrated ovens to make
roasts similar to the *sous-vide* method that is so popular today, cooking
them for hours at super-low temperatures so as not to sacrifice tenderness or moistness. By doing so much ahead, we could focus on
putting the pieces together all at once when the moment of truth
came. In Stocker's giant warming ovens, we could reheat sixty vegetable plates at a time, and then transfer them to the long counter that
ran down the center of the kitchen while the line cooks sliced meat or

finished sauces. From the second that first plate hit the kitchen counter to the last waiter placing a finished plate in front of a guest out in
the ballroom, no more than eight minutes had elapsed.

THREE WEEKS AFTER I'D ARRIVED AT VICTORIA, I was in my room during
afternoon break when someone came to tell me I had a call at the
communal pay phone at the end of the hall. *"Hej, Marcus. Det här är
Jens, Christina's pappa."* Why would he be making such an expensive
international call to his daughter's ex-boyfriend? The minute I got on
the phone, I sensed trouble. Christina wouldn't get out of her bath-
robe, her dad explained. She had been depressed ever since I left and
he and Aiko, Christina's mother, were worried. The only thing that
might lift her spirits was if she came down to Interlaken for a visit.

To be honest, I didn't want her to come. But I had been raised to
be respectful of my elders, so I couldn't find a way to say no. At nineteen, how do you tell a man that your relationship with his daughter
had been little more than a fling and that the fling was over and that
you were working now and no longer found his nice but kind of clingy
daughter to be very much fun?

"I'm working fourteen-hour shifts," I said in a feeble attempt to
dissuade him, but he was insistent. It'd be a short visit, he promised.
We hung up the phone with the agreement that she'd arrive by the
end of that week.

When I got back to my room, I paced back and forth trying to
sort out my thoughts. (In my room, that meant three steps one way,
three steps back.) What had I just said yes to? What kind of message
would it send to the management of this elite Swiss resort that I was
trying to desperately convince that I was more than an able kitchen
laborer? I needed them to see me as a chef in the making, not a black
Swedish kid with a girlfriend and one foot back in Gburg. That would
not be a good look. Not a good look at all.

Christina came and, unexpectedly, I was happy to see her. Somewhere between home and Interlaken, she'd climbed out of whatever

funk she'd been in, and I have to admit: It was a kind of relief to be around someone who knew me well, who could speak Swedish and catch me up on life back home. And, of course, to sleep with each night. But I also didn't want anything or anyone to get in the way of my work commitments, and I told her as much. She had to lie low. "If you go out, use the side exit," I told her. That was the door least likely to put her in the path of one of my bosses. "Or wait here and do your thing. Whatever. Just be cool, OK?"

I'd half hoped Christina would stay in the room, writing letters and reading. But she was too curious, and she headed out almost every day to wander around the town or take day trips: a boat across Lake Brienze one day, a funicular ride up to the view-filled Harder Kulm the next. Half the time, when I came back to the room during my afternoon break, she would be gone, and I wouldn't see her until after my shift, when we'd either hang out in the room or head over to Balmers, the bar popular with English speakers, where she charmed everyone we met.

One afternoon on her seventh or eighth day, after I'd put my laundry in the dorm washer, Christina dropped her bombshell.

"By the way," Christina said, "I'm applying for a job here."

I flipped. "You're kidding, right?"

"I talked to this nice girl in human resources, and she said they'd be very interested in hiring someone who spoke Japanese." At least 20 percent of Jungfrau Victoria's guests were Japanese; how perfect to have on hand a pretty girl who spoke French and Japanese, not to mention English and Swedish.

Christina searched my face, waiting for it to mirror the excitement she felt, but I was having a hard time faking enthusiasm. I was on a carefully plotted path to finding success as an international chef. I was on rung two of more than two dozen I'd have to climb before I reached my goal. I couldn't bear the thought of being thrown off course. This is not good, I thought. This was not the plan.

"Fine," I said, finally relenting. "But no one here can know we're together."

Christina was not daunted by my tepid response. "OK," she said. "I'll come back in the fall and put in a formal application."

MOST OF THE LETTERS that came to my wooden mail slot outside the Chatterbox that summer were from Christina or my family. I wrote to them, too, but most of my correspondence was devoted to job inquiries. I sent letters inquiring about kitchen positions all over the world. This was in the pre-computer days, and word of mouth was the way job news traveled. A new *commis* would come in with glowing reports of the last place he'd worked, and ten eyebrows would go up as his peers made notes to themselves to follow up. Anywhere I saw racks of tourist brochures, I picked up pamphlets from hotels and applied for work. I had my rules, though: only three stars or more.

"Why set the bar so high, Marcus?" my father would say. "*Three* stars? Why not take something easier to get into and work your way up? Why make it so hard?"

My logic was simple: I wanted to learn from the best so I could be the best. The letter writing, my painfully slow typing, the proofreading all felt like a nightly round of *mise en place*. Everything had to be just so. And yet, for every twenty I sent out, I'd get one response, usually a curt "not right now." I'd file those away for later, taking them at their word and keeping a flicker of hope alive, resolving to try again and maybe get a different response. Whenever I retrieved an unfamiliar envelope from my box, that flicker turned into a flame. So when I saw the stationery from Nice's famous Hotel Negresco, I immediately put it in my back pocket and counted the minutes until afternoon break, when I could open the letter in the privacy of my room.

"Monsieur Samuelsson," it began, and right away I could tell this letter was much better than a "not right now." If I were to find myself in Nice, it said, I was welcome to come to their kitchen and see what positions were available. The Negresco was home to Jacques Maximin, the executive chef who had made the hotel's reputation and produced scores of great young chefs: Alfred Portale, Joachim Splichal, Alain Allegretti, and the chocolatier Jacques Torres.

As soon as I could score a couple of days off, I hopped on a train and headed south. All along the way, I alternated between reading the French cookbook I'd brought along and calculating my next steps. Once I got the Negresco job, I would not cut short the Victoria contract—that would be a no-no. But as soon as it was up, I'd go to Nice, and from there, maybe I'd head for Paris.

I walked from the Nice train station to the palm-tree-dotted waterfront Promenade des Anglais. The Negresco sat at the center of the Promenade, among a strip of art deco palaces, all of them looking out onto the Cote d'Azur and its brilliant blue waters. In the late afternoon light, the sun low enough to illuminate the building's magnificent belle epoque facade and its unmistakable pink dome, I steadied my breathing and reminded myself to put one foot in front of the other.

Once I was inside, in carefully practiced French, I asked for the kitchen.

"The chef is not here," one cook said. "Come back in an hour."

I wandered along the beachfront, too distracted to appreciate the women sunbathing topless in their rented beach chairs, waiters bringing them cool drinks and fresh towels. When I returned, I got the same answer.

"Chef is not here. Come back in an hour."

The third time I walked into the kitchen, I was steered to an imperious man in his midforties with a half-buttoned chef's coat and a tremendous beak of a nose that he raised up in order to look down at me.

"Who are you?"

"I'm Marcus Samuelsson, here from Victoria Jungfrau." I showed him the letter. "I'd like to work for you."

His expression bordered on amusement.

"*Non*," he said. "We don't have anything." And then he walked away.

Common practice was to humor the *commis* who'd traveled from so far with a tryout for a day or two—kitchens could always use an extra hand—but I wasn't being extended even that courtesy. What made it worse was that now I was without a tryout and a warm bed—as a room for the night was the usual exchange for the free labor.

I left, devastated. There were other beautiful hotels along the Promenade des Anglais, but I wasn't willing to take second best. Or maybe it was that having spent all my bravado on the Negresco, I couldn't risk being rejected by a second-tier hotel just because of the color of my skin. Fuck it, I thought, and caught the next train back to Interlaken.

I made it a point not to dwell on the matter of race. I believed in my knife skills, and my sense of taste, and my capability to listen and to get things done. I was never afraid of hard work. Every place I'd worked in so far was a success for me because once I had my whites on and started working, there was no doubt that I would be the last man standing, regardless of whom I was up against. One ignorant chef who couldn't see past the color of my skin was not going to stop me. I'd go back to Victoria, learn everything I could, and, eventually, people would have no choice but to say yes.

WITH CHRISTINA BACK HOME and out of the picture, I had been able to return my full focus to work, and my reward was to be moved to a new station frequently, exactly the kind of exposure I'd hoped for. *Entremetier, viande, pâtissier*—these were not simply descriptions anymore, they were essential elements of a magical experience that started when a guest checked in. During my stint with the *entremetier,* I learned to make a delicious summer avocado soup, creamy with coconut milk, garnished with pink grapefruit and pink peppercorns. When I was on *viande,* I sautéed a knuckle of veal with carrots, onions, and garlic, deglazed it with white wine, then cooked the juices down into a rich, meaty syrup. With *pâtissier,* I made hundreds of raspberry and champagne mille-feuille, each one garnished with a scoop of champagne sorbet, each plate adorned with a swirl of buttery caramel glaze. *Mormor* always asked me what was it like to dine in a five-star hotel restaurant. I told her that I still didn't know. But I did know that to cook at Victoria was to go to bed every night with a taste of perfection on your tongue that lingered, even after you had brushed your teeth.

No matter what my assignment, that was the prevailing code, and when I finally settled in to a more permanent placement in the kitchen, I joined the honor guard. The *garde manger sous-chef* was a cantankerous, exacting Brit named Paul Giggs.

Mannfred liked to say that if you wanted to make it in Stocker's army, you had to match your heartbeat to his. Stocker was a Picasso in the kitchen: gifted, egotistical, bullish, and brutal, but an artist through and through. Giggs, on the other hand, was a heat-seeking missile. It just so happened that he was a chef, but one imagined that the experience of working for him would be the same if he ran a basketball team or a crew of bank robbers: You did what he said, and you did it quickly. If you wanted in with Giggs, you had to buy into more than his vision, you had to fall in, lockstep, with his methods. What Giggs excelled at was breaking staff the way cowboys broke down wild horses. This put him in good standing with Stocker, but almost no one else. The cheese manager did not appreciate Giggs reducing the cheese girl to tears when she wrapped the Stilton and the aged cheddar in the same plastic wrap. She thought she was conserving materials; he thought, and he told her quite publicly, that she appeared to have been born without a brain, and was putting the hotel's very reputation on the line, besides. We chopped, cooked, and tasted our way to perfection because we ran on fear: fear that the chef would not like our work, fear that the chef would not like us, fear that a single misstep could get us humiliated or, worse, fired.

Giggs combed through the kitchen staff and picked out all the outcasts and English speakers for himself. Our crew had Jews, Asians, women (still a rarity in the kitchen), and me, a black Swede. Maybe he figured that if we'd made it that far without the advantage of being in the majority, there was a chance we had both resilience and ambition, both of which he demanded. Since we all had obstacles to overcome, most of us worked our asses off to stay where we were. He knew how to ride that, to push us to the very edge without losing us. He would forgive inexperience, but he had no patience for laziness, and there was no room on his team for drunks or druggies. He would dismiss you just as easily for the hint of impropriety as he would for shitty performance.

To join Giggs's ranks was an honor and a risk. There were already plenty of warring factions in the kitchen: The Germans and the Swiss hated each other, every one of the sixty people who staffed the kitchen was in competition for Stocker's attention, and pretty much all of the other *sous-chefs* couldn't stand Giggs. If Stocker had any problem with Giggs's abrasive personality, he overlooked it because he understood that it was in service of his goal. Stocker was worldly but so was Giggs. He had traveled widely and spoke several languages, including Swiss-German, and if foreign guests needed a special meal, Stocker turned to Giggs and our station prepared it.

Working *garde manger* was part finesse and part butcher shop. The first time I volunteered to break down a whole lamb, Giggs laughed at me. But none of the other *commis* had volunteered, and I could tell he was impressed, at least enough to let me fail on my own initiative. On the next meat delivery, I went into the meat locker and asked for help, working step-by-step under the watchful eye and loud mouth of Franz, Giggs's *chef de partie*. When Franz revved up the chain saw and handed it to me, the buzz of the motor brought back the turbot incident at Belle Avenue, but wimping out was not an option. When he wasn't calling me an idiot, Franz actually imparted useful information, like why it was important to cut in the refrigerated room so that the fat would stay firm. If it warmed up enough to melt, that's when blades could slip. How we saved the restaurant money by doing this work ourselves and not paying a premium for the discrete parts of the animal. He showed me how to remove the filet, kidneys, and sweetbreads with a small knife and how to saw down the bones for stock. Everything had a purpose and a destination. The finest cuts, like the filet, went to La Terraza, the shanks would be braised for Stube, and the fat went with the trimmings for sausage. (La Terraza was the hotel's fine dining establishment, Stube the more casual pub.)

We got to the leg, which needed to be deboned, filled with thyme and garlic, and set aside for the saucier. I plunged my knife into the flesh, rooting around for the bone.

"*Scheisse! Dümmling!*" Franz yelled. "What's in that woolly head of yours? I know it's not a brain!"

He took the fillet knife from me and cut *along* the leg muscles rather than through them, lifting out a miraculously clean bone at the end. I loved this part of my time in Switzerland. There was so much knowledge in Stocker's team, from the top on down to the line cooks. A guy like Franz could talk smack all day about my Afro, my lack of brains, my mother, her alleged lack of virtue. I didn't care because I was learning to butcher from one of the best and once that knowledge was in me, it belonged to me.

OF ALL THE KITCHEN'S STATIONS, the *garde manger* did the heaviest lifting when it came to banquets. Other stations had their responsibilities, but we prepared the bulk of the food: platter upon platter of sausages and cured meats, sliced cold calves' brain on beds of lettuces and herbs, chilled cream of asparagus soups, smoked halibut with horseradish cream, and eggs in aspic, all of it beautifully laid out on tiered, linen-covered tables. Giggs had a special eye for flourishes, so we also learned how to chainsaw ice blocks into eagles, mold sugar gum paste into flowers, and carve elaborate designs into the rinds of melons.

The first time Giggs handed me a felt-tipped marker and told me to cover a plate in plastic wrap, I thought he'd gone off the deep end.

"Draw your food," he commanded, by which he meant he wanted the vegetables artfully arranged. "If you've arranged your veggies beautifully," he explained, "when it gets to the meat guy, he will respect the plate more. He won't just push everything aside to get his filet on there."

I'd been wrong when I said Giggs was merely a drill sergeant who served Stocker's vision. I would eventually learn that all chefs worth their mettle have their own styles and their own passions, but every single one of them can go from zero to asshole quicker than the average Joe. You have to be willing to be a jerk. Otherwise it's not worth it, the years of apprenticeship, the never Wall Street–level money, the ungrateful diners, the misfit miscreants you count on to execute each service flawlessly, not to mention the prima donna behavior of all those raw ingredients—the coquettish egg whites that may or may not fluff properly for you today; the potatoes that may decide that today is the day that they will burn, not crisp; the tomatoes that didn't ripen because of an unexpected heat wave. As a chef, you are at the mercy of the farmer, the butcher, the fishmonger, the weather, and God.

Giggs was a bruiser who came from humble roots, working-class Sheffield, an English city south of Manchester. He'd killed and sold chickens in the local market at age twelve, and the closest thing to fancy food he knew growing up was a can of blood pudding. It was his inherent love of food and an ability to work harder than anyone around him that got him out. His biggest break was to get a job on "Lizzie," the RMS *Queen Elizabeth* luxury ocean liner that ferried passengers across the Atlantic until 1968. His exacting standards, withering sarcasm, and penchant for publicly ridiculing his staff always had, at their base, a loyalty to upholding quality. His arrows stung, no doubt, but they were shot democratically; he picked on everyone equally. With one exception. As someone who'd earned every penny he ever spent, he had even less patience for wealthy guys who had no drive. As far as Giggs was concerned, to grow up awash in opportunity and then *not* do something with yourself was a sin of the greatest proportions. The rest of us committed more common crimes, which he relentlessly policed.

Giggs would send you back to your room if your shoes weren't polished.

"You're not respecting me!" he'd shout.

If we had a banquet coming up for 124 Mercedes executives, and someone was foolish enough to round the number up to 130, he'd scream about his food costs being jacked up for no good reason.

"What the fuck makes you think you're prepared for a five-star establishment such as this? Whatever it is, you're sorely fucking mistaken!"

If Giggs had kicked our butts once too many times in a given week, we'd go to Mannfred's parents' on our day off. His mother would cook for us and coddle us until we were fortified enough to return. Mannfred was one year younger than I was and nowhere near as experienced in soccer, but we played for the hotel's team and helped them win the local hospitality league tournament. Little by little, I could see my grown-up life come together—a lot of work, a little play. My friendship with Mannfred helped me keep the balance.

I CLEANED UP THE STATION after service one night, and when I was done, I reported to Giggs so he could sign me out.

"You're done?" he asked.

This usually made me think twice, but on this night, I'd been extra careful, so I stuck to my guns.

"Yes, Herrn Giggs."

"You're ready? Really? You think you're ready?" he kept asking as he inspected each shelf of the walk-in. When he got to a plastic tub of aspic that I'd carefully wrapped and rewrapped, he stopped.

"Are you sleeping, Samuelsson?" he asked. "Were you out too late last night or something?"

I'd dated the tub, as we did with all perishables, but I got the day's date wrong and had put down the twenty-second instead of the twenty-first. A ten-minute rant ensued, in which Giggs accused me of wanting to poison the guests when we served them bacteria-ridden aspic. He let me know that I was a lazy son of a bitch, and maybe that's how we did it in Sweden in our backwoods, pissant country restaurants, but poisoning the guests was not the policy at Victoria Jungfrau. About the fourth time he mentioned the idea of poisoning, he lifted the tub off the shelf, ripped off the plastic wrap, and tipped it over onto my feet.

Giggs continued at full volume, and in another minute or so, Stocker stuck his head through the doorway to see what the commotion was. This did not quell Giggs in the slightest.

"Herrn Stocker," he said, switching from English to German. "Mr. Samuelsson has decided to be lazy today." Stocker glanced at the pink gloppy mess around my feet and then turned to Giggs.

"We need to go over the menu for tomorrow. I'll be in my office."

I spent the next hour recleaning the walk-in, and rewrapping and redating each container, then enduring a second thorough inspection, which ended in a grudging dismissal.

To endure such humiliation didn't get easier after months of working with him, but I did learn to make fewer mistakes—and every day started off with a level playing field, which is to say that everyone else who worked for Giggs had just as much of a chance as I did of being on the losing end of a shitstorm. I also understood that Stocker needed his *sous-chefs* to be paranoid sons of bitches so that he didn't have to micromanage each station. If Stocker spent all his time in the trenches, no one would be keeping an eye on winning the war.

The thing that made Giggs my hands-down favorite boss was that he protected his own. If he had chosen you for his team and you pulled your weight, he made sure you got promoted, even if it meant leaving his crew. If openings came up on another station and with a *sous-chef* he respected, Giggs would go straight to Stocker and make a case for one of his own to get the spot. This was rare.

By November, I was slipping up only enough to be chewed out once a week. Since some guys were getting berated hourly, this was a huge improvement. I was finishing a lunch shift one afternoon when I got called into Mr. Stocker's office. Now what, I wondered. As I walked—fast but not so fast that I could be accused of running—I scrolled through my last few shifts the way people say the dying watch their lives flash before their eyes. I knocked.

"Herrn Stocker?" I said.

"Mr. Samuelsson. *Wie geht es Ihnen?*" How are you?

I said nothing in response. How was I supposed to answer? Mr. Stocker had never asked me how I felt about anything before. There was more than a desk between us. He sat there with his gold spoon and his tall pleated hat, his crisp pants and jacket. I had certainly learned how to be cleaner, but I was still a mess, and I couldn't stop thinking about the fish salad I had left out in my rush to get to his office. So much for going a week without Giggs yelling at me.

Stocker cleared his throat and then spoke. "Mr. Samuelsson, *sie sind ein guter chef.*"

I translated and retranslated what he'd just said. Was I getting it wrong? No. He'd told me that I was a good chef.

"We have watched you be able to work with others and your effort is good. When you come back from the winter break, Victoria would like to hire you as a *demi chef de partie.* I have suggested you. I am not sure if you are going to make it but I'm willing to give it a go. Go to human resources and they will handle the details." He picked up a pen and looked down at the papers on his desk.

I did nothing. I said nothing. Twenty seconds must have passed and he looked up at me.

"That is all. Why are you still here? *Raus! Raus!*" Out! Out!

I walked out in a daze, and all I knew was that I needed to double-check with Giggs. If he told me this was true, that I was getting promoted to *demi chef de partie* of the fish section at twenty years of age, then I would actually believe it.

I got back to the *garde manger* and when Mannfred looked at me, he raised his eyebrows. "Uh oh," he said. "What happened?"

"Not now," I said, looking for Giggs. I found him by the walk-in.

"So what did Chef say?" he asked.

"I think he wants me to be *demi chef de partie.*"

"Of course he does. I told him to give it to you. What? Do you think this stuff just happens? As far as I'm concerned, you owe me. And I'm gonna hold you to it."

The plan was that I would work through New Year's Eve, and then leave Victoria until the spring. I had to exit the country to renew my visa, and while I probably could have filled the time by working at Belle Avenue, being in Switzerland had made clear for me that I only wanted to work abroad and in kitchens with truly international staffs.

In anticipation of my six-month Victoria contract ending, I'd been sending letters up to my Göteborg connections every week looking for help with where to go next. Stocker himself offered to find me a placement between my Victoria contracts, but I wanted to show that I had juice—at least a drop or two, in my Göteborg world. Finally a Belle Avenue line cook hooked me up with a placement at Nordica, a Swedish-owned hotel in central Austria. I'd bracket Austria on either side with a week of R & R back home, just enough time for Mom to wash my clothes, to let my grandmother stuff me to the gills with her cooking, to hang out with Mats, and to pick up a few shifts at Belle Avenue. After all, I wanted to show off what I'd learned.

TWELVE A SHORT STAY IN AUSTRIA

(THAT WILL CHANGE MY LIFE)

A SERIES OF NIGHT TRAINS TOOK ME NORTH AND EAST TO BAD GASTEIN, an Austrian spa town with a long winter tourist season, thanks to its radon-rich springs and ski slopes that held a snow cover long after the other resorts had melted down to dirt. Unlike Interlaken, Bad Gastein didn't attract much of an international crowd—no former higher-ups from the Marcos regime or Gucci-loafered Ferrari owners in sight. Bad Gastein was an Austrian destination for Austrians—the richest Austrians, but the ones happy to vacation within their own borders.

As soon as I walked through the doors of Nordica, the hotel where I was supposed to work, I knew something was wrong. There should have been the clatter of silver and glass in the front of the house as waiters set tables and refilled condiments for lunch. But there were no waiters. No linens on tables, no silverware, not even any salt and pepper shakers. I found the manager, a distracted Swede who told me that the renovation had "fallen off schedule"—something to do with the plumbing. No one could tell when the restaurant would reopen.

My interim gig was gone.

I now had three months to fill before my second Victoria contract started and only enough money in my wallet for a night or two in a hostel. Even more urgently, I had the sense that if I didn't fill my time with cooking, the guys back at Victoria, including Mannfred, would pull ahead of me. Three months was a lot of learning time, and goofing off would only hurt my prospects. It was like soccer drills: There were a thousand ways to skate by, to fake your way through them without giving 100 percent effort, but you were only cheating yourself. No one was going to chart my course for me; the cooking world didn't work like that. I had to find my own way.

I walked down the hill from the hotel to the center of the village, down the winding streets lined with four- and five-story buildings that stood shoulder to shoulder as if huddling against the bitter winter winds. I can figure this out, I told myself; I just need to think.

I wandered around town until I spotted the Elisabethpark, a gigantic yellow-stucco hotel with four stars on the plaque by its front door. The building had a regal yet worn quality to it: The twenty window frames on each floor held sparkling panes of glass but, if you looked closer, the white paint on their frames was chipped and fading. The domed awning over the front entrance showed fatigue where the metal frame had rubbed too long against the fabric. I saw no obvious staff entrance—it would turn out to be down a hidden alley—so for my first and only time, I passed under that awning and entered through the front door.

A bellhop and two desk clerks looked at me when I walked in. In the few extra beats of their gazes, I sensed that familiar shift from "Who's this young guy?" to "Who's this young black guy?" A small, middle-aged woman in a brown dress and black pumps, with reading glasses on a gold chain around her neck, crossed the lobby to intercept me. She used the formal form of address, *Ihnen*, not the familiar *dir*, to ask if she could be of assistance. At least she respected me enough to throw me out politely.

"I'd like to work in the kitchen," I answered in German, and mentioned what had just happened up the hill. By chance, I was speaking to the owner of the hotel, Frau Franzmaier, who ran Elisabethpark with her husband. She took the Victoria Jungfrau reference letter I pulled out of my bag, held up her glasses without bothering to rest them on her nose, and read.

"I can start right away," I said.

"You speak German and you're not afraid of work," she answered. "OK, then. We'll give you a try."

MEMORY IS FUNNY AND, of course, comparative. In a matter of hours, life under Stocker and Giggs began to seem positively cushy. At Elisabethpark, fifteen people did the work of sixty and I worked six days each week, not five. I started at eight in the morning, worked straight through till four, downed a quick staff meal, and zipped up to my room to rest. By 5:30, I was back in the kitchen in a fresh uniform— which would be damp and dirty by the time the kitchen closed at midnight.

The payoff for those fifteen-hour shifts was that I jumped several rungs up the ladder. I was given the vegetable station right off the bat, which meant there was no one between me and Mannfred, the executive chef. I was Chef's right hand and Heidi, a talented young woman from Berlin who worked the grill, was his left. By the end of the first week, our trio had established a rhythm: How much we spoke correlated to how fast the orders were coming in, and when Chef asked if we were ready—"*Bereit?*"—I could tell from his inflection whether he was cueing me up to fire a new order or asking me to step in and plate with him.

Frau Franzmaier was our bridge to the front of the house. She burst through the swinging door to the dining room a hundred times a night, plucking a white smock off a hook and putting it over her nice clothes as soon as she came into the kitchen. If it was slow, she'd have a few sips of wine from a straight-sided juice glass and gossip with Chef about this purveyor or that competitor. If it was busy, she would call out orders through the small microphone across the counter from Chef or dip into the back room to retrieve fresh napkins, then shed the smock and head back out to charm the guests.

At Elisabethpark, we did not look to France as the core of our cuisine. We didn't bow down to truffles or put foie gras on a pedestal. Instead, we looked to Austria itself, to goulash and dumplings and noodles and freshwater fish like lake trout and perch. This was a revelation.

I learned the regional variations in Austrian cuisine, from Vienna's *beuschel* ragout made from calf lungs and heart to the local *krutspätzle*, a side dish of flour noodles made with sauerkraut, pressed through a strainer and sautéed with butter. *Salzburger Nockerln* became my favorite dessert: Its meringue peaks echoed the surrounding Alps, and the warm vanilla sauce spooned on top was said to be the melting snow. We put flecks of smoky Tyrolean bacon into dumplings and, of course, served loads of *tafelspitz*, the dish that all Austrians loved the way Swedes loved their herring. *Tafelspitz* was aged sirloin, preferably from a young ox, simmered with parsnips and carrots and spiced with paprika, dry mustard, and cayenne, then served over buttered noodles. I liked it instantly, but I couldn't help wondering how much better it would taste if it had lingonberry sauce to cut through the rich, savory broth.

My shifts may have ended at midnight, but the buzz didn't wear off for another few hours. Some nights I staggered back to my room to record the day's menu in my journal. If I'd learned a new technique for poaching cabbage, I wrote it down. If I'd watched Chef roast a pork belly over potatoes until the drippings practically caramelized them, I wrote it down. If I saw him make button-shaped spaetzle noodles and wondered how they would taste with dill rather than caraway, I wrote down that idea, or made up the recipe and recorded it, step-by-step, amount by amount.

Of course, I was also a twenty-year-old guy, not a monk. I found a way to exist outside of this cycle of work and reflection. A couple of times a week I'd go out with my Austrian comrades to a local bar, drinking beer or *most*, a local hard cider, while we argued over whose job was harder, whose burns were more serious, and who almost went down during service. My story of the Aspic Massacre definitely won me a spot in the Fuck-ups Hall of Fame.

One night, I ran into a band of Swedish guys at Gatz, an après-ski spot on the ground floor of Hotel Gisela. I was not so interested in pounding schnapps shots the way my countrymen clearly had been doing all evening, but it was such a relief to speak in my native tongue that I hung with them for an hour or two. Some had come to work in the kitchen at Nordica and had, like me, arrived to find that the place wasn't open. They were drinking through the two weeks before the restaurant was slated to open.

"What could we do?" one of them said. "We went skiing!"

I was reminded again that while I may have shared a heritage and a language with my fellow Swedes, most of my countrymen lived much more luxuriously than I did. Maybe it was because of my race, maybe it was because I was adopted, maybe it was simply because I was Lennart and Anne Marie's son and they suffered no fools, but all this talk about not working and no real plans struck me as kind of pathetic. I went back to the table with my buddies from the hotel.

A couple of Austrian girls eventually wandered into our crowd, and I recognized one from the workers' entrance at Elisabethpark. Brigitta worked as a chambermaid. She was a few years older than me and lived above the laundry room. She didn't seem to mind my kitchen German and, like everyone I met in Austria, she seemed intrigued by this black Swede who'd dropped into their midst. Brigitta was beautiful like an old-fashioned movie star; she reminded me of the women in my mother's photo albums from the 1940s. She was from a tiny village in the part of the valley that grew apples and pears, and she paid attention to me as I struggled to make myself understood. We talked for a while, and then a band started playing and it was almost impossible to hear.

"Do you want to come over and listen to some music?" she asked.

I followed her back to her apartment and spent the night.

THE THREE MONTHS IN AUSTRIA instilled in me a deep appreciation for hard work, and the power of a regional cuisine. In some ways, those Austrian dishes were my first real experience with soul food. Elisabethpark may not have been a five-star restaurant, but I saw that warmth and camaraderie and dedication could produce outstanding food just as well as the cutthroat competition that fueled Stocker's kitchen staff. With fewer resources, we pulled off a different five-course tasting menu each night, as well as a new à la carte menu, handwritten by Frau Franzmaier, every day.

In late March, on one of my last days off, I sat in a coffeehouse by the town's waterfall, at a table by the front window. Swedes may drink more coffee than any other Westerners, but Austrians know how to serve it. Waiters bring a glass of water and a chocolate to go along with your order, and the coffee is always beautifully presented, served in a glass on a saucer, the foam peaked just so. A *Franziskaner* was a latte made with whipped cream and a double espresso was called a *kleiner schwarzer*. I could never order *schwarzer* without butting up against the memory of *"schwarzkopf,"* a slur I'd heard growing up from Swedish skinheads back home.

I had laundry to do and I was overdue to write a letter home, but I was there because Brigitta had left a note under my door that morning, asking me to meet her. I hadn't seen her since the night we hung out at Gatz. We'd had a lot of sex that night and the next day, and when we finally left her room, we had to walk through a laundry room full of white-scarved women who giggled at us. They knew what was up.

Maybe she wanted to hang out some more, I thought. Maybe I was that good.

I didn't see her come in, so I was startled when she put her hand on my shoulder. She was as pretty and elegant as I remembered: light green eyes and long brown hair with bangs that came down almost to her eyelashes. She had deep dimples when she smiled, but she was not smiling now. She didn't even sit down.

"Ich bin schwanger," she said. "I am pregnant."

If there was any conversation after that, I don't remember it.

After Austria ended and before my second contract with Victoria began, I'd scheduled ten days at home in Sweden, and I now dreaded every one of them. I had gotten a girl pregnant, and as much as I wanted to pretend it hadn't happened, it had. This was, of course, a predicament that many of my friends back home had faced, but in Lutheran Sweden, abortions were more the rule than the exception. It usually played out like this: Once a guy found out his girlfriend was pregnant, maybe he'd go with her to the appointment or maybe not, but he always arranged a place for her to hang out for a few days afterward, maybe a friend's apartment, and he'd stay with her there until she was OK to go home. It sounds harsh, but that's usually how it went. That was the routine.

The mess I was now in was anything but routine. I had gotten a Catholic girl from a Roman Catholic country pregnant. The outcome was far less clear.

When she broke the news to me in that café, I felt hammered. I was stunned into silence. My brain worked overtime, trying to wriggle out of the reality: Why did this happen to me?

For a second, I considered "doing the right thing"—marrying Brigitta, this woman I hardly knew, and spending the rest of my life in Austria, not a place where many black Swedes from Ethiopia have been known to put down roots. I'd get a job as a line cook somewhere, maybe at Elisabethpark, and that would be it. But before I could even finish articulating that scenario in my head, I was past it.

I couldn't do it.

I also couldn't work up the guts to ask Brigitta if she had thought about terminating the pregnancy. She wasn't asking for my opinion. Or, for that matter, my money or my time; she had a big family and they would be supportive of her as she raised the child.

"I thought you should know" was pretty much all she said.

"OK," I said. "Thank you."

By the time I got back to Gburg, I was no clearer than I had been in the moment. And I was pissed off: I'd done everything in my life not to become a statistic. I'd done everything I could to avoid the negative stereotype of an irresponsible black man, but there was no disputing my part in the situation. Or my stupidity.

"You seem so tired, Macke," my mother kept saying. "I think they work you too hard."

"What's on your mind, son?" asked the father who usually welcomed my rare silences.

I tried to calculate the damage my news was going to cause, but I couldn't. Brigitta could not have been more than ten weeks pregnant when she told me. She didn't look the slightest bit heavier. This is what I told myself, to feel better.

"Maybe something will happen," I thought. "Maybe she'll change her mind."

THIRTEEN **SECRETS**

SUMMER WAS ONE LONG PANIC ATTACK. SOMETIMES I FELT LIKE I WAS going to die . . . or at least that the career I'd worked so hard for was about to die and I was standing by its deathbed, watching helplessly. I said nothing about the pregnancy to anyone at Victoria, not even Mannfred. Not even Christina, who started her job at the same time I returned. She and I were given a small apartment in the dormitory—a step up over the monk's cell I had during my first stint—but despite the daily contact and nightly intimacy, I kept mum.

The only way I managed to keep up the lie was that the restaurant kitchen was such a refuge. My job had changed, but everything else, including Giggs's incessant sarcasm, was just as I had left it, and I happily dove back in.

As *demi chef de partie* for the *garde manger*, I now had more responsibility, more independence, and more of a public face. I not only butchered without Franz standing over me, I was now the one who stood over the new batch of *commis* and came down hard on them when they cut through muscle. I showed them how to fillet fish and how to prep oysters by slitting apart the shell without fully disengaging the flesh. When we had breakfast buffets, I worked the omelet station, taking orders directly from a long line of guests and cooking their eggs in front of them. This sounds simple, but we were cooking over portable gas burners that gave out uneven heat. Stocker wouldn't hear of us using nonstick pans; he wanted us to use only the beautifully polished copper pans. He believed that an omelet should be cooked through but never, ever have "color," which meant any omelet with a browned edge was to be immediately discarded. On this point, he was adamant. Finally, you had to have enough polish to be able to do all this while chatting up the guests, most of whom couldn't have cared less if their eggs were a little brown.

After Stocker's meeting broke up one morning, Giggs came back to our station and made a beeline right for me.

"He wants to see you," Giggs said.

I hesitated, feeling a wave of panic rise up. What had I done?

"Now!" Giggs barked.

Stocker barely looked up from his desk when I walked in. I didn't dare sit down in the chair across from his desk unless I was asked. I was not asked.

"You speak English well, Mr. Samuelsson," Stocker said in German. I wasn't sure if he meant it as a question or a statement, but I decided to answer in English.

"Next to Swedish, it's my best—"

"I have a colleague in Gstaad," he interrupted. "At the Grand Hotel, which is very busy in the summer. He needs cooks. Victoria is Switzerland's leading hotel, as you know, and as such, we must also lead the way in staff. I am sending you for twenty-five days. You will go tomorrow and when you arrive, you will ask for Herrn Muller."

I stood, frozen, while it sank in that I was not in trouble. In fact, to be sent away was a reward. "Thank you, Herrn Stocker," I said. I prepared to launch into how much this meant to me, how honored I was, how grateful, and—

Stocker had no interest in compliments. "Do not embarrass me," he said, and picked up his telephone, dismissing me from the room.

Gstaad was only forty-five miles away, still in the Bernese Alps and so similar to Victoria in its no-nonsense professional atmosphere that within two days, I felt like I'd been there forever. The Grand Hotel had half as many rooms as Victoria and its banquets didn't serve more than a hundred people, so the pace was manageable, and I never felt overwhelmed. As an extra hand, I worked in the *garde manger* and also helped out in the meat station. Because the staff was more Swiss and less international in its makeup, people were even more formal in their interactions with me, but I also noticed that I was treated with more deference and respect, as if the Stocker stamp of approval bumped up my status automatically.

WHEN I GOT BACK TO VICTORIA three weeks later, my status went right back down to its previous level; in fact, it almost seemed like the *sous-chefs* and line cooks above me were now determined to keep me from getting a swelled head. They loaded me down with grunt work and, whenever the opportunity arose, reminded me that I was not out "in the country" anymore, but back in the real world. I didn't care. I knew I had held my own in Gstaad, I hadn't embarrassed Stocker, and I'd successfully added one more notch to my chef's belt.

But the better I got at my job, the less I liked it. Let me rephrase that: I loved working for Giggs and Stocker. Stocker's innovation with technology and technique made all of our lives in the kitchen easier, and his expectation of peak performance was one I admired and aspired to. Giggs, despite his crankiness, was a great teacher, and he rewarded effort and talent with extra attention and time. Even

Victoria itself had a personality—of grandeur and tradition, all of which was anchored in a beautiful landscape that I was taking full advantage of, thanks to the hiking, biking, and skiing I did with Mannfred and his friends. But I longed to work in a kitchen where the chef's passions ruled. Stocker and Giggs held to the highest standards in the industry, but they worked from a playbook set in stone. French stone.

Giggs, who had traveled so widely on his cruise ship days, offered clues about his own palate preferences when he added lemongrass to staff meals or threw together fried rice between service. He'd talk at great length about the difference between Thai and Indian curries, but I never saw him developing his food while on the clock. He followed the script. The potential of our kitchen seemed so vast, too. That's what killed me. We had dozens of foodways within reach, from the Portuguese and Spanish dishwashers to the northern Italian and American waiters. And the more I mastered the basics, the more I longed to shake up the routine.

Sprinkled throughout the international kitchen staff were the rich kids who were never going to cook as professionals but wanted the Swiss hospitality pedigree. You could tell this group instantly: They strolled along when the rest of us dashed. Their hands were baby soft—no calluses, cuts, or burns. You'd never see them pull something out of a deep fryer with their fingers, as seasoned line cooks did. And they didn't want to help, either—they were completely up front about having come to Victoria with no hands-on experience, and also clear about the fact that their futures as hoteliers or managers wouldn't include any cooking. The rest of us watched in awe as they said hello to Stocker when he passed by. They actually looked him in the eye, which seemed to confuse him, and he usually just grunted in response and kept walking. Still, we also had interns from Tehran and Colombo and Seoul who loved to eat, and even more, loved to entertain. They rented small houses around town, and the big benefit for me was that those houses had kitchens. Those of us who lived in the dormitories would get invited over for meals, and we'd have Indian naan bread, Chinese fried rice and glazed spareribs, Japanese *nabemono*. The foods we'd eat at those informal dinners were alive with heat and flavor; they had a vitality that spoke to me instantly and far more persuasively than the thrice-reduced cream sauces that took days of careful tending to render just so. Why was there no room at Victoria for those tastes?

I wrote in my food journal almost every night. I tracked what I was learning, but I also started to ask questions, to play with the what-ifs of dishes that were taking shape in my mind. What if you matched turbot with a miso-based stock? What if you put seared salmon into crisp spring roll wrappers? It was not my place to suggest these things openly, but the ideas kept coming, so I kept scribbling them down.

Meanwhile, Christina and I got along on the surface, but we were mismatched, too. She wanted to see us as having a future; my cooking dreams and my secret threw up a wall that couldn't possibly be broken down.

By the fall, that secret was about to burst at its seams. Any glimmers of hope I'd held on to of this issue magically going away were finally extinguished when I got a letter from Brigitta. She was coming along, she wrote, and due in November. She enclosed a set of paternity papers for me to file with the Austrian consulate in Bern. She asked no involvement from me, but she would not pretend that she didn't know the father of this baby.

I filed the papers during a day trip to Bern with Mannfred.

"Where are you going, man?" he asked when I said I'd meet him back at the station in a couple of hours. Splitting off on my own was completely uncharacteristic of our adventures together.

"I just need to go do something," I said.

In late November, the news came. A baby girl, born on the sixteenth, five days after my twenty-first birthday. Both mother and daughter doing fine. I was not fine, though, and every time I looked at Christina, every time she told me she loved me, I felt like a bigger jerk had never existed.

The news of the baby arrived just before Christina and I were scheduled to go on holiday with her parents. They were driving down from Göteborg, and would pick us up for a trip to France, then take us back to Göteborg for winter break. I'd picked the destination, Monte Carlo, thinking that I might try for a spot at the famed Hotel de Paris while I was there, which would be a perfect conclusion to my apprenticeship stage.

The night before her parents arrived, I burst. Christina asked me something simple, like whether she should pack this sweater or that sweater, and I spilled my guts. The one-night stand, the lying, the pregnancy, the baby. She cried and screamed all night; I apologized, got defensive, and then apologized again.

"Hey," I said, at one point. "This is completely fucking with my dreams, too."

"Why did you wait until *now* to tell me?" she asked, over and over again. *"Why?"*

I had no answer for that.

Her parents, Jens and Aiko, pulled up to Victoria at eight the next morning, as planned. We threw our bags into the trunk and for most of the drive south, Christina and I sat mute in the backseat, staring out opposite windows. When we did speak, it was not to each other. Our three days in France passed peacefully, if quietly, and I imagine Christina's parents assumed we were burnt out from work and perhaps a little tired of our dip into domesticity. When we got to Monte Carlo, I felt too anxious and mixed-up to walk into the Hotel de Paris and ask for a tryout. I'll write a letter, I told myself.

As soon as we got back home to Göteborg, I headed over to Mats's house. Lots of boys in our neighborhood went to Mats's dad, Rune, for advice. We felt close to him because he'd coached us in the local peewee soccer league, but he was also just an all-around solid guy who'd listen, tell you what he really thought, and get you out of a jam if he could.

"This is one I can't help you with," Rune said, after I finally spat out my news across his kitchen table. "Go to your parents, Marcus. I can't make this go away."

I went home and confessed to my parents.

"OK," Mom said.

"OK," Dad said.

This is going well, I thought. I didn't need Rune's help after all. I'd practiced on my sisters just minutes before breaking the news to my parents. (Anna and Linda had squealed with delight. Not helpful.) Now I was in the living room, doing it for real. My father looked down at the pipe he held in his hand, fingering its smooth stem. My mother had shifted from lounging in the overstuffed chair that sat at the end of the sofa to sitting up straight, letting her knitting rest in her lap. The silence lasted too long.

"I know a guy who works at La Toscana," I said, trying to show that I'd been thinking things through, "who doesn't have to pay child support based on economic hardship or something."

"No, Marcus," my mother said, in a hard-edged tone I rarely heard from her. "You are going to pay. You are going to pay every month."

"I don't have any money—"

"That's OK," she interrupted. "We will pay until you do, and then you are going to pay us back and start paying it yourself. And you are not going to miss one month. I guarantee it."

I'm sure I looked confused; up until now, earning money had been last on my list of career considerations.

"You can still go back to Switzerland and cook where you want to cook," Mom said. "But this is your responsibility, and while we will help you now, that little girl is yours to take care of. Always."

WHEN I GOT BACK TO SWITZERLAND, Giggs bumped me up to *chef de partie*. At twenty-one years of age, I oversaw ten guys at a time, and I attended Stocker's morning meetings, which were always held in German. I also became a master compartmentalizer, pushing Brigitta and the baby, a girl she'd named Zoe, back into the farthest reaches of my mind, focusing only on the job at hand. I tracked food costs for my station, calculated orders for our various purveyors, and evaluated the new *commis* who streamed through. Who had "it" and who didn't? I was brutal in my judgments. After all, there was a woman and a baby—my baby—in Austria who were proof of just how much I'd been willing to sacrifice for my career. I'd always had plenty of ambition to spare, but the secret awareness that I was now a father, that there was a little girl who would someday need me, drove me harder.

Herrn Richter, Giggs started to call me when I'd tell him that one guy was fucking up and would be out in a week, or another guy was going to go far. "Mr. Judge."

Stocker's assistant passed out the day's menu at the start of the morning meetings, along with a list of upcoming special events. I stood in the back of the room as we looked over the sheet one morning and saw a giant corporate banquet—a black-tie buffet for nine hundred—scheduled for the next weekend. For such big events, part of the personnel deployment discussion was always how many runners would be needed. Runners were the lowest rung on the serving ladder, and one that would gather in busboys, porters, and *commis* as needed.

"Twenty-one," Stocker calculated. "We'll need twenty-one *nègres* for this." He used the French kitchen slang for underlings, which literally translated to "blacks," and which also meant "negroes."

I froze in my spot. I was the only *nègre* in the room. Not even the darker-skinned Tamils were represented in Stocker's small office, not even an Italian. No one looked over at me. Was it good or bad that I was so invisible? Was it actually a compliment that no one made the connection between the term for a near-worthless employee and this newly promoted *chef de partie* who stood among their ranks?

My industry was far from perfect, but it was my industry now, the place I had chosen for myself. For all its shortcomings, it met most of my needs. I'd proven to my father that I could make something of myself and on my own, and now that I was twenty-one, I had officially aged out of the Swedish military obligation. I had made many small mistakes and one very big one, but I was still moving forward. I would keep writing letters to restaurants all over the world—it had become an obsession—but for the moment, I was exactly where I needed and wanted to be.

WITH CHRISTINA NOW OUT OF THE PICTURE—she'd broken up with me after the trip to France—my social life in Interlaken revolved around Mannfred and his friends. When it came to skiing, Mannfred and his friends had me beat.

Fortunately, I couldn't have cared less: Getting out of town and working out the kinks of a stressed-out body were more than satisfying. One weekend, seven of us decided to take a ski trip to Zermatt and ski the Matterhorn. Mannfred brought along Sascha and Jorgen, two old friends of his from school. The rest of us were from Victoria: Martin, a waiter from southern Germany, and two cooks, Klaus and Giuseppe.

We needed two cars to fit the lot of us. Giuseppe had an old Fiat and Mannfred commandeered his sister's new car. We left early on a Thursday morning, and in the two-hour drive south, we seemed to be driving straight uphill to the little mountain village of Zermatt. The old Fiat strained once we reached the town of Visp, and Giuseppe worked the clutch heavily as he negotiated the hairpin turns. When the roads narrowed to one lane, we pulled over to the very edge of the mountain every time an oncoming car passed by, and I made the conscious choice not to look down. Instead, I daydreamed. I wondered where I'd go next after Victoria, felt bad about how the years with Christina had ended, but was also relieved to be back on track, career-wise. I wondered if my parents were disappointed in me because of the baby, and I thought about how work, with all its pressure, was now the easiest part of my life, the one place where I could drop every other concern and just learn and taste and cook.

Mannfred hit me on the shoulder. *"Nicht mehr schlafen,* Samuelsson." No more sleeping. We were there.

I was a decent skier by Swedish standards. I'd dabbled in it as a kid and watched ski competitions on television religiously—at that time, one of my countrymen, Ingemar Stenmark, was considered one of the best in the world. But now I was standing at the top of the same slopes he'd sped down, and what had looked steep on television looked like a perfect vertical in real life. The other guys, who'd grown up on mountains like this, took off in straight lines while I launched into a cautious slalom. Mannfred stayed back and skied with me, never mocking, never teasing, and we'd regroup with the others when we reached the bottom and do it all again.

At night, we ate sausage, pounded cheap wine and cold beer, and made fondue. As we drank, we also talked shop: We all decided that Mannfred would one day be the chef of Victoria and the rest of us would work for him. (First, though, he and I would get Giggs to hook us up with a *stage* on a cruise ship so we could see the world.) We argued about which *sous-chef* was the biggest hard-ass and speculated on why there seemed to be a sudden influx of East Germans on staff. We tabulated how many of the waitresses Klaus had dated and which of the interns was his next victim. We skied six hours straight each day, and after a couple of hours of drinking and winding down, we hit our beds hard.

Driving back on Sunday, I jumped in the front seat of the Fiat with Giuseppe. Klaus and Sascha climbed in the back. We were in a hurry: We had to get the other car back to Thun in time to catch a train to Victoria, and the Swiss guys said the Sunday train schedule was spotty. Driving downhill was just as tricky as driving up, with the additional challenge of ice slicks that could combine, dangerously, with the downhill momentum. Jorgen had won the poker game on our last night, so his prize was to drive Mannfred's sister's car. No one else cared who drove, but Jorgen had just gotten his license, so every turn behind a wheel excited him. Giuseppe passed Jorgen whenever he had the chance, then Jorgen would make a comeback on a wide flat stretch and overtake our car. The rest of us shouted and pointed whenever one car passed the other. We stopped to gas up and while our tanks filled and a light rain began to fall, we stood under the tank shelter. Giuseppe and Jorgen got into a playful pissing match over whether Italians were the best drivers in the world.

With full tanks, we climbed back into the cars and the game began again. I settled into the front passenger seat, thinking about the stiff muscles I'd be taking into work the next day. Giuseppe and I had a perfectly unobstructed view of the other car as Jorgen sped past us to get in first place. Jorgen was still at an angle to the main road when a large sedan suddenly appeared, coming straight at us. Neither car could stop or slow down in that millisecond of visibility, and the sedan slammed into the new car. Mannfred, unbelted, flew out the side window on impact and the car spun three times before coming to a stop, wedged up against the side of the mountain. I saw him land at an awkward angle, his body making the dark equivalent of a chalk outline in the snow. He was hurt. It was bad. But he was alive.

It took thirty terrible minutes for the ambulance to arrive. Each minute was a bomb, in which our lives slowly ticked away, exploded, and then slowly began ticking again. I knelt by Mannfred while we waited and he lay still, taking shallow, awful breaths. We alternately screamed for help and cried. Blood and glass were everywhere.

Martin, who had been in the backseat, stumbled out of the car in shock. He'd have many stitches but came out with no broken bones. Jorgen would never walk again. The driver of the other car died on impact.

Mannfred died in the ambulance.

I got back to Interlaken at two in the morning and somehow fell instantly asleep. When I woke up, it was noon, and as I remember it, there was no sun, only gray and dark. Stocker was in his office, and I sat and talked to him. For the first and only time, we had a long conversation that had almost nothing to do with work. We talked about the accident and about Mannfred.

"It's time for me to leave," I said at the end, and Stocker did not argue.

"Take a couple days off for the funeral, then come back for a week to finish up," he said. "I am very sorry about this, Marcus."

I had no idea he knew my first name.

MY PLANE TOUCHED DOWN AT NEW YORK'S JOHN F. KENNEDY INTERNA-tional Airport, and when I stepped into the terminal, the first thing I noticed were all the black people. They were everywhere. Black gate agents, black flight attendants, black baggage handlers, black cashiers, black cab drivers. Black people, everywhere I turned. The second thing I noticed was that no one was looking at me differently. No, scratch that: No one was looking at me at all.

Right then, I knew I'd come to the right place.

In the weeks after my grief-stricken departure from Switzerland, I'd scrambled to find another restaurant placement. I was still aiming for France, but while I looked for a three-star spot that would have me, I needed to keep moving forward, not to mention keep some money rolling in. I followed up on every lead except for the ones that would have kept me in Sweden. Ironically, the apprenticeship I finally secured was in a Swedish restaurant . . . in New York. In fact, this restaurant was more Swedish in its menu than any I had ever worked in. Aquavit, housed in a former Rockefeller mansion, had opened in 1987, back when I was still a student at Mosesson. It was the brain-child of a food-loving Swedish businessman named Håkan Swahn who had settled happily in New York some years before but had missed the flavors of his homeland. In collaboration with the famous Swedish chef Tore Wretman, Håkan opened a restaurant that would be the first in the United States to serve more than smorgasbord and meatballs. Aquavit found a receptive audience among adventurous patrons who appreciated the pairings of sour, sweet, and savory that were, on the one hand, slightly exotic but, on the other, crafted from ingredients familiar to the European palate.

I'd landed the job at Aquavit thanks to my old friend Peter, a for-mer *commis* at Belle Avenue. Peter had gone on to do well, and now he was a *sous-chef* at Aquavit. He got the executive chef, Christer Lars-son, to offer me a nine-month apprenticeship, and so here I was at the airport, with nothing more than a telephone number and an address.

I threw my two duffels into the luggage hole of the bus, handed my ticket to the black bus driver, squeezed past a black woman nod-ding along with whatever was streaming out of her earphones, and sat by a window. I was more well-traveled than the average middle-class Swedish kid, thanks to soccer and my apprenticeships, but I'd never been anywhere that seemed as exotic as this. Over the course of the half-hour drive in from Queens, the enormity of the city started to sink in. There was just . . . more of everything. More congestion, more cars, more people, more skyline, more garbage. I don't think I looked away until the bus emptied out at Grand Central.

My first apartment was on the east side of the island, on Fifty-second Street and Third Avenue. Peter was not only my direct boss at work, he was my roommate, generously letting me bunk with him and his brother Magnus, a massage therapy student at the Swedish Institute College of Health Sciences, in their second-floor walk-up. Technically, the apartment was in midtown, but really, it had none of the business-world cachet of that label. We were more or less on the edge of the world then, in a tenement apartment so small I slept on the massage table set up in their living room.

"You can stay as long as you like," Peter offered, and while I knew he was generous enough to mean it, I also knew I should find my own place as soon as I could.

Peter's apartment was not far from the restaurant, which was then half a block west of Fifth Avenue and between Central Park and the Museum of Modern Art, all easy landmarks. But even with clear directions and a city laid out on a strict and logical grid, I got lost on my first day. I was distracted by everything. Especially the street people. In Göteborg, there was only one man who slept in the street. Everybody knew him and knew that he was rich—he *chose* to sleep there. In New York that first day, I saw homeless people on every block, stationed outside ATM lobbies and supermarkets, some holding Styrofoam cups, some passed out in entryways and alleys. I saw people smoking covertly, which meant, I figured, that they were not smoking tobacco. In Sweden, even though we had drugs, they were done in private, not out on the street. I was so turned around and discombobulated on the first day that even though I'd left the house after lunch and the commute was only a twenty-minute walk, I didn't arrive at the restaurant's doors until after my three p.m. shift start time. Not a good start.

Aquavit had two levels, a booth-filled ground-floor café adjacent to the bar, and a formal dining room downstairs. The dining room felt like a solarium: It was the one-time courtyard of the house, now closed in by glass, and its central feature was a Zenlike waterfall against one wall, which kept the mood of the room subdued and soothing.

The kitchen was smaller than any I'd ever worked in, a dozen cooks crammed shoulder-to-shoulder, pot racks overhead and screwed onto every available inch of wall. Manhattan real estate was too expensive to waste on the back of the house; there wasn't enough room for a kitchen with discrete stations and a traditional *chef de partie* system. We had Chef Christer and a couple of *sous-chefs* overseeing the rest of us, who were simply called line cooks. The other distinction was the smell, which was different from any kitchen I'd ever known. No matter how diligent we were in our cleaning, one odor lingered underneath: roach spray.

In many ways, Aquavit was the most comfortable work environment I'd had in years. I now had the skills to do most tasks automatically, which allowed me to pay attention to the overall rhythm of the kitchen, to the way Chef Christer worked through a week's worth of inventory, putting a glazed salmon with potato pancakes on Monday's menu and, by Friday, offering a tandoori-smoked salmon. The kitchen languages were English and a sprinkling of Swedish; the social culture was Swedish and American, a combination of familiar and relaxed; the flavor palate was in my bones. The informal café stuck to traditional Swedish fare: meatballs with mashed potatoes and lingonberries, vegetable and cheese-filled blini, rolls from the northern regions. In the dining room we used classical French techniques, with Christer applying Tore Wretman's brilliant philosophy of taking regional and folk specialties and elevating them to a more sophisticated plane. We'd make venison just as my mother's people did in the Skåne region, but instead of smoking it, we'd pan-roast it with olive oil, aquavit, thyme, garlic, allspice, and juniper berries. Instead of serving it with the traditional cream sauces, we'd lighten it up with a fruit and berry chutney. In another house favorite, Christer paired avocado and lobster, a melding of two worlds that worked so well it was hard to imagine no one had done it before.

On the line, I was able to hold my own from day one. I was more precise and probably a better cook than a lot of the guys, but they were fast and I had to get up to speed. We would churn out ninety covers for the pre-theater crowd, something I'd never seen before. In Göteborg, Belle Avenue was practically next door to the concert hall and city theater, but no self-respecting Swede would have considered eating until after the shows. At Aquavit, we got the ticketholders in and out in under an hour, then turned around and fed another ninety people right after that. The first few times I was on a pre-theater shift, I thought, Holy shit. I was drowning, constantly behind, constantly playing catch-up to the guys around me. So what if I was cleaner? It was speed that counted.

WHEN I WAS AT WORK, I gave everything I had to Aquavit, but when I was off the clock, I was a full-time student of New York. Here, it seemed, was everything I ever wanted. At first, I tried to make my $250 weekly paycheck go further by buying a used bike to get around. It got stolen almost instantly, which led to my first big American purchase: a pair of Rollerblades. I hardly rode the subway after that. The energy of the city was infectious, and I took to Rollerblading all over town on everything but the wettest and iciest of days. Skating was a way to save money and satisfy a lifelong addiction to exercise, but it was also a way to learn the map of the city, its architecture and topography, its neighborhoods and, most exciting of all, its foods. To get to work, some days I'd skate uptown first and cut back through Central Park, sailing through the aromas wafting from the chestnut-roasting vendors, the hot dog and shawarma carts, the syrupy burnt sugar of the peanut and cashew men. Other days I'd dip down into the thirties so that I could skate through Koreatown, with its smells of kimchi and its modest barbecue joints in the shadow of the Empire State Building. All those years of playing hockey on bumpy pond ice were finally paying off.

If I worked the early shift, I'd take off after lunch service and skate down the east side of the island, stopping in the Indian groceries to wander through the spice aisles, once in a while treating myself to something unfamiliar, like the pungent, gummy asafetida, which went from having a truly objectionable stink when raw to a pleasant garlic-meets-leeks vibe when cooked. One week I'd try yellowtail sushi in the East Village, and the next week I'd save up money to sample the tamarind-dipped crab rolls at Vong.

My favorite of all the ethnic-food areas, though, was Chinatown. Manhattan's was the biggest enclave I'd ever seen (at least until I ventured off the island to discover the South Asian neighborhoods of Jackson Heights, Queens), and I had my first dim sum at Golden Unicorn, a two-floor restaurant a couple of streets below Canal that was so vast and well-trafficked that it will probably outlast any other on the island. Chinatown's curbside stalls reminded me of the fishmongers in Göteborg's Feskekörka and along the Bryggan up on Smögen Island. There weren't just snails on offer here, but five different kinds of snails that had been graded into three sizes each. Some of the fish I could recognize, but many vendors didn't know how or didn't bother to translate their signs into English—besides, the bustling shoppers that jockeyed for service suggested that language was not a barrier to commerce. I went into basement supermarkets on Mott Street where I found entire aisles of dried mushrooms, and varieties of ingredients that I'd never known came in more than one version, like sea salt, which I now saw packaged in different grinds—fine, coarse, and flake—and in colors from white to pink to black.

My old boss Paul Giggs kept me company on many of these adventures—in my mind, at least. I'd look at the dish section of the supermarket, noting the graceful curves of teapots, the thousands of chopstick designs, and I'd recall his instructions to draw our food, to study the gemstones in Bern. "Food is not just about flavor," he'd lecture us. "It has countless dimensions, and one is visual. What do you want it to *look* like? What do you want the customer to *see*? Your job is to serve all the senses, not just the fucking tastebuds, OK?"

In the aisles of Kalustyan's, a spice market on Lexington Avenue that continues to be one of New York's best exotic food sources for everything from *farro* to Kaffir lime leaves, I'd hold different dry curry blends up to my nose, committing their distinct aromatic structures to memory, but also remembering that they wouldn't release their full powers until they met up with heat.

"Toast your spices in the pan first or don't even bother," Giggs would say when he made a curry for Victoria Jungfrau's staff meal.

One spring day, I skated by a greengrocer in the northern corner of Chinatown, a block from the part of the Bowery where lighting supply stores alternated with restaurant equipment warehouses, chandeliers and exhaust fan hoods spilling onto the sidewalks. The unusually patient and orderly line of patrons stopped me. They were watching a woman with a large knife who stood at a makeshift counter between bins. Wearing a thick glove, from a stack by her side she picked out a green, spiky orb the size of a soccer ball, then sliced it open and into wedges, sliding her knife between the thorned skin and a milky interior flesh. In one fluid motion, she dropped the flesh into a plastic bag, secured the bag with a knot, and exchanged the bag for cash, only to start the process over again.

I watched for a minute or two, trying to locate a sign that would tell me the name of this object that resembled a medieval weapon. No luck. Was it a melon? A squash? I was upwind of the counter, but now and then I caught a whiff of something that cleared my sinuses. I smelled something nutty and fetid. The odor was repellent, but so tantalizingly strange that I couldn't break away. Finally, I tapped the shoulder of the last person in line, a young woman holding the hand of a toddler who looked to be her son. In her other hand, she held a bouquet of plastic shopping bags, pinks and greens and blues, all spilling out with leafy vegetables and paper-wrapped packages.

Not knowing if she spoke English, I combined raised eyebrows, pointing fingers, and speech.

"What is that?" I asked.

"Durian," she said, in an English far less accented than my own. "Green durian. It just came in this week. You like the smell?" She smiled as she asked this, but even as she wrinkled up her nose in shared disgust, I could see she wasn't about to give up her spot in line.

Again, Giggs's voice spoke to me.

"Cat piss," he'd once said, describing durian, a popular Asian fruit he'd first had in Singapore. "Smells like cat piss mixed with garlic, but the custardy texture is pure velvet and, if you hold your breath while you eat it, the flavor is sublime."

I slipped my hand in my pocket to make sure I had some bills, then took my place behind the mother and her son.

THE MORE GROUND I COVERED in New York and the more people I met, the more I came to see the difference between international and diverse. Interlaken was international, and I got off on the energy of being around so many different cultures and languages there. But in the end, they were all going back to where they came from. The American waiters would head back to LA after one too many cold winters; the Portuguese dishwashers would be allowed work visas only as long as Switzerland needed their labor; the hoteliers and chefs in training, like me, would learn how to make fondue and *röschti*, then go on to the next kitchen, the one with more stars or a more famous executive chef. New York was different. There were divides along lines of race and class, but whereas the ethnic Swiss owned Switzerland and the ethnic Swedes owned Sweden, everybody in New York had a stake in where they were. Maybe you had to have a place this big to allow there to be a hundred different New Yorks living side by side, but almost everyone I saw seemed to move with a sense of belonging. This was their city whether you liked it or not.

I had an Italian-American friend named Anthony, a kid a couple of years younger than me whom I'd first met in Switzerland. Anthony was a good kid, if a little rich and bratty, the son of a hotelier who came from Garden City, a classic Long Island suburb. Sometimes I'd go visit him on a day off, which was like going back to the quiet of Partille or any other Swedish suburb, except even more removed. Anthony and his buddies drove everywhere, the girls sprayed their bangs into place and wore Reeboks, and when they weren't listening to Taylor Dayne, they listened to black music, even though they didn't have any black friends. I knew that Anthony genuinely liked me—I had his back the whole time we were working for Stocker—but I also knew that I was something of a prize he could parade around his friends to up his coolness factor. Almost none of Anthony's buddies ever went into New York City, except the adventurous few who'd snuck out one night to go in and hang out under the bright lights of Times Square.

All in all, I couldn't have asked for a better launch pad into the United States than Aquavit. My friend Peter watched out for me. Chef Christer was kind to me. The work, the food, the familiar culture, and the easier languages gave me a serious comfort zone, but I came to America to be with Americans, not Swedes. I was still working on getting to France, but I had an inkling that I might come to live in the United States someday, and this was my chance to check it out and make sure.

Apparently, I made my enthusiasm and curiosity plain, because I quickly made friends who volunteered to show me their versions of New York. One of the most influential was Casey, a line cook at Aquavit who was the only African American there. He came from a working-class background, and in the summer, he'd take me to family cookouts. His parents lived in the city of White Plains, a short train ride north from Grand Central Station, and I felt like I was entering an MTV video set when I saw their backyard table laden with fried chicken, coleslaw, and potato salad, with the guys my age able to drop in and out of any song lyric blasting from the DJ mixes on the stereo, everyone joining in when their girl from Mt. Vernon, Mary J. Blige, came along. *"What's the 411? / What's the 411? / I got it goin' on . . ."*

Every experience Casey showed me was hardcore. He took me to late-night hip-hop clubs in distant corners of Queens. We'd change trains three times so that we could see every kind of act, from unknowns to Run-DMC. New York wasn't as polished back then as it is now, and those three a.m. train rides home felt like scenes from *The Warriors*, where a gang rides subway after subway in its quest to get back to Coney Island. Casey's friends either worried that I was some kind of cop or were amused by me: I was black but not black. I played soccer and they played basketball. I had darker skin than almost all of them but poor command of their language and even poorer command of style—my Levis were too close-fitting, my Doc Martens were not Tims, and it took me a while to shift from my blown-out Hendrix fro to the fade I finally adopted for the rest of my stay.

The more time I spent with Casey, the more I realized how quaint my own upbringing had been. From the outside looking in, I was fascinated that these guys who lived inside the law and weren't broke still related to the hip-hop world where everyone was on the lam and out of work. Casey's buddies identified with that world and stuck with it the way I've since seen the alumni of black colleges or fraternities stick together.

We'd go to the outer boroughs to hear music but also to play basketball. I'd say, "There is basketball in Manhattan," but they never wanted to play there. Manhattan was where they worked. They called it "money-making Manhattan," and they didn't know anyone who lived there, except for maybe in Harlem. When we went to parties in Harlem, I realized their whole world was completely black. Maybe there'd be some Puerto Ricans involved, but otherwise, it was all black. On the one hand, that was opposite from my own upbringing. On the other, it was just as homogenous.

Casey became my window into African American experiences, and I was so happy to be invited along; this was what I came to America for. At times, it felt like a cultural test: What would it take for me to belong? Was the color of my skin enough?

Casey had a serious side, too, and he knew more about the Black Panther movement than anybody I've ever met. We would have these big arguments about how to fight for racial equality—MLK or Malcolm, early Malcolm or late Malcolm, violent or non-. Casey was intrigued by Sweden, and listened to my stories as if I were telling him about living on Mars. I realized how his world, so full and rich in some ways, was also like my pal Anthony's in that it was so completely cloistered, cut off from the rest of the world. As cosmopolitan as Casey and his homeboys seemed to me, they were also sheltered. It was 1993 and we didn't have the Internet; they didn't see black movers and shakers outside the classic professions of entertainment or sports. They had very little in the way of role models aside from Biggie Smalls and Tupac Shakur, men who, right or wrong, came across as powerful and self-made.

ANOTHER NEW YORK came to me through Aquavit, the New York of Central Park. I found it through Carlos, the Guatemalan fry guy who had fingers made of asbestos and would reach into the fryer to pull out pieces of fish and remain unscathed. Carlos turned out to be a serious soccer player. Plenty of guys in Aquavit's kitchen came from soccer-loving cultures. They had a favorite team or strong opinions of who was or wasn't worth shit, but not too many actually played with any regularity. Carlos was good.

"I'll show you where you can play," he offered, and the next day we both had off, he took the train into Manhattan from his Red Hook apartment, where he lived in close proximity to twenty or thirty people from his hometown of Guate, or Guatemala City. "We have better teams in Brooklyn, but this is easier for you."

We met at a field in Central Park, just above the Ninety-seventh Street transverse and in the lower part of the North Meadow. It was a series of fields, actually, all of them in use and with squadrons of players waiting to take over when any match finished.

I towered over many of my Central American teammates, which was the exact and pleasant opposite of my lifelong Swedish soccer experience. Even though I had no Spanish and some of them had no English, we were all fluent in our sport. We held our own against a crew of well-practiced Brazilians, then trounced a team of American yuppies whose training was no match for those of us born to the sport.

Afterward, I was with my teammates, shooting the shit, goofing on each other's mistakes and re-creating the great passes and goals. I got so worked up about a bad call that I started cursing in Swedish. *"Värsta* fucking *domare någonsin. Du måste vara jävla blind att ha missat det!"* Worst fucking call ever. You'd have to be fucking blind to have missed it!

I saw a group of black guys headed toward me. The smallest of the bunch, a light-skinned guy with a shaved head, looked me in the eye.

"*Svenne?*" Are you Swedish?

"Yeah," I said in English. "Are you?"

Teddy told me he was an Ethiopian raised in Sweden and Israel, and the guys with him were equally international, some part Swedish, some Somalian. The tallest one, a guy named Mesfin, was from an Ethiopian family that had moved to Stockholm. Mes was an aspiring photographer in New York, currently working at a coffee bar and schlepping backdrops at a fancy photo studio in the West Village.

Teddy, Mes, and I started hanging out right away. They were more like me in terms of experience and culture than anyone I'd ever met, and they also knew how to navigate the city. Mes had a coworker at the coffee bar, a handsome Somali Swede named Sam. Sam and Mes roomed together in a quirky arrangement they had with a model friend. The model let them stay in her apartment for free when she was doing the seasons in Paris and London, and it was several steps up from anything they could have afforded on their own: a doorman one-bedroom on Twenty-fifth and Park. At that point, I'd left Peter and Magnus's to stay in a series of word-of-mouth apartments with roommates I didn't know and where my stuff, what little of it there was, constantly went missing. When Mes suggested I join him and Sam in their one-bedroom, I packed my bags and went.

We rotated sleeping arrangements; one person got the couch and two shared the bed. At first we were suspicious of the doorman, as-suming he knew we were not legitimate tenants, but he didn't seem to care and opened the door for us just as promptly as he did for the little old ladies with their little old dogs. That apartment was my first home in New York, a place where my Swedish-English patois was the common language.

My new roommates brought me into their world, which was every bit as exotic as my adventures into Queens. This was the era of the supermodel, and Mes's studio would regularly bring in Christy Turlington or Naomi Campbell for shoots. Eddie Murphy would be in one day, TLC the next. Often, the shoot day would end with a party, and under the guise of being staff, I'd join them behind the bar, pouring coffee and beers. If we didn't have a posh party to crash, we'd go to the one-dollar beer place in the Village where we could play pool and the jukebox gave you seven songs for a buck. We loved going high and low, and between the three of us, we had enough charm to get in almost anywhere. In Manhattan at the time, there was an ongoing underground party called Soul Kitchen that played soul music and switched locations every Thursday or Tuesday. One of us always figured out where that party was going to be. We'd go to Nell's on Fourteenth Street, a club that had live bands upstairs and hip-hop on the floor below, and where you got in not by wearing a suit, like so many clubs these days, but by wearing an attitude.

None of us talked about it—we were guys, after all—but we all felt freer in New York than we had at home; we were no longer such oddballs. We all had other black friends and other people of color as friends and everybody did his thing. Everything we moved to New York for was happening for us: diversity, music, excitement, creativity.

Not everything went my way in New York, of course, and some of those disappointments were greater than others. On the lighter side of failure, my attempts at love, American style, flopped. I had this idea, when I arrived, that I wanted to date a typical American girl. (Whatever that was.) I wasn't more specific than that in my desire; I was just ready to change up from the Swedish au pairs I'd met through *Svenne* buddies at work. Casey hooked me up, of course—I'd have had no other way into that world.

The deck was stacked against me from the start, since I knew almost nothing about dating, much less American dating. In Sweden, we hung out in groups, and whoever ended up as couples still traveled as part of the group. Whoever had money paid; there were no expectations, and no one kept track. Once I got to America, my Garden City buddy Anthony filled me in on the high school prom rituals of the boy asking the girl, the corsage, the limo, the bow tie having to match the dress.

"For a high school *dance*?" I kept asking him.

When I met up with my first proper American date, an African American woman a couple of years younger than me, she seemed ready for adventure.

"Let's go places," she said. Cool, I thought, and headed for the nearest subway.

"No, I can't," she said, looking down at her high heels. "Not in these."

So we cabbed down to the Village to have a drink and some food at a skanky place on Bleecker Street. Then she wanted to go uptown to the Shark Bar, so we cabbed up to the Upper West Side and had another drink. Then she wanted to go back downtown to listen to late-night music, and when we stepped out onto Seventh Avenue, I counted out the fare for our third taxi of the night and I realized I had only eight dollars left. I panicked, then I got mad. Screw this, I thought.

"This has been nice," I lied. "But I have to get up early tomorrow."

It's not in my nature to give up easily. I met another girl and came up with what I figured was a surefire plan. One of Aquavit's Brazilian waiters had gone back to Rio for vacation, and I was apartment-sitting for him. He had a nice place, so I figured, OK, rather than go on a date to some bad restaurant, I should invite the girl over so I can cook for her. I get to show off what I'm good at, and we'd eat better and cheaper than any restaurant I could afford. I called and proposed the dinner.

"What are you talking about?" she said, as if I were crazy. For me that wasn't a weird thing, just to invite someone over and cook a big meal. She finally agreed to come—as long as she could bring a girl-friend/bodyguard.

"No problem," I said.

I did a four-course meal, with appetizer and soup and a potato-wrapped salmon.

The girls oohed and aahed at every course. I figured I'd put the girl I liked at ease, but as soon as dinner ended, and I asked if she wanted to hang out, she and her friend announced they had to go. I guess they'd figured they'd eat with me and then go hang out with the guys who were serious prospects, guys with enough loot to wine and dine them.

That wasn't me. My salary wasn't going to increase anytime soon, so I had to figure out how to have fun on the cheap, and find girls who would go along with that. By the end of my nine-month stint, I'd tracked down the best hot dog stand in the city, and that's where I'd take my dates. Afterward, if a girl hadn't given up on me yet, I'd invite her to take a walk with me through Central Park. You'd be surprised how many New Yorkers have never really *been* to Central Park—or if they have, haven't visited it in years.

I love Central Park like only an immigrant could. It's an American masterpiece. I explored every corner of it: I'd skate up to 100th and Fifth to sit in the rose garden or hang out at the east-side plaza where roller skaters of every shape and size danced all day long. People were making out, picnicking, jogging. There was every color and ethnicity. Back then, you'd see lots of Vietnam vets, too, guys who'd checked out of society and made their home there. On the soccer field, I'd play one day against some of the best soccer players I've ever competed against in my life, and the next day, I'd be playing against some bum who would drop out to go smoke weed and then come back in. No one cared. No one was there to judge.

Being broke and living in a city like New York was no problem, once I realized you could still find plenty of stuff to do if you knew where to look. If I was going out and had fifty dollars to spend, I'd grab the *Village Voice* events calendar, scoping out whatever was cheap or free—concerts in the park, clubs with no cover, off-off-Broadway shows that needed butts in the seats. I got it down to an art form: how to have a good time for forty-nine dollars or less.

The best place to start was Chinatown, which was busy and energetic, with a sidewalk scene that provided plenty of visuals and smells and a totally exotic soundtrack. I found spots where my date and I could get a tasting menu for five dollars each, if you ordered right, and since I was the cook, I always ordered. We would share noodles, dumplings, steamed buns, barbecue ribs, hot and sour soup, and one noodle dish for the grand sum of ten dollars. Add in some really bad plum wine and a tip: sixteen dollars and you were good to go. For me, the best dish of all was the sweet pork buns, which were such a new combination of textures and flavors. The big white buns were light and airy with a slightly toothy skin caused by the steaming process. I watched as the cooks loaded up bamboo steamer baskets with buns, put on their lids, and then set them over heats much higher than we ever used at Aquavit. At the center of the bun was a filling of roasted pork and a sweet sauce.

It came with a side dish of soy sauce, and into this I'd mix every condiment on the table: mustard, chili sauce, and a bit of chili vinegar. We'd dip the buns in the sauce and get through the obligatory first bite—all dough—to get to the mind-blowing second bite, which combined dough and filling. It's still one of my favorite dishes to eat. I always wondered who created this dish, how it came about.

The whole experience of the Chinese restaurant was so intriguing to me that I never minded being treated rudely or made to wait. And yes, the lighting was usually operating room fluorescent and the floor was linoleum and the service would have gotten you kicked out of restaurant school, but if you were lucky enough to be able to see into the kitchen, even glimpses through swinging doors, you saw a fury of activity, cooks working at top speed putting out tremendous volume and quality. That work ethic, along with a price I could afford, kept me coming back.

Chinatown was just one of a hundred food destinations I'd discovered, and almost day by day, my desire to stay in New York grew stronger. I was intrigued by what I was seeing in the American approach to food. It clearly started with the traditions of Europe but was not bound by them. Europeans I'd worked with scoffed at American cuisine, claiming it was nothing more than burgers. I knew that was bullshit. I was having one unbelievable food adventure after another, and I didn't want that to stop.

In New York, I was surrounded by people who were on their way somewhere. I wanted to be on my way, too, but it turned out that the rest of the New York cooking world wasn't quite as easy to crack as Aquavit had been. While I was still waiting to hear from places I'd written to in France, it seemed silly not to explore some American options while I was in the country. I aimed high. Jean-Georges Vongerichten was at Lafayette and Daniel Boulud was at Le Cirque, and while they were clearly geniuses, they were not at center stage. Center stage, at that moment, belonged to David Bouley, a chef from Connecticut who had made his mark in the city when he ran the kitchen at Montrachet, a TriBeCa restaurant owned by the then fledgling restaurateur Drew Nieporent. Bouley won raves for stuffing cabbage rolls with foie gras one night and pairing red snapper with a tomato-and-coriander pasta the next. Both Bouley and Nieporent were about to build food dynasties, but due to mismatched temperaments, not together. In 1987, Bouley opened his own restaurant— Bouley—on West Broadway and Duane, practically around the corner from Montrachet. He knocked it out of the park, too, earning four stars from *The New York Times*, repeatedly coming in at number one in the reader-driven *Zagat Survey*, and winning awards from the industry's benchmark-setting James Beard Foundation. Customers reserved months in advance to taste Bouley's locally sourced fingerling potatoes or his roasted wild salmon with sesame seeds in tomato water.

I wanted to work for David Bouley.

I took the subway down to Canal Street one afternoon to see if I could secure a *stage* with him. I was fairly sure Christer Larsson would let me off for a couple of weeks; it was a kind of gentlemen's agreement among chefs to let your hard workers train with someone else when the opportunity arose.

The first thing I noticed about the restaurant was a crate of fresh apples sitting out on the sidewalk, waiting to be taken inside. I made my way back to the kitchen and recognized in every detail—the decor of the dining room, the freshness of the herbs that an intensely focused *commis* was chopping, the quiet seriousness of the staff—the same level of commitment I had known at Victoria Jungfrau. I found the *sous-chef*, a German guy who would go on to have his own successful restaurant in the West Village some years later. I told him my history and asked if they'd let me *stage*.

"No," he said, and I realized that his gaze had stopped short of actually focusing on me, that he wasn't putting any effort into seeing beyond an instantaneous judgment he'd made that I was not worth his time. It was the look. I'd seen it everywhere from Gburg to Nice. "I don't think so."

"You could let me do a tryout before you decide," I suggested, feeling emboldened by my recent successes at Aquavit. I was offering a couple of weeks of free, skilled labor. If they let me work just one shift, they'd see what I could do.

"I don't think so," he repeated, and turned his back.

Had they ever had a black cook in that kitchen? Would they ever?

It was becoming clearer and clearer to me that black people were almost by design not part of the conversation about fine dining. In New York, I'd only heard of one black man to pull a chair up to that table, and that was Patrick Clark, a second-generation chef from Canarsie, Brooklyn. In 1980, when he was only twenty-five, Clark brought nouvelle cuisine to TriBeCa via the Odeon, and *The New York Times* gave him two stars in its very first review of the place. Clark would go on to do stints in LA and DC, he'd turn down an invitation to become the White House chef for the Clinton administration, and he'd eventually be named executive chef for Central Park's iconic Tavern on the Green restaurant.

Sometimes, when Christer Larsson took me along to swanky cooking events, I would see Clark there. He seemed like a nice guy with a big personality, built like a boxer. A well-fed boxer. He was always, without fail, the only black man among his peers, but he seemed at ease in any environment, confident that he deserved to be in the room, on equal footing with other food-world luminaries who left me starstruck, like Park Avenue Café's David Burke and Aureole's Charlie Palmer. Clark always seemed to be accompanied by people of color, people who probably would never have gotten into the room without him.

Back then, as a black man in the world of fine dining, Patrick Clark was truly the exception to the rule. His food was solid and well-executed, his passion and personality were larger than life, and yet he would never get more than two stars. I wanted more. I wanted four stars. The upper echelon among chefs was still reserved for white men, but I knew, in my heart, that that could change. I was the Lion of Judah, as Ethiopians sometimes referred to themselves, born into one of the oldest, proudest civilizations on the planet. And I was raised with the truth of equality, by white parents who lived out their belief in racial equality through their love and protection and support. I believed in myself as a chef. I just needed to get through the door. The key, I knew, was to have the one credential that still mattered above and beyond anything else: France. If I could get to France, then even a jerk-off *sous-chef* couldn't afford to ignore me.

I HAD TO GET TO FRANCE. ANYONE WHO WANTED TO KNOW GREATNESS had to go to France. Yeah, I found French food too heavy and rigid and fussy sometimes, with technique overshadowing flavor, but there was no question that it embodied excellence, history, and craft—three qualities that appealed to me. Plus, I needed that pedigree in my pocket.

Starting at Belle Avenue and then whenever I went home between jobs, I'd go to the library to look up French restaurants. I didn't even know enough French to write the letters, asking for work; I had to find someone to help me translate. Plenty of places didn't bother to respond at all, many said no, and the first one that wrote back with possibilities was the Paris branch of a Swiss hotel chain, no doubt impressed by my time at Victoria Jungfrau.

"Take the job," my father said, a firm believer in going with the bird in hand. I was holding out for a place that had earned top honors, which meant three stars in the Michelin guide.

"No way I'm taking that," I said.

"Marcus," he said, in a tone that meant he was trying to appeal to my sense of reason. "Even if it's a one star or a zero star, just take the job. At least you'll be in *France.*"

He had a point, but I wanted to hold out. If I kept working hard, there would be a payoff.

In the summer of 1993, two events conspired to catapult my cooking to a new level. First, after thirty polite rejections to the letters I'd sent to three-star restaurants in France, one finally said yes. The family-owned Georges Blanc restaurant in Vonnas, halfway between Dijon and Lyon, offered to take me as an intern the following May, and if everything worked out, I would be allowed to stay for nine months. They would cover room and board, but as was always the case in restaurant apprenticeships, the higher the level, the less you got paid. At Georges Blanc, I'd get squat. I'd have to save up for my transportation and living expenses, which might have been possible if I hadn't had to make the monthly payments for my daughter.

The second event, which ended up being a kind of solution to the challenges of the first, happened on a hot August day during the break between lunch and dinner services, when Paul Giggs walked through the doors of Aquavit. My old boss from Victoria Jungfrau had left Switzerland and gone back to working for cruise ships, this time a highly rated Norwegian cruise line. His ship had docked in New York, and he decided to look me up. He was sitting at the bar when I came out of the kitchen, and I did a double take at seeing him perched on a barstool. He had come to visit, but he also happened to be look- ing for a cook. Was I interested?

"It's hard work," he warned. "There's no such thing as a day off." Paul's timing couldn't have been better. My contract at Aquavit was almost up and cruise ship work paid incredibly well, many times over what I'd ever earned. I agreed to sign on for a four-month stint, a run that would take me from Fort Lauderdale to South America. This was the adventure Mannfred and I had talked about so many times back in Interlaken. Going through with it would be a kind of tribute to my lost friend.

I ended up doing two stints for Paul, back to back, filling the months between New York and France and wiring my earnings to my mother to bank for me. I made enough to finally pay off what I'd borrowed from my parents, salt away six months of child support payments for Zoe, and pile up a good chunk of change for France. I also got to see the world, albeit in four- and five-hour doses when we docked in ports from Venezuela to Saint Petersburg.

In a creative sense, work on the ship wasn't that challenging or rewarding. Paul was giving customers what they wanted: nothing too complicated. We'd make crab cakes on a "haystack" of fried leeks, minute steaks, and lemon garlic roasted chicken, day in and day out. What mattered was consistency and service, pleasing the passengers who had paid a thousand dollars a day to be on that ship. It was a little like being an actor in a Broadway show, having to be on time and do your best six days a week, except we did it for seven. Every day, we had two hundred guests to feed and we cooked them breakfast, lunch, and dinner. I learned how to bang it out, and I remember thinking that if I ever had to do pre-theater dinners again, I'd be able to do them with my eyes closed.

Guests usually came aboard for one week, and they rated the food at the end of their trip: Paul went apeshit if we got anything less than top marks. Fortunately, we rarely did.

He was fair and he rewarded talent, but if you messed up, he was not nice. My worst moment on the ship was near Acapulco. I'd recently gotten Paul to hire my buddy Susan, a Swede I'd worked with at Aquavit.

"I don't know about bringing women onto the boat," he said, but I vouched for Susan and she worked so hard and was so talented that

Paul accepted her instantly. Unfortunately, from swimming or eating something ashore, Susan fell horribly sick. Either we had to cover for her, or she had to go home.

"No problem, we'll pick up her slack," I promised, but taking over a second person's station in an eight-person kitchen turned out to be too much. I was handling her fish station *and* the grill, and I started to lose track. Was that lamb order rare or medium rare? How many tenderloins was that again? It was too much. I was going down. Marcel, a Swiss cook who was in charge of the *entremetier* station, had to step in on fish while I dug myself out on the grill. I started screaming out orders, totally out of control, and when Paul saw how lost I was, he screamed louder, berating me all through service.

"You ugly fucking piece of shit," he'd say every time a well-done steak came back from a customer who'd asked for rare.

Service that night felt like it went on forever, although I'm sure it was just as short or as long as it always was. Afterward, I got off the ship as soon as I could and went into an Acapulco bar for a drink. I sat on a terrace overlooking the wide curve of the bay, nursing my beer and alternately feeling sorry for myself—I was just trying to help out a friend—and cursing Giggs for being such an unforgiving hard-ass. Like one New Year's Eve at Victoria Jungfrau, I'd messed up big time, ruining a ton of dinners and throwing off the entire kitchen's rhythm in the process. I decided I could quit first or let Paul fire me, but if I quit, then I was letting him win. I wasn't going to be the one to buckle first.

I'm not sure why Paul didn't fire me. Maybe in the scheme of things, I took my mistake more seriously than he did. Maybe he kept me on because Susan came back to work the next day and he knew I wouldn't be in a position to fuck up again. He carried on; I carried on.

For me, the privacy of the single berth on the ship was all about putting on my headphones and listening to French language lessons. Georges Blanc wasn't going to be like Victoria Jungfrau, where I'd had a kind of grace period to get up to speed with my German. I needed to hit the ground running. I also continued to dream on the page, in my journals. In order to progress, I felt that I had to develop new dishes, to take all I was seeing and tasting and make it into something that was *mine*. As committed to excellence as Paul was, I never saw him putting energy into developing his own cuisine. He seemed to have the attitude of, basically, Fuck it, I'm just going to make Italian food for the Italian customer. He had become an extended arm of the clientele.

I didn't want to do that. I knew I wouldn't be good at it, other guys would be better, and I had zero interest in it. I was interested in chasing flavors. I wanted to shake things up and see what happened. What if I took this piece of turbot, put Parmesan on top, put it in the salamander to speed-melt the cheese, then finished it with an orange chutney? I didn't know if mixing French fish, Italian cheese, and Indian Caribbean flavors would be good, but I wanted to try it.

Those were the ideas I'd write in my journal, everything I'd tasted or wanted to try. I'd write down an idea and if it didn't even work on the page, I'd let it go. I was my own gatekeeper; I had to fall in love with an idea before I would take twenty minutes and try to make it. First of all, twenty minutes was a precious amount of time in any kitchen, but especially on the cruise ship. Weeks might pass between chances to experiment, but you did it when you could because you never knew when the chance would come again.

"OK," Paul might say during a morning planning meeting. "I need another entrée for tonight."

"I got it," I'd say, and offer up one of my latest inventions, one I'd already tested on the page and in the kitchen. After a while, when Paul needed to fill in a gap in his menu, he automatically turned to me.

"Marcus, what have you got?" he'd say.

LIFE ON THE SHIP DEMONSTRATED yet one more way in which a kitchen staff could be divided up into factions. Cooks sat with cooks, of course, and officers with officers. I was the only black in the kitchen, but I was considered European and therefore given a middle level of status. The Norwegians were at the top of the heap, and the Filipinos who cleaned and actually ran the boat were at the bottom. There were plenty of onboard romances, but it went without saying that a Filipino dishwasher should never touch a Swedish chambermaid. The Filipinos lived four to a room and if the Europeans and Americans thought a nonstop five-month schedule was tough, it was nothing compared to theirs—eighteen months with not a single day off and not a single second of privacy. What the hell was that? They were hardworking people. The only benefit, as far as I was concerned, of the separate-but-unequal world on the ship was that the staff mess hall featured two menus, one for them and one for the rest of us. I always ordered theirs. Their food showed traces of the country's Asian location, its Spanish colonizers, and its importance as a European and Arab trade route, and the results were richer, spicier, and tastier than anything else on offer. I would have been happy to eat the stewed chicken adobo over rice every day, but my absolute favorite was a jellyroll-style beef dish called *morcon*, filled with the unexpected but tasty combination of hard-boiled eggs, cheese, sausage, liver, and strips of pork fat, all tied together with string and simmered in a vinegary sauce.

New flavors were what I was after, and in almost every port of call, I smelled or tasted something I'd never tasted before. I'd have four hours to go ashore, and I'd go by myself unless Paul or Susan wanted to tag along. Ports are, as a rule, the seediest area of a city, and the captain often issued warnings to the crew to be careful. For a change, my color was an asset in terms of blending in; in many of our layovers, only my blond shipmates got the stares and hustles. Under the protective layer of my skin, I went unnoticed, which allowed me to observe and relish the most beautiful aspect of port culture: the street food.

Funny when you imagine how a certain food should taste, and then you experience the authentic version. In the middle of a food market in Acapulco, I ordered four tacos: two pork, one fish, one chicken. I watched a small brown woman with long black braids make the tortillas right in front of me, patting the masa dough into flat circles much smaller than I thought they would be. The pork was simply roasted and pulled apart; the fish was a version of grouper that had been pan-seared and tossed with a little oil and chopped cilantro stems—not the leaves, just the stems. The chicken was shredded leg meat roasted with chilies and tomatoes and red onions. Doritos were about as close as I'd ever come to Mexican food, so my expectations were all fabricated from stereotyped images I'd gotten who knows where. I expected the tacos to come in crisp-fried tortilla envelopes, but instead, they were little pyramids of layered ingredients on top of soft flat pancakes. They were garnished with sliced red onions and jalapeños, lime wedges, and, on the side, green and red salsas and a dish of yellow rice. I spooned as much rice and salsa as I could into each taco, squeezed lime over the whole thing, and dug in. Fantastic.

The *pata negra* I tasted when we stopped in Spain, on the other hand, wasn't love at first bite. The fat in the ham was too pronounced for me, but its distinctive flavor, coming from the black Iberian pigs that'd been fed a strict diet of acorns, caught my attention. It was an acquired taste, and I knew I'd try it again. For breakfast in Spain, they took ripe tomatoes, peeled them, and crushed them on top of toast, adding a grind or two of black pepper. It was so bright, it was almost blinding. I still do a sandwich like that, almost twenty years later.

In Jamaica, I had a grilled fish sandwich on the beach, the simplest preparation, but it was fresh and completely connected to the beautiful surroundings, the best damn sandwich I'd ever had. A waitress in Puerto Rico saw my surprised look when she set the *camarones de mofongo* I'd ordered in front of me. I probably wasn't the first foreigner to be disappointed with a plate of grayish porridge, but she told me to dig inside with my spoon, and underneath the velvety plantain puree, I found a spicy blend of chopped shrimp and pork. Now that I've come to understand something about African cuisines, I see the dish as a blend of Africa's plantains and Caribbean spices, but all I knew then was that it was delicious and filling. Borscht in Russia tasted better after I'd spent the afternoon Rollerblading through Saint Petersburg's Palace Square under the shadow of massive buildings that had played a role in the Russian Revolution, but borscht, let's be honest, can be only so good.

When my second contract with Paul took me to Asia, all the flavors of the staff dishes Paul had made at Victoria went from black-and-white to Technicolor. I tasted coconut milk and lemongrass in hundreds of preparations, sweet and savory, and I thought, This is it: This food has as much integrity and power as any French food I'd ever eaten. Why did people fly in Dijon mustard when they could make their own, fresher and better? I started to ask myself, Who lied? Who started the lie that France had the greatest food in the world? That question ran through my head every time I bit into something new and that changed my notions of what "good food" is. Then that question was replaced by a second: Who's going to make the people realize that food dismissed as "ethnic" by the fine-dining world could be produced at the same level as their sacred bouillabaisses and veloutés?

It wasn't just the flavors that knocked me on my ass. It was seeing different people holding it, preparing it, serving it. Sometimes the chefs were not in the white jackets, and it wasn't only men, it was women, it was children, it was everyone. There were Indians, blacks, Koreans, mixed people. When I had my own restaurant someday, I thought, I would never rule out someone based on race or sex or nationality. I wouldn't do it because it was egalitarian, I'd do it because cutting people out meant cutting off talent and opportunity, people who could bring more to the table than I could ever imagine. I felt like I was climbing aboard a new food train, one that I'm still on to this day.

SIXTEEN **THE PRICE**

I WAS IN THE CRUISE SHIP KITCHEN, OFF THE COAST OF VENEZUELA ON Christmas Eve, when the telegraph came through that my grandmother Helga had died from a stroke. True to her personality, it happened while she was cutting down a tree with a hand saw. A bursar brought the news to Paul, who hesitated before he told me. We were about to go into dinner service, and Paul worried I'd be too upset to make it through my shift. He was not unfeeling; I would have had the same worry. He did choose to tell me, after all, and I took the news and then kept working, no faster or slower than I would on any other day. *Mormor* was one of the most important people in the world to me. I was heartbroken, but I was also proud that I was able to finish my day at work. Although I could not even afford to call her on a weekly basis during my many apprenticeships, I felt like her hands always shadowed mine in the kitchen—she had the instinct, I had the technique, and together we were unstoppable.

No one at work had any idea about my daughter Zoe. On one level, I didn't want people to think I was nothing more than a cliché—the absentee black father. On another, I was afraid the information could somehow hold me back or limit my opportunities in a way that would, in the end, not only harm me but make it harder to meet the slim responsibility of financial support that my mother had assigned me. I told myself that when the time was right—which, for me, meant when I'd achieved what I wanted in my career—I would make my presence known in Zoe's life. Next year I'll be better, I would tell myself. Next year I'll have time.

In the spring of 1993, I left to do my *stage* at Georges Blanc, the name of both the chef and the restaurant. Blanc had virtually taken over the village of Vonnas, not far from the Swiss border in the fertile stretch of grape-growing valley that produced Beaujolais, burgundy, and Rhône wines. Among chefs of my generation, Georges Blanc was a fixed point in the constellation of stars we looked up to. A fourth-generation restaurateur, he'd moved his family's restaurant, also called Georges Blanc, from Michelin's highly respectable two stars to three. He was a major player, the first globally renowned chef I'd ever been around. He had a helicopter pad out back so he could be flown to do lunch in Amsterdam before setting off for Dubai or Singapore or Japan. I'd never seen a celebrity chef before; I hadn't even heard the phrase. While Stocker was a serious, hardworking chef, Georges Blanc had a French flair and an eye for opportunities. Tourists and guests loved meeting him: Blanc laughed easily and kissed women's hands; he toured people through his kitchen, a winning, generous tour guide. His restaurant was especially popular among Americans, who came in as couples or on business, and wealthy Japanese, who arrived in busloads. Many of the Japanese saw Georges Blanc as a key stop on a string of the region's three-star restaurants. If it's Tuesday, it must be Alain Chapel. If it's Wednesday, it must be Georges Blanc.

When I arrived, Blanc was fifty years old and at the peak of his career. To aspiring chefs like me, he was one in a small handful of master chefs considered among the best in the world. Another was Paul Bocuse, who was almost twenty years older than Blanc. Bocuse was the ne plus ultra of twentieth-century cooking, credited with transforming haute cuisine into nouvelle cuisine. There was one of Bocuse's students, the Austrian Eckart Witzigmann. There was Joël Robuchon in Paris and Frédy Girardet in Switzerland. The Roux brothers, Albert and Michel, were in London, changing the culinary reputation of the entire city, and Marc Haeberlin was launching a global food empire from his L'Auberge de l'Ill in Alsace. Notably, there were no Americans on the list. No Italians, even. France was the standard setter on the world stage, and back then, if you looked in their establishments, they were all, more or less, doing the same thing: exquisite execution of French cuisine, some of it modernized or lightened, but in terms of a flavor palate, they were all speaking the same language.

I knew my path would be different—the cruise ship travels had confirmed it—but I respected that language the way a modern composer might respect Bach. The better I could speak it, the freer I would be to create my own.

In broad daylight, I could see that Georges Blanc owned the town of Vonnas. Almost literally. He had bought up much of the real estate on the town square and, in addition to the quaint, half-timbered, luxurious hotel/restaurant I was headed for, he had created a somewhat more affordable, casual eatery called L'Ancienne Auberge. He'd also established his own vineyard some years before, just beyond town, and had transformed many in-town storefronts into specialty shops that made Vonnas into a food lover's paradise.

I went into work the next morning with first-day jitters. I had replaced my Converse sneakers with Dr. Martens boots, my pants and jacket were fresh and crisply ironed, and I was wearing a simple dark tie. I had finally made it to Division One in the cooking world; there was no higher for me to go. Division One is an elite club. Once you're inside, you have established yourself, but that doesn't mean you can slack off. Everyone at Georges Blanc worked with a palpable commitment to excellence. Everyone from the boy polishing glasses to the woman arranging flowers moved at a fast clip, no time to sit down, all of them preparing for the common goal of knocking each guest off his or her feet.

We were in constant competition, with ourselves, each other, and the other three-star restaurants. We had to be on our toes at all times. It didn't take long for me to be grateful that I hadn't gone straight from Belle Avenue to France. When I left Göteborg, I was still a novice. At Georges Blanc, you had to fight for your place every day. It would take everything I had to hang in France.

That first day, I crossed the perfect square filled with shops, which were all redone in a medieval style, with facades of plaster and exposed wood framing. I had the feeling of being in a gourmet theme park done in the best of taste. I thought I was just passing through the square on the way to Georges Blanc, but when I got there, the HR person pulled out my file, checked it against a list, and simply said, *"Boulangerie."*

Back outside I went, walking over to one of those shops on the square, a bakery that was to be my home for the foreseeable future. I wasn't working in the actual restaurant kitchen, but I still felt a part of the team, and just as I'd found working in the garden at Victoria Jungfrau, there was plenty to learn. I'd never tasted bread like this. A croissant fresh from the oven is a beautiful thing, and now I know how they're made, how much butter they require, and how fresh the butter has to be to give them their lightness and flake. Our shop also made small takeaway snacks and meals that sightseers could pick up on their way out into the countryside, where they'd drive through cornfields and visit vineyards and tour the farms that raised *poulets de Bresse*, a local chicken so special that it got the distinctive appellation AOC, a guarantee of authenticity given to such specialty items as Roquefort cheese and Le Puy lentils.

My favorite prepared dish in the shop was the lobster lasagna. This wasn't like any lasagna I'd had before. We started with fresh lobster. Lots of lobster. The tail was reserved for restaurant use, but we got the claws, the body, and the legs. We dug out every bit of meat from them and used the shells to make our stock. Then we made our own lasagna sheets and layered them with sautéed spinach from the garden, lobster, and just-sweet oven-dried tomatoes. The results were brilliant.

I kept my head down and did what was asked of me, knowing that if I did a good job, someone would notice and I would be moved to the kitchen. It was a mutually beneficial arrangement: I was there to learn, but I knew they were also sifting through the stream of *commis*, looking for whom to pluck out of the group and add to their team. A friendly American I worked alongside, a big boulder of a guy named Jeremy, didn't see this same big picture. He'd been stuck in the *boulangerie* for more than a month and still wasn't cooking. He was pissed.

"Why won't they let me go on the line?" he'd say. "It's bullshit. I'm going to ask them why."

"Don't," I said. "Don't draw attention to yourself. I know it sucks, but try to be as small as possible."

He would never get on the line, I could tell. He wasn't going to last. A lot of Americans had this problem in the European kitchens. It wasn't that they didn't love cooking, it wasn't that they didn't have the skills. They'd done their research and paid their dues and worked just as hard as I had to get to restaurants like Victoria Jungfrau and Georges Blanc. But to get ahead in that culture, you have to completely give yourself up to the place. Your time, your ego, your relationships, your social life, they are all sacrificed. It's a daily dose of humility that a lot of Americans find difficult to swallow. Guys like Jeremy could never fully tamp down the desire to be seen and heard, to stand out and make his mark, to go up to the chef and get noticed by chatting: "I just want to say hi and thank you."

The thing is, small talk with a *commis* is the last thing on a chef's to-do list.

Correction: It's not even on the list.

Many of the European kids who were going into cooking at that time came from blue-collar families; maybe their parents were farmers or had run small hotels. They understood what it meant to give yourself up. The European mentality was that if you were in town and happened to see the general manager, you crossed the road, you didn't say hi. If you saw even a headwaiter coming toward you, you'd wait until he passed by. You hadn't done anything wrong; it was just common sense to stay out of the way. Nothing positive could come of an interaction.

"Why do you think he doesn't like me?" Jeremy would ask me when one of the *chefs de partie* came into the shop and ignored him.

"I don't think he *knows* you," I said. "I don't think he has any idea who you are. Try to make sure it stays that way." Time and time again, the Americans didn't realize the benefits of invisibility until it was too late. Being noticed often led to being fired.

THE GUY WHO CAME to deliver truffles drove up in a Mercedes-Benz. He sat with our chef at a table in the empty dining room, and over a glass of wine, they made their deal. Then he drove off to another three-star Michelin and did it again. The same thing happened with the duck guy, the chicken guy, the cheese guy, the woman who sold us our asparagus and haricots verts. I'd never seen food so fresh or treated with such reverence. For the first time, I realized what was missing back home. Fishermen in Sweden didn't go straight to the restaurant, and Sweden didn't have enough agriculture to support such direct relationships between growers and chefs. At Belle Avenue, we relied on shipments of shrink-wrapped or frozen specialty items, and that resulted in a chronic separation between our product and seasonality. We cooked foie gras all year round because that was what we thought it meant to be a French restaurant. But in Vonnas, when the spring harvest of asparagus came in, we'd feature it in five different dishes each night. In the fish station, we never opened scallops during prep, even though that required stepping out of the fast-paced service to shell them for each order. It was a trade-off, but Blanc placed the highest value on keeping them fresh up to the very last minute. And because they came to us alive and in their shells, they were nothing like the ones that came to Belle Avenue in jars. The experience of cooking the two was completely different, too: The fresh scallops had a dryness to them that made the caramelization process significantly faster. Searing them off took seconds; if you didn't pay attention, they were easy to overcook.

At Georges Blanc, we did not take shortcuts. Animals came in whole and we did everything but slaughter them ourselves. It took a while for me to learn how to clean a wild duck, and if you're too slow, the duck's fat warms to room temperature and you end up pricking the skin as you pluck it, rendering it useless. To clean truffles, we used toothpicks and toothbrushes to remove the dirt, never water. We'd store the cleaned truffles in dry rice, and once the truffles were used, the rice was boiled into the most aromatic side dish on earth. If Blanc microwaved a vegetable, it wasn't to save time, as Stocker had done in Interlaken; it was to retain flavor by shortening the cooking time.

If any corner was cut, it was the corner they didn't quite under-stand, the corner that included the rest of the world's cuisines, so many of which were unknown to or considered beneath them. If those flavors had been included in a more forceful way, I think they could have created at an even higher level.

As it was, the restaurant produced impeccable dishes it had been serving for generations. We were famous for *poulet mère Blanc*, a chicken braised in cream. To make it, we used only the select local chickens, never more than three pounds in weight. We plucked and then blanched each bird, which separated the skin from the meat. Then we skinned and butchered it, separately simmering breasts and dark meat in chicken stock and cream, until the legs and thighs were tender, and the breast was still moist. We let the chicken sit overnight in its liquid, then lifted out the meat and reduced the remains into a wonderful, even *heavier* cream sauce. Labor alone makes this one of the most expensive chicken dishes I'd ever seen, but it also showed me that chicken can hold its own on a menu with lobster and truffles and other expensive ingredients if you take a lot of care and treat it with respect and elegance. On the (barely) lighter side of the menu, Georges Blanc would roast endives, basting them with butter and honey, then put a steamed lobster on top and finish it with butter, mustard, and lemon. It might not sound light, but the absence of a cream sauce was practically revolutionary.

Georges Blanc built his cuisine on three pillars: to preserve the honest and rustic heritage of his ancestors; to maintain the level of elegance that had earned him his third Michelin star; and last, a distant third, to look into the future, exploring new techniques and ingredients.

One dish that spoke to this last category was an appetizer of frog legs in curry sauce with pea puree. When the frog legs came in, we had to clean them, skinning them and then trimming down the legs into pearlescent drumsticks. We'd sauté the legs in garlic and onion until the pale flesh turned golden brown, then debone the meat, using the tip of a knife and being careful not to do a hatchet job that would leave us with mush. We served it with a simple, bright green pea puree. For the puree, we used a pre-blended Indian curry powder that came in a large saffron-colored tin, and we mixed that with garlic, salt and butter, frog leg bones, chicken stock, white wine, cream, and peas. Once we plated the puree, we laid down the frogs' legs and drizzled curry froth across the top.

This appetizer was very popular and somewhat surprising to find in Vonnas. It showed me that Georges Blanc had paid attention when he traveled beyond his world, and he looked to bring those flavors in as long as he could make them have some relationship to French traditions. His example would be invaluable to me when I unexpectedly took over the kitchen at Aquavit a year later. At Aquavit, I found that I didn't have to deny my interest in the flavors I'd tasted while traveling the world, but I also had a duty—and a sincere desire—to uphold the restaurant's Swedish identity. Georges Blanc had shown me how to achieve a balance between those conflicting aims.

By the time I got to Blanc, I'd pretty much gotten past my ritual of throwing up before a big shift. I still had stomachaches from time to time, but even in the intensely competitive and demanding world of that kitchen, I had come to a point where I felt I deserved to be there. I wanted to learn but also to make a contribution, to prove that they had made the right choice by inviting me. I was so intent on doing a good job that I passed up nights out with the staff, even tempting offers to play soccer on the inter-restaurant league. As much as I loved playing soccer, I didn't want to turn France into a soccer trip. I didn't want to stand out for any reason other than my work as a chef.

In New York, I'd reveled in making new black friends. But in France, I hardly spoke to the other black man in the kitchen, a dishwasher from Africa. Other than my giving soiled pans to him, we had no interaction. I was, to be honest, afraid of overfamiliarity and stereotypes. I didn't want him to call out to me, "Oh, African brother . . ." and then end up with both of us in trouble for wasting time. The truth was I chatted with no one, but it particularly sticks with me that I didn't chat with him. We were, after all, part of an underclass, objects of a prejudice that showed up in the common vernacular of the kitchen. Just as in Switzerland, the French term for a low-level kitchen assistant is *negre*, which directly translates to "black." I'd heard people use it countless times, people whose politics are straight up, people who consider themselves worldly and unprejudiced. But there it was, and every time I heard it, the word was more than a word, it was another wall I had to climb.

I had to find my own ways of letting off steam, and I was too strict to let myself experiment with drugs or drink excessively the way so many cooks I knew did. Running became my release. Some of my best moments in France were when I had a day off and I went running in the cornfields or through vineyards. Everywhere I looked, I saw where the food we cooked came from. The farmers seemed to be living very simple lives in direct contact with the earth; the men wore knickers and boots, and the women wore flowery dresses and aprons, much like my grandmother. I felt the high of the serotonin that running released into my brain, but also I was just happy to be there, in that moment. It was a time of no women, no money, and hard work, but I knew that I was lucky to have it all.

Georges Blanc and his wife, Jacqueline, who worked the front of the house, often brought favored customers through the kitchen. As staff, we never made eye contact; we knew we were expected to conduct ourselves in a dignified way, to speak, if it was absolutely necessary, in a subdued tone. Once Georges Blanc saw that I was there to work, that I could handle the tasks I was assigned, and that I spoke English well, I started to go along on cooking demonstrations. He was not one to overlook an asset. For most of these outings, I stood to the side and translated for the chef who was doing the actual cooking. Or I'd go along on a catering job for events at Blanc's winery when he knew there'd be a lot of English speakers there. I was not merely taking omelet orders as I had in Switzerland; I was responsible for communicating concepts, for true interaction.

When things got tough, I'd think about Mannfred and how he was so good at always moving forward. I tried to do the same, to take nothing personally, to see opportunity in every moment. So what if I had to cook for Georges Blanc's dog? A *stage* is a *stage*, and I did my best. That old, ill-tempered retriever ate better than anybody: I'd take a piece of tenderloin, salt and pepper it and sauté it off quickly, then maybe put mustard on it. The end result reminded me of beef Rydberg, the classic Swedish dish that we'd often make at Aquavit. The dog didn't care about the dish's provenance: He wolfed it down the minute the plate hit the floor.

Commis were also responsible for making our afternoon staff meals. We weren't given instructions or recipes, and I suspect that this was the one chance to shine that the higher-ups gave us. If we did a good job, they let us know.

I sometimes made *röschti*, Swiss comfort food, in an iron pan. The dish made me think of Victoria—Mannfred, Giggs, Stocker—the place where I went from being a *commis* to a budding young chef.

Other guys would do more elaborate dishes, but I had learned how to deliver absolute rustic comfort with this. I built the flavors slowly, thinking about how the bacon adds salt, and how the apple and caramelized leeks add sweetness. When I served the table, they made all the universal signs of approval—smacking lips, kissing their fingers, waving a fork, grunting. These guys knew food. They knew flavor. So when they told me the dish was good, I knew they meant it. I knew I had something. More than a few of the dishes I served to the staff in Vonnas landed on the menu years later at Aquavit.

When Georges Blanc offered me a full-time job, I knew it was time to go. To me, that was equivalent to a diploma, proof I had been successful. But I was headed for different frontiers, ones with bolder flavors, to be made and consumed by a cross section of people who more accurately reflected the larger world and, for that matter, me.

It was tempting to say yes to Blanc; I had fallen in love with the spirit of the place, and with working with foods that were organic and seasonal before either became a trend. But the day he made his offer, I got caught in the walk-in refrigerator with a chef who decided to go off on his Japanese *commis*. The chef was a few years younger than the *commis*, and the *commis*, like most of the Japanese who came to work for Blanc, was an excellent worker, meticulous and fast. The chef was just a cocky guy showing that he was boss. He had not only called him a fucking idiot and an amateur, he had upended the *commis*'s *mise en place*, creating a holy mess inside the refrigerator. And when his screaming wasn't enough to fully express his rage, he punched the guy in the stomach. Right in front of me.

The *commis* didn't say a word. He'd flexed his stomach in anticipation, practically breaking the chef's hand. The *commis* was going to be fine, but I remember watching this and thinking, OK, I've gotten all the training I need here. Time to go.

This was the dark side of the French tradition. All of the chefs had come up through that same brutal system, where only the upper echelons had any sense of job security. Even the *chefs de partie* didn't know if they were going to get punched or fired the next day. Besides, if you put a lot of guys in one room, they are going to fight. Ask any of the top chefs and they will tell you that they've all seen violence in the kitchen. It's not what I do; it is not how I treat people, but there's no denying that this is the way it was. By the end of the nineties, this nonsense started to disappear because cooking became so competitive. Good cooks are hard to come by: They have plenty of options now, and if you treat someone that way, they'll leave. It is, thank God, a different time.

I left on good terms, even though I turned down Blanc's offer. How do I know the parting was positive? Because I've subsequently sent a couple of my own guys there to *stage*. One was a black kid, and I'm proud that I paved the way for him, that Georges Blanc gambled on something new by having a *negre* come, and the *negre* turned out to be an asset.

SEVENTEEN **ANOTHER GLASS OF AQUAVIT**

As my time at Georges Blanc came to an end, I sat down and wrote three letters. The first was to an American talk show host I'd watched during my Aquavit internship. He was edgy and funny and, more than anything else, smart.

"Dear Mr. Letterman," I wrote, "have you ever considered branching out into restaurants?"

I wrote a similar letter to Oprah Winfrey, who was already much more than just a TV personality and would surely see the wisdom of partnering with me.

"Dear Ms. Winfrey," I wrote. "Nothing could be a better accompaniment to the conversations you have on air every day than a restaurant. . . ."

Just to be safe, I also wrote to Aquavit's founder, Håkan Swahn. "If you hire me," I promised, "I will make Aquavit one of the top ten restaurants in the city."

Only Håkan wrote back.

I was twenty-four years old and I didn't know what the hell I was talking about. I didn't know how American rating systems worked, I didn't know the difference between *Gourmet* and *Bon Appetit*. I just knew that of all the places I'd lived, New York was where I fit in best, and I was willing to give everything I had to get back there.

Aquavit had opened its doors in 1987, about the time I walked through the entrance of Tidbloms in Göteborg as a culinary student casting about for my first internship. Håkan Swahn and his chef Tore Wretman quickly distinguished their restaurant from the smorgasbord houses that had, for so long, been the face of Swedish food in America. They paid tribute to the spirit and ingredients of Swedish cuisine, but they also understood they were in New York where sophisticated diners prized bold flavors and fresh ingredients.

Over the years, Aquavit ran into trouble finding the right match for the kitchen's helm. All of Swahn's executive chef choices were Swedes, but that was no guarantee they could maintain the level of excellence to which Swahn aspired. One was dutiful in the execution of Swedish classics but lacked initiative to break new ground; another was *too* Swedish, paying almost no attention to the tastes of the American customer. The August before I returned, Swahn had made a risky move by hiring away a *sous-chef* from Bobby Flay. This was years before Bobby became famous for his *Throwdown!* television show, before *Iron Chef* and *Boy Meets Grill*, but he had already made a mark with his two restaurants, Mesa Grill and Bolo, as well as by winning the Rising Star Chef of the Year Award from the James Beard Foundation. Flay may have been a fourth-generation Irish-American New Yorker, but he had fallen in love with southwestern and Cajun cooking, both of which distinguished him then and still. Maybe because his own story was so unorthodox, Bobby didn't see any problem in hiring Jan Sendel, a young Swede who'd come to New York to be an actor and had no formal culinary training whatsoever. Bobby had his hands full with Jan, whose passion was a blessing and a curse. Jan loved food and was a devoted student of the craft, but he also got bored quickly. Still, the two worked together well enough that after eighteen months, Bobby promoted him to *sous-chef*.

The New York fine-dining world is a small one, and Håkan got wind of Jan's impressive performance down at Mesa. When he needed a new chef to infuse Aquavit's menu with energy and freshness, he approached Jan. This was a bold move on Håkan's part, since Jan was only thirty-two and had never run a kitchen before, but Håkan wasn't afraid to gamble on a guy who radiated talent, and Jan couldn't resist the chance to be an executive chef. Jan arrived at Aquavit in August, and when I came in five months later, he had already begun to turn things around.

ON DECEMBER 31, 1994, I left a New Year's party in Göteborg before midnight. My mom drove me to the airport, I slept on the plane, and I woke up in New York on January 1. The day was dead, as it probably is all over the world, but I didn't care: I had three hundred dollars in traveler's checks in my pocket, and a new life.

I started at Aquavit the next day. The minute I stepped into the basement kitchen, I sensed a new vibe. There were fewer Swedes on staff and the radio was turned up louder. Christer Larsson had been a quiet, calm boss and Jan was the opposite, with his shaved head and high-topped Doc Martens, in the way he rapped his wedding ring against the steel counter whenever he wanted a waiter's attention, and in how he would call cooks out if they fucked up, yelling and cursing until his voice went hoarse. He loved the limelight, to be sure, and if there was none shining on him, he'd create it. The Swedes—who'd made up at least half of the line before—had been replaced by guys from Mesa Grill, so the influence of Bobby hung around us, a constant reference point for how things should be done.

None of the Mesa guys was more critical to Jan than his

forty-year-old Bronx-born *sous-chef* and right-hand man, Larry Man-heim. Larry was a good cook, but he was also like the kitchen's super: When the garbage needed to go out, Larry got someone to take it out. When the fish guy came by, Larry talked to him. This left Jan free to concentrate on developing new dishes. A growing buzz in the city about Aquavit's new chef was starting to make everyone on the team hopeful.

I got hired on to join this ragtag band because Håkan had the wisdom to see through the naive bravado of my letter. I was talking shit for sure, but at least my goals were in line with his, my love for the city came through, and, underpinning it all, I had demonstrated my ability to contribute during my internship there the previous year; now that I'd been on the cruise ships and in France, I would be only a stronger worker, and my European training would be something nei-ther Jan nor Larry could offer.

Jan didn't come from a standard fine-dining point of view, and he didn't give a shit about France. Instead, he looked to Latin America, the Southwest, and, to a lesser extent, Asia. He didn't make classical stocks; as a go-to herb, he used cilantro instead of thyme. Avocado was a staple. If the best flavor was to be found in a jar, Jan took the jar. If he could have done Mesa Grill with a Swedish flair, he would have, but the problem was that those flavors were often too far away from each other. There were dishes where you could meld them, like a blue corn pancake with gravlax, but the balance he sought was a challeng-ing one to strike.

What I loved about Jan's food was that it was relentlessly flavor-driven. He might never have been to France, but the upside of that was that he wasn't hamstrung by tradition. He relied on his palate, and he was gifted with a brilliant one. He loved the bold chilies of the Southwest, but he also embraced Asian flavors like miso and galangal, and those seemed to be a natural match with Swedish ingredients. Having been to the source countries for those ingredients while on the cruise ships, I often felt like I had a closer understanding than he did of the flavors he played with, but I was not there to challenge Jan,

I was there to work for him. I came in early, worked hard, and kept my mouth shut.

Jan seemed to like me from the start. Maybe it was because I was black; before the end of our first conversation, he made sure to let me know that he was married to an African American woman. I smiled politely, but thought, So what? How is that relevant to me? You wouldn't believe how often people say things like this. What really impressed me about his wife was not her color, but that she did the window displays for Bergdorf Goodman. I had passed that store almost every day the first time I lived in New York. For a broke but style-conscious guy, Bergdorf's was a fantasyland, and I knew every inch of those windows, studying the fabrics and colors and silhouettes as they changed from season to season. One day, I'll go inside, I thought.

Or maybe Jan liked me because he saw I was totally comfortable in my role as a supporter, and he needed support big-time: Jan hadn't become a name yet, and that made it hard for him to draw experienced cooks. Aside from Larry and Jan and a few of their Mesa Grill friends, Aquavit's line relied on recent culinary school grads, young guys who might someday be good cooks, but who came to the restaurant with no chops whatsoever.

In my first weeks, Jan regularly invited me out after work to party with him and the rest of the Aquavit crew. "C'mon, Marcus," he'd say. "Join us for one round."

I went out a couple of times, while I was still learning people's names, but I cut that off almost right away. I liked the people I worked with, but I wasn't into the expensive champagne or the coke that often found their way into late-night escapades. I wanted to be taken seriously, and going out to bars and clubs and strip joints and getting trashed seemed like a good way to end up in an unprofessional situation. Plus, the last thing I needed was to make an ass out of myself in front of my employer. It seemed particularly crazy to me when waiters and cooks would go out with Jan and get wasted. That promised way more downside than upside. If I went out at all, it was with my old crew of Mes and Sam and Teddy. If I acted the fool with them, so be it. They didn't sign my paycheck.

I'm glad I drew that line, too. It made everything simpler. I liked where Jan was going with his food, and we talked a lot about how he was going to tweak the menu for spring, what dishes to start introducing in March. My classical training came in handy when we were figuring out how to put a new dish into production, and he was always willing to test a recipe that I'd come up with.

"Show me that duck dish you've been talking about," he said one night after service.

"I'll have it for you tomorrow," I said.

The next morning, I plunged a couple of duck breasts in salted water and weighed them down with a plate to keep them submerged, exactly the way my grandmother taught me to cure meat and fish. Six hours later, I took one breast out of the brine and sautéed it in honey and soy. I served a slice to Jan, and he chewed it, closing his eyes and frowning a little as he chewed.

"Nice, but let's try adding another layer," he said, and we sautéed the second breast, this time adding in lemongrass and Kaffir lime leaves. It was fantastic.

"This goes on the menu," Jan said.

Things were going well for all of us. Jan posted every article that mentioned Aquavit on the bulletin board outside the changing room, and the mentions were consistently positive. Valentine's Day fell on a Tuesday that year, but we were full to the gills, and that put everyone in a good mood. Two days later, Jan came into the kitchen carrying a curly piece of fax paper. "Check it out, man," he said as he handed me the page. It was an advance copy of a *New York* magazine article about Jan and the restaurant, praising his leadership after only six months at the helm. His charisma had come across to the journalist, too, who dubbed Jan an "MTV-style" chef. Jan was glowing.

We had a big pre-theater seating that Saturday night, and our middle station cook called in sick at the last minute. This was a problem. Middle station is sometimes called the *friturier* or "fry cook," and he not only does the frying but also helps out the guys on either side of him, who are usually meat and fish. We were short-staffed so Jan tapped a kid named Allen to take his place. Allen was a culinary student doing an internship with us. He was probably nineteen years old, and on a good day, he would have been the third-level helper over in the *garde manger* station. He probably saw this as his shot, and besides, how could he possibly say no?

"You can't fuck up," Jan warned him. "Not tonight."

"I got it, Chef," he said, a little too eagerly. "I got it."

Allen did not have it. He was too young and inexperienced to hold it together, he got swamped, and he went down hard during our early service. He hadn't done enough prep, and he was running out of supplies while diners started to worry about whether they'd make it to their seats before the curtain went up. Allen lost track of his orders, and if he stopped cooking to catch up on prep, a dice that would take a practiced cook three minutes took Allen fifteen, and that was twelve minutes we didn't have to spare. The meat and fish cooks stopped asking for Allen's help, and the rest of us tried to help dig him out, but it was no use. For a good half hour, we couldn't get meals out the door in any semblance of order. Guests complained; pissed-off waiters brought dishes back that weren't cooked right. When that seating finally cleared out, and we had a half-hour lull before regular dinner service heated up, Jan exploded.

"What the fuck are you trying to do to me?" he yelled at Allen, who stood in front of the walk-in with his shoulders bowed, trying to take up as little space as possible. Jan kicked at the refrigerator door with one of his Doc Martens. The handle of the walk-in broke off and clattered to the floor. That only unleashed a new torrent of curses, some now in Swedish, capped off by Jan grabbing fistfuls of Allen's shirt and slamming him into the stainless walk-in door.

"Why doesn't Chef just fire him?" one of the meat cooks muttered. "It would be a lot less painful for everyone."

The rest of service was no less disastrous, and when we finally finished breaking down the kitchen for the night, I was more than ready to clock out. Our chef and the usual crew were headed out for drinks, but I politely declined. I was going to sleep.

"See you Monday," I said to Jan on my way out.

Sunday was my day off and that Monday, I headed back into work, as usual. Aquavit was across the street from the Peninsula hotel, and on my way in, I said hi to my pal Joey, the hotel doorman.

"Yo, Marcus," he said as I passed by. "I heard there was an accident at Aquavit."

I didn't pay him much attention, went in the front doors, and signed in. Two cooks came out of the service elevator, heading for the exit—the opposite direction from where they should have been going.

"Where are you clowns headed?" I asked.

"Jan died, man. The restaurant's closed."

Died? The words didn't sink in. I kept moving.

I got in the elevator, went down one flight, and walked numbly through the dining room. The seven-story atrium was as beautiful as ever, with water purring down a sculpted copper surface against one wall and a giant mobile suspended above, a colorful smattering of kites borrowed from the Museum of Modern Art. Once I stepped into the subbasement, I saw Adam, the restaurant manager and one of Jan's closest friends, sitting on a stool, alone. Adam never sat still, but there he was, staring blankly, holding a cup of coffee in both hands but not drinking it, tears running down his cheeks. Then I got it. Jan was gone.

EIGHTEEN **LIFE AFTER DEATH**

"*VI SITTER ALLA I EN KNEPIG PLATS HÄR,*" HÅKAN SAID AS THE TWO OF us sat in the empty restaurant. We are all in a difficult place here. It was only late afternoon, but grief and winter's dark blanketed the room. Someone had brought us a basket of crispbread and a ramekin filled with caviar spread. Håkan dipped a knife into the putty-colored roe and smeared it across a cracker, then left it on his plate, untouched. I pulled the napkin from the place setting in front of me, folding it and refolding it.

Håkan didn't waste words: No one in-house was in a position to take over. It was enough to have gambled on Jan, a thirty-two-year-old first-timer, so Håkan would be going to Sweden in search of someone to fill the position. Could I deal with a new boss?

"Yes."

In the meantime, Larry was going to hold down the fort. He was older, and a natural manager. As for me: Jan had come to Håkan only a few days before his death to say he wanted me to become his *sous-chef*. They hadn't gotten around to telling me, but now, here it was. I could take the promotion, but only if I were willing to take marching orders from Larry.

"No problem."

We reopened the next day. Larry, who was probably Jan's best friend, tried his hardest to set aside his feelings and work as if nothing had happened. He kept the team together by writing up the shift schedule, ordering the food, and showing everyone that it was OK to keep pushing forward. For the first couple of days after Jan's death, the rest of us were in shock, distracted, going through the motions. The food suffered.

"Get your shit together!" Larry shouted. "We've got people to feed."

I honestly believe the restaurant wouldn't have survived if Larry hadn't stepped up and taken charge. He was so steady that Håkan worried he was in some kind of unhealthy pattern of denial, and suggested he take a few days off so he wouldn't crash and burn. Larry brushed off Håkan's suggestion, reminding him that when you come from a rough neighborhood like he had, tragedies happened.

"Listen," Larry said. "Most of my friends from growing up are dead or died when we were kids. This is bad, but I've been through it before. I need to keep working."

Larry was a rock, but there was no way to completely smooth over the loss of his talented, charismatic friend. Without Jan at the helm, the other Mesa guys started heading back to Bobby's kitchens—slowly at first, then like rats fleeing a sinking ship. We lost people every week, and we didn't have the pull in the job-hunting market to bring in anyone new. The staff grew leaner and leaner, and we eventually turned every dishwasher and porter we had into a line cook. I spent a lot of time teaching people how to chop onions without hurting themselves.

To any visitor passing through over those next couple of months, it would have looked like Larry was running the show with me as his right hand. But there were three of us heading up the kitchen, the third person being the ghost of Jan. We'd be working on the spring menu or trying to streamline the workflow, and somebody would always bring him into the discussion.

"But Jan would never . . ."

"I don't think that's where Jan was going. . . ."

"Jan didn't really like . . ."

Larry ran the show and talked to the press and the fish guy and the dishwashers; I worked on the menu and filled in wherever he needed me to. We fell into a good groove, but even though I respected him tremendously, I sometimes felt he didn't understand Swedish cuisine. In fact, he'd never been to Sweden, which made it hard to come up with new dishes. Larry would go on years later to have a great career in Las Vegas, but it wouldn't be in a Swedish place. Sweden wasn't in his soul.

Larry's reference point was New York, and after a month or so, it was clear he was headed back to work for his fellow born-and-bred New Yorker, Bobby Flay. Larry said he'd stick with us until Håkan found the new guy, but then he would be gone. I could have left, too, but I didn't want to quit on a place that had been so good to me. Plus, what would I go back to? I didn't have a green card yet, so I would have had to head back to Sweden. I was here, why not try to make it work? Håkan had tremendous business smarts and a huge passion for the restaurant, and I wanted to see who he came up with to fill Jan's spot. I kept my nose to the grindstone, working with the younger cooks, developing a menu with Larry, and solving problems as they came up.

Around the end of April, Larry decided he couldn't wait any longer, and officially left to go back to work for Bobby. Håkan still hadn't found Jan's replacement.

"Can you keep it together for another month?" Håkan asked. "Even without Larry?"

"Yes," I said, not knowing how in the hell I would live up to that answer. Håkan flew over to Sweden, Larry left, and I kept the kitchen going, counting heavily on two young guys, Nicholas and another Marcus. Somehow, we kept the walls from crashing down around us.

When Håkan got back, he called me into his office.

"Have you found your chef?" I asked.

"I believe I have."

"Who is it?"

"You, Marcus. I want you to be the new executive chef of Aquavit."

WE NEVER TALKED ABOUT it with the press but Jan's death was drug related. He had had a heart attack and he was only thirty-two years old. In many New York restaurant kitchens, the nineties still felt very much like the eighties. Jan's crew partied hard.

In France and Switzerland, we went out drinking after work, but nothing like what these guys did. Giggs wouldn't have tolerated us not being clear the next day. But with Jan and some of the people he hired, the late nights and drugs brought with it the usual tolls: mood swings, spotty attendance, forgetfulness; sometimes a guy would totally blank on the specials. So I had to not only rebuild the kitchen but send a message that Aquavit was no longer a party kitchen.

My one condition for accepting the job was that I be allowed to hire the *sous-chef* of my choice. I took inventory of everyone I'd ever worked with, thought about where they were and how well they'd blend into the somewhat chaotic picture at Aquavit. In the end, there was only one person who fit the bill: a Swede named Nils Norén. He was a couple of years older than I and an up-and-coming chef in Stockholm. He worked at an excellent restaurant called KB, the first Swedish restaurant ever to earn a Michelin *macaron*. Nils had come to *stage* at Aquavit earlier that year, and in the two weeks he spent in New York, we developed an unusually good rapport; I knew we'd be able to work together. We not only had Sweden in common, we were both classically trained, so Nils understood how to use France as a

Marcus, age five, stops to pick flowers on a family hike through the countryside (1975)
Collection of the author

Marcus and his mother, Anne Marie, enjoy the sun during a lakeside picnic (1974) *Collection of the author*

Marcus's father, Lennart, at his fiftieth birthday party in Göteborg (1982) *Collection of the author*

The summer after his adoption, Marcus enjoys the sun in the backyard of the family's house in Göteborg (1974) *Collection of the author*

Three years after their adoption, Kassahun and Fantaye are officially baptized as Marcus and Linda Samuelsson (1976)
Collection of the author

Marcus and his sister Linda, in their Easter Saturday outfits, outside the family's summer house in Smögen (1974)
Collection of the author

Marcus sits on his mother's lap, next to his sisters, Anna (*middle*) and Linda (1976)
Collection of the author

The Samuelsson family gathers at *Mormor* Helga's on Boxing Day for a traditional roast turkey dinner (1974)
Collection of the author

Marcus and Linda on the northwest coast of Sweden, with the Carlsten Fortress in the distance (1976)
Collection of the author

Marcus and Linda decorate buns for the holiday season in *Mormor* Helga's kitchen (1974)
Collection of the author

Marcus, age twelve, in the portrait his parents had taken to announce his confirmation ceremony (1982)
Collection of the author

Marcus (*second from left*) and his classmates performing in a school-wide ice show (1975)
Collection of the author

During the summer in Gburg, pickup games of soccer were a daily event. *From top left:* Peter, Klaus, Marcus, and Mats (1983)
Collection of the author

Marcus, age thirteen, shows off his new bicycle (1983) *Collection of the author*

Marcus preps for the dinner shift in the kitchen of Aquavit, in the historic townhouse building on 54th Street (1999) *Paul Brissman*

Marcus, with film crew in tow, does some shopping in his favorite food neighborhood, New York City's Chinatown (2000) *Paul Brissman*

The last tables of the night finish their meals as Marcus takes a well-earned break in Aquavit's dining room (1998) *Paul Brissman*

Marcus's adoptive mother, Anne Marie, and natural father, Tsegie, meet for the first time in Abragodana, Tsegie's village in Ethiopia (2009) *Collection of the author*

Marcus (*second from left*) with his father, half sisters, and mother, Anne Marie (2009)
Collection of the author

Ashou, Marcus's second-youngest half sister, outside her father's house in Abragodana (2009)
Collection of the author

Anne Marie and Tsegie stand with Marcus and his new wife, Maya, at the altar (2009)
Collection of the author

Maya and Marcus just before their wedding ceremony (2009) *Collection of the author*

Michelle Obama, Marcus, and local schoolkids harvest vegetables from the White House organic gardens as part of the First Lady's Let's Move! program (2011)
Eddie Gehman Kohan for ObamaFoodorama.blogspot.com

Marcus brings a group of students from the local YMCA over to his home in Harlem for an impromptu cooking class (2010) *Paul Brissman*

Students from a local school in Harlem stop by the Rooster for lunch (2011) *Eden Fesehaye*

Marcus in the patio area of his new restaurant, Red Rooster, which looks out over Harlem's Lenox Avenue (2011) *Paul Brissman*

reference point but not the end game. We also shared a frustration with the Swedish attitude toward fine dining, which generally hadn't opened up much beyond traditional French and traditional Swedish.

A *stage* usually entails observation and schlepping, but Aquavit was short-staffed, so Jan put Nils on the middle station right across from me while I held down the fish station. That proximity gave us a chance to observe each other under pressure. Nils was controlled and specific in his work habits and he was extremely dedicated, but he was also a free spirit; he listened to reggae and had traveled to many places, including Asia and South Africa. That balance struck a chord with me, so as soon as Håkan gave me the thumbs-up, I placed the call. I expected Nils to give a measured, Swedish response, to thank me and tell me he'd consider the offer and get back to me shortly, but he said just one word.

"Absolutely."

It was my first hire and it turned out to be a great one; we worked together for ten years. We never once fought. Nils shared my desire to bring new flavors into the restaurant, and yet we both knew we had to do it without freaking out Håkan or the regular customer base. One of the burdens of taking over the kitchen was that Aquavit was known for many classic Swedish dishes: Herring, gravlax, and meatballs were never going to come off the menu. I hadn't cooked this kind of classic Swedish cuisine since Belle Avenue, and as I spent more time with these dishes, my fondness for them returned. I also felt a need to bring them up-to-date.

The liberation of being in New York was that the customers who made up our base didn't have extensive knowledge of traditional Swedish food—they just knew what they liked. I saw that as my opportunity to turn the menu around. I could make the herring less salty; I could add a peppery heat to the smoked salmon; and even in the case of the *hovmästarsås*—a sweet dill mustard sauce, served with gravlax, that was almost a religion in Sweden—I made adjustments, aiming for a deeper, nuttier flavor. Adding actual nuts would have been costly and introduced textural challenges, so I used brewed espresso instead. I started testing out the sauce in dining-room specials, and the response was strong. Eventually, it became the sauce we used for both herring and gravlax. Later, I even took away the chopped dill that had always been a given on the plate. I felt it was a cliché.

As excited as I was about bringing the restaurant back up to its past status, I knew I couldn't fix everything at once. There were two kitchens to manage: for the upstairs café, which had a heavy flow at lunch, and for the dining room, which drew more covers at dinner. For the time being, I decided to leave the café alone. I shifted most of the Swedish cooks upstairs because they knew how to do the home cooking that the café was known for and they could manage its day-to-day operations.

As for the dining room, Nils and I poured all our creative energy into developing new dishes. I started by looking through my old food journals, remembering flavors and pairings and preparations from everywhere I'd ever worked, everywhere I'd ever been: I wanted to find ways to incorporate the efficiencies of Switzerland, the soulfulness of Austria, the reverence for ingredients I learned in France, but I wanted to do it with a Swedish accent. The key was to keep seafood at the front and center of the menu. I kept some of Jan's dishes, like his lobster wrapped in pear slices, and began adding my own as soon as I could develop, test, and refine them. We fell into a routine of sitting down after lunch, talking through new ideas and then splitting up to go and work on them individually. Every idea was run through a gauntlet—not only did we talk about how it would taste, but we broke it down into distinct components: How would it look? What was the ideal temperature to serve it at? What kind of mouthfeel did we want it to have?

We both looked beyond food for our inspiration, which was key. I might build a recipe on the idea of being on a boat off the shores of Smögen; Nils would read a book about architecture and start out a concept based on shape. Each of us would take the lead on certain dishes; others were pure collaboration. Nils came up with an amazing counterpoint to our salty, spicy fish dishes: a goat cheese parfait. I rolled salmon in parchment paper and served that with an orange-fennel broth. I made a salmon tartare using a barely smoked salmon, then served it with crispbread and a mustard we'd created. I knew right away I wanted to do a tomato soup with crab at its center. So I slow roasted tomatoes in salt, sugar, black pepper, and garlic, then filled each tomato with crab salad and placed that in the center of a low flat bowl that held a ladleful of a gingery tomato soup that had the citrus notes of lemongrass. I just knew these flavors would work together, and they did.

Nils and I used every spare moment to keep pushing into new territory, always with flavor in mind. For example, once I'd toppled the *hovmästarsås* god, the door was open for me to try more. From my Rollerblading adventures, I knew which Pakistani and Indian stores on Twenty-seventh and Lex would have mustard oil or purple and black mustard seeds. If I wanted to make a jackfruit sorbet, I'd take the D train down to Grand Street, do a lightning shop, then zip back up to the restaurant, carrying everything in my backpack. I'd try whatever caught my eye; because these weren't fancy French ingredients, I never ran into cost problems. Bitter melon looked like a cross between okra and cucumber, but it was most definitely neither; lychee fruit, when peeled, looked like translucent eggs; sliced lotus root reminded me of the doilies *Mormor* put on the back of chairs to protect the upholstery. Some things I recognized from a market in Singapore or a stand in Hong Kong, but when it came to more mysterious items, I'd buy anything once, as soon as I'd established from the seller that it wasn't going to kill me.

Every time I went down to Chinatown, especially in the early morning, the beauty and insanity of the neighborhood seduced me. In summer, the streets were already packed and smelly, even though the sidewalks were freshly hosed down. At a dim sum cart I could buy five cakes for a dollar. At a fish stand, I'd get giant prawns. I could see old people in their street clothes tucked into pocket parks doing tai chi, following the syrupy slow motions of a guy with a sword in his hand, red tassels hanging from its handle. With most of my interactions, there was no common spoken language, and definitely no fabulousness. It felt direct and honest: You pointed, you paid, you stuffed your purchase into your bag, and you moved on. I'd go back uptown and try making jackfruit sorbet one week, then the next week experiment with wonton wrappers. Then and still, Chinatown was a tremendous source of inspiration.

When Nils and I found a way to use a new ingredient, the next step was figuring out how to package it. I knew that a word like *galangal* on the menu would make Håkan go bananas, so we had to find a way to hide it. We'd make salmon brushed in miso and wrapped in Thai basil, then serve it with fennel and a broth that used Kaffir lime leaves, lemongrass, galangal, and the Japanese citrus fruit called *yuzu*, and on the menu we'd call it crispy salmon with orange broth and grilled fennel. Wasabi was horseradish; ponzu was citrus vinaigrette. The key was presenting these things in accessible, understandable terms, which kept customers in their comfort zone. I had a responsibility to the restaurant not to confuse the diner, but I had an even greater responsibility to upgrade the food. It was a delicate balance.

At the same time I was trying to reimagine the menu, I was developing as a chef, and I had more than my share of failures. You could make a mistake back then without it sinking you. Reviewers always came more than once before they wrote their reviews, and food bloggers—who take the pulse of a restaurant every thirty seconds and sound the death knell if they don't like the feel of a napkin—didn't yet exist. One of my more notable disasters was a beef tenderloin dish. Aquavit never was and never will be a steakhouse, so I thought I'd replace the boring, straight-ahead grilled New York strip we offered with something more sophisticated and gentle. I poached the beef in milk and served it with potatoes and sorrel, a vegetable that seemed just right for late spring and early summer. It is a really great dish—if you have an all-star team in the kitchen. We didn't. To begin with, poaching is a far more delicate process than grilling. It's easy to miss the mark and end up with dried-out meat. With grilling, the texture and flavor that come from charring over high heat cover up a multitude of sins. I was aiming for something more feminine, but the process requires close attention and periodic checking—in other words, a little too sophisticated for a busy Saturday night and the twenty-one-year-olds we had on the line.

After a week of failing miserably, Nils and I agreed to go back to the grilled New York strip.

Throughout the summer, we kept banging and pushing. I had so much food in me that I launched six- and seven-course tasting menus, changing them almost every day. It was an ambitious if not slightly crazy idea for an understaffed restaurant, and we kept at it for the better part of a year, until we started to settle into a rotation of dishes we felt worked, and also when I could see that it was unfair to expect the waitstaff to fully understand and represent the food when dishes flew in and out the door so fast. Håkan knew that we couldn't and shouldn't sustain so many changes, but he also knew the restaurant needed positive energy. I don't regret pushing so hard because in the back of my mind, I knew this was my moment. Out of the tragedy of Jan's death had come an amazing opportunity to communicate the diverse flavors I was so passionate about.

If Nils and I went too far, it was because we were there to kick ass, and anybody who didn't fall in line either left of his own accord or got pushed out. Håkan put everything he had into supporting our efforts to turn things around, too—he renovated the restaurant's interior, brought in a restaurant consultant, and hired the leading food PR company in the city, the same people who were representing established chefs like Alfred Portale and Bobby Flay. Between the consultants and the flacks and the press, I felt like I was undergoing interrogation: What's your philosophy? What's your food mantra? What's your vision? Where do you get your inspiration?

"I'm just working," I wanted to say, but of course that wasn't enough. I had achieved my dream of becoming the *koksmastare*, the head of the kitchen, and I had to accept the corporate stuff that came with it. Through their efforts, I started to develop ways of talking about my food—that I liked it highly seasoned, that my anchors were

Sweden, France, and the world, and that I wanted to create something *different*.

Word started to get out. Editors from *Food & Wine* came in to eat, and so did the great Chicago-based chef Charlie Trotter, who instantly took a liking to our new direction and became an ally and a friend. Our consultants drew on their deep connections to the American dining scene: They arranged for us to host the meetings of the city's most prominent wine society, to partner in a charity event for the James Beard House, to participate in a wonderful antihunger project called Taste of the Nation. Håkan dealt with most of the schmoozing, but he'd bring me out to this person or that group to shake hands and say a few words. Gradually, a buzz was building.

No restaurant ever succeeds solely on the talents of its chef. There has to be a good business model, someone keeping careful track of food costs and management. This was where Håkan excelled. Håkan and the consultant, Richard Lavin, who was serving as the restaurant's general manager, taught me how to be accountable to those points. At our Thursday morning meeting, the three of us would sit in Håkan's elegantly appointed office and talk about long- and short-term goals. I walked in to the first meeting without a pen and paper, but never made that mistake again. If linen costs were up, we discussed why. If I wanted new plates in the dining room, where was I going to cut back in order to free up that money? If we talked about a challenge we faced, it wasn't enough for me to say I'd take care of it. *How* was I going to take care of it?

We all pressed on and then, boom, one day in late September we found out we were going to be reviewed by Ruth Reichl, the top critic for *The New York Times*. The night before, a few of us gathered in Håkan's apartment to watch a local news channel that gave a preview of the review. The minute they announced that Reichl was giving us three stars, Håkan and the rest of my coworkers jumped out of their chairs and shouted. I would have been thrilled with two stars: Three was beyond anyone's expectations. There were toasts, there was back-slapping, there was some fist pumping. I was happy because they were happy, but the import of the review didn't sink in.

The day after the review came out happened to be one of our wine society dinners. The head of the society stood up to make his opening remarks, and after attending to the society's announcements, he brought up the review.

"When I met Marcus," he said, "I knew he would be the one. I knew when I picked this place for our dinners there was magic in the air."

I thought, This is great; let's all just get back to work. But the truth was that as soon as the review came out, it *was* magic. I had dreamed of success for so long. I'd left restaurant after restaurant, from Belle Avenue to Victoria to Georges, because I knew I could do better.

But the truth is that I had no idea what success would look like, feel like, taste like.

When you're the new twenty-four-year-old chef at a relatively low-profile Swedish restaurant and you get a three-star review from *The New York Times*, it's like taking a small indie movie to Sundance and walking away with all the awards and a major distribution deal to boot. The whole world shifted on its axis. In two days, our reservations doubled. The congratulations cards and calls and flowers were endless. Everything opened up in ways big and small. I used to have to argue with my fish guy over our order, which always came last on his list of deliveries; now we got our fish at 9:00 sharp and it was always the best. I didn't have to argue with any of my vendors anymore; in fact, they began to send new products for me to try, gratis. I was flooded with invitations to all sorts of cooking events and for the best tables at restaurants. We started to get calls from Sweden, from cooks who wanted to come over to work. Wow, I thought. This is the way it is supposed to be.

"*Vart du vill åka*," Håkan said. Anywhere you want to go.

Håkan decided we should celebrate our three-star review in proper fashion, so he was taking me out for dinner, along with Adam, Aquavit's manager. Aside from my grandmother, I've never met anyone who kept a tighter rein on the purse strings than Håkan, but he would never pinch pennies when it came to a great meal. In the years to come, we would fly around the world together just to try out restaurants. We made special trips to Paris, eating at Ducasse and Taillevent, and we flew to Spain to try the thirty-five-course tasting menu at El Bulli, the temple of molecular gastronomy.

I was still getting used to my position as head chef, so I must have looked uncertain when he asked me to pick the place.

"I mean it," he said. "This deserves the best."

I chose Lespinasse, the four-star restaurant in the St. Regis hotel that I'd been reading about for some time. It was helmed by Gray Kunz, who was raised in Singapore by an Irish mother and a Swiss father. Kunz was my kind of chef: He made his mark by chasing flavors, by not only working with a broad palette of ingredients that spoke to his global citizen upbringing, but knowing the properties of each one intimately and combining them in fresh ways.

As much as I looked forward to the meal, for me, the evening presented several problems, the first being that I was going out with my well-dressed colleague and boss to the top restaurant in the city and I didn't own a suit. As a matter of fact, I didn't own a single pair of pants other than jeans. I went out and bought some black pants. In the back of my closet, I had a greenish jacket that would probably do, and a white shirt that would be OK if I ironed it and never took the jacket off. The shoes I would have to borrow.

At 7:25 that night, Adam, Håkan, and I walked through the doors of the St. Regis, the flagship in a fleet of luxury hotels that had been built by one of the Astors. The Astor family came as close to local royalty as New York would ever know, and the hotel, while designed to make guests feel at home, was palatially appointed, down to the eagle-topped gilt-and-glass mailbox mounted to the wall of the lobby.

We made our way to the bar, an underlit and opulent space that would have made the king of Sweden uncomfortable, much less a *blatte* Swede in borrowed shoes. Håkan and Adam ordered dry martinis on the rocks, so I did, too. I took a big swig and began to cough. Håkan and Adam laughed; it was obvious I'd never had a martini before. I let the ice melt a bit before taking a second, more cautious sip, only to confirm that I'd never be ordering a martini again.

I hated the fussy decor and I was clearly not cut out for cocktails, but I will never forget that dinner. Never. The food that came out of the kitchen that night was all classical—salmon, filet mignon, duck— but the flavors, the spices, and the approach were unlike anything I'd had before. Kunz's personal experience of East-meets-West showed up in his use of the Asian flavorings I was coming to love, the galangal and lemongrass and red curry, but he wrapped them in the elegance of French traditions. In the kitchen, Kunz's bench was deep, full of young chefs who would make names for themselves in the near future: He had Troy Dupuy as his executive *sous-chef*, along with Rocco DiSpirito, Floyd Cardoz, and Andrew Carmellini. It was like a nuclear reactor of talent, and it produced an unbelievable dining experience: French wines, French service, but the flavors of Singapore. I said to myself: That's it. I can live without the mausoleum decor, but *this* is the direction I want to go.

At the end of the meal, we were invited to the back of the house. The kitchen was spotless, as if an army of workers cleaned it with toothbrushes every night, and the equipment was even more state of the art than Victoria Jungfrau's. Håkan estimated later that we were looking at a $4 million job, if you added together renovation and equipment. It was so clean it sparkled; the room was literally humming. Everyone worked with an intensity that was completely self-contained.

As I walked down the center aisle, with the grill on my right and the salad station on my left, I was reminded of the kitchen tours at Georges Blanc. There, I had kept my eyes lowered at all times. Now, I could look everywhere, at everyone. We were shown everything, including the walk-ins and the pantry. This was a ritual that dated back to the way Michelin judges would tour a place that they were evaluating. A great restaurant should be proud to show what happened behind its doors, and clearly, Lespinasse was proud.

To SPEND THE EVENING eating a meal worth thousands at Lespinasse and then head back to a seedy rent-controlled apartment on the West Side was very much my life. People always talked about how my neighborhood, Hell's Kitchen, was going to be the next hot area, but when I lived there, the streets were still full of junkies and hookers. I didn't have a doorman at the entrance to my building, but I did have a heroin addict who hung out, day and night. You heard fights in the parking lot across the street, and of course wherever there are prosti-tutes and addicts, you're going to find pimps, pushers, and crime; but for the most part, if I didn't mess with them, they didn't mess with me.

Friends from Sweden would come to stay—the apartment turned into more or less a hostel for *blattes*—and they would freak out about the street scene.

"Just keep moving," I'd tell them. "Just leave it alone."

The people on the street weren't the only ones running scams. I shared that apartment with Magnus, the Swedish masseuse I'd lived with when I first came to New York. He was a great roommate, and the only reason we went our separate ways was that he wanted to move in with Jake, his American boyfriend. This was a problem for Magnus, because he was in the United States on a student visa. His solution: Marry Jake's sister. In every circle I belonged to, from my *blatte* buddies to the restaurant crew, there was always some kind of hustle going, from buying a green card off the street to paying a year's rent up front, and in cash, to get around not having a bank account or Social Security number. None of us judged each other; we were all hardworking guys doing what we needed to do.

I was one of the lucky ones. I was an immigrant, first of all, here by choice and not a refugee escaping persecution. Not only was I here by choice, but Håkan was sponsoring my immigration process, and because I had a particular professional talent, as a Swedish chef com-ing to work in a Swedish restaurant, I moved to the front of the line in terms of processing citizenship. Still, I'd have to wait more than a year for the papers to go through, during which time I wasn't allowed to leave the United States, but my parents supported me and we agreed that missing a few holidays at home seemed like a small price to pay. Even though my own situation was relatively stable, many of my friends were on edge.

I remember going up to the Bronx late one night with a few of the African guys I'd met through Central Park soccer. One of them had arranged to pay $200 for a fake green card, and he'd gotten a call that it was ready for pickup. Three of us hopped on the Seventh Avenue express train and rode up into the Bronx to Grand Concourse, where we switched to another train. When we got out, it was about ten p.m., and we followed directions that led us to a small bodega with a red sign and blazing yellow light bulbs outside. The guy who had business to conduct went into a back room, and I hung by the counter, where a middle-aged Puerto Rican woman with hair pulled back into a ponytail perched on a stool, flipping through a Spanish-language version of the *National Enquirer*.

At the end of the counter sat a glass hot case, with three shelves inside. The top shelf held a tray of half-moon-shaped pastries.

"Excuse me," I said to the woman. I pointed to the turnovers and raised my eyebrows.

"*Empanadillas,*" she said. Mini beef turnovers.

The second shelf had a tray of what looked like fried skin. I pointed at them.

"*Chicharrones,*" she said. Fried pork rinds.

The bottom shelf held a slow-roasted pork shoulder that had clearly been heavily rubbed with spices. Its skin was crispy and big chunks of it had been hacked off and sat next to it, the flesh looking tender enough to fall apart in your mouth.

"*Pernil,*" she said. Roasted suckling pork.

"*Por favor,*" I said, nodding at the roast. I dug into my pocket and pulled out a five-dollar bill, and handed it over. She pulled out a Styrofoam container and, with a fork, began poking through the tray. From what I could figure, she was making me an assortment, equal parts crunchy skin and interior flesh, some fatty parts, some lean. I saw streaks of spices that had been pushed way down deep into the flesh. When the woman finished her careful selection, she reached for a bag.

"No, no," I said, and pantomimed raising a fork to my mouth. For the first time, she smiled, and she rifled through a gray tub behind her, pulling out a white plastic fork.

Who knows how long that roast had been sitting in the warming case? I didn't care. The skin still crackled between my teeth. The meat, tender and moist, fell apart in my mouth, and I instinctively started to break down the components of the flavors involved. Garlic, of course, right up there in the front. Cilantro, peppers, tomatoes, but what else?

"*Que?*" I said, pointing to the little deposits of seasonings that had sunk into crevices in the skin.

"*Sofrito,*" she answered, then pointed to herself, identifying herself as the chef. "*Mi sofrito.*"

THE YEAR THAT FOLLOWED the *Times* review was full of learning curves, none steeper than figuring out how to staff a kitchen team. I didn't have a following like David Bouley or Daniel Boulud; Culinary Institute of America grads weren't lining up outside my door, begging to work at Aquavit. No one was lining up outside my door, actually. On top of that, the pace Nils and I set was too much for some of the employees already in-house, and every Friday for six months, it seemed like I had to fire someone who couldn't keep up. One ethnically stereotypical but true fact: I never had to fire any of the Latinos on my crew; they worked harder than I did.

The guys I booted from my kitchen were mostly the entitled culinary school types who thought they could pick and choose their tasks. One exception was a kid named Paulie from Bensonhurst, Brooklyn. He was an Italian American kid, big gold jewelry, Brooklyn accent, cursing in Italian, the whole central casting deal. But Paulie had an enormous love for food. He always stayed focused; when everybody else went down, he stayed afloat. Paulie was ready to work for me every day of the week and he hinted that he preferred the life of a restaurant kitchen to, as he put it, "the family business."

"If I'm not working here," he told me after volunteering for two double shifts in a row, "then I just have to go work in my uncle's butcher shop, which doesn't sell much meat, if you know what I mean."

Another kid I respected was from Saint Lucia, a guy named Nelly.

More than one of Nelly's brothers were drug dealers, but Nelly was clean, and he worked his ass off. For these guys, working in a kitchen was a relief, a refuge. I understood. I had never been a boy from the hood, but I'd found life in Göteborg to be stifling in its own way. Anyplace where people do exactly as their fathers and brothers have done, it's hard to make your own way.

Over time, more Swedes came to work for us, and they almost never had an issue when it came to their work ethic. They were talented chefs and hungry to go beyond the narrow confines of Sweden's fine-dining world, so they were game for whatever Nils and I asked. Like me, a number were the children of academics, but where many of them felt they were breaking the mold of their parents, I felt like I was simply trying to live up to being the man my father was, a man who pursued his deepest passion. Only one of the *Svenskar* was a bad apple, a kid from Stockholm who'd come across the Atlantic in search of the world's biggest party. I followed Paul Giggs's example and tossed him right away. The rest aspired to make something of themselves, to turn this experience to their advantage once they got home. Sure enough, a number of those guys have gone on to have great careers all over the world, starting restaurants in Sweden and cooking at great hotels throughout Europe.

Our crew took shape as a band of misfits who probably wouldn't have fit in anywhere else. That, in itself, made us tight.

BY THE MIDDLE OF THE FOLLOWING SUMMER, I was starting to feel pretty well established. Our staff was solid, business was good. Paulie had worked super hard for me over the last six months, and I wanted to reward him by sending him out to *stage*. *Stages* are one of my favorite traditions in the restaurant world. First of all, half of who we are as chefs has to do with the chefs who came before us. So the *stage* shows respect for wisdom. Second, the fact that if you do well for your chef he'll send you away still strikes me as one of the most generous professional acts I've heard of. If you were at a law firm and they wanted to reward you, they'd probably give you a bonus or some time off. But in cooking, serious cooks understand that there's nothing more valuable than the chance to learn something new.

"How would you like to spend some time working for Bobby Flay?" I asked Paulie.

"Are you fucking kidding me?" he answered.

I took that as a yes.

I called up Bobby and told him I had a young guy who was really good; would it be OK for him to spend a week in Bobby's kitchen?

"Let me think about it," Bobby said. "I'll get back to you."

A few days later, I got his answer. "No."

I hung up the phone in shock. I thought I had pull. I had no pull. Not only did I not have pull, but I had to go back to Paulie and explain how much pull I didn't have. It took me a long time to realize that a great review from Ruth Reichl had signaled only that I was a talent to watch. In order to be a fixture on the New York dining scene, to be able to call someone like Bobby Flay and ask him for a favor, I needed to show I had staying power. Sure enough, a year later, when Felicia Lee wrote a nice piece about me and my food for *The New York Times*, Bobby was the first to call and congratulate me. I was solidly on the scene now, he said. Only then did other chefs begin to approach me at events—including Patrick Clark, who'd always seemed to steer away from me before the article appeared—but Bobby had led the pack.

"You're here, man," he said. "You're here to stay."

I've gotten to know Bobby really well since then, and he is one of the coolest, best chefs in New York. He is honest about his food, takes a lot of pleasure from his work, and has been extremely helpful in guiding my career. I can't fault him for thinking, back then, that I hadn't earned the right to ask what I was asking for.

This was before Las Vegas had its mega–restaurant boom, where regional chefs could supersize their efforts in the Nevada desert with corporate backing and high-rolling customers. All Bobby had were a couple of restaurants in Manhattan. All David Bouley had was his place in TriBeCa. I'm not saying this to minimize their talents; I'm just pointing out that the world was smaller and, in some ways, the competition was fiercer. Making it in New York was The Shit. Capital *T*, capital *S*. And I had to work my way up, just like everybody else.

I'd overreached with Bobby, but I'd made Paulie a promise and I intended to make good on it. I had no choice but to throw a Hail Mary: Georges Blanc. I wrote a letter, sent it off, and to my amazement, they said yes. Small problem: Paulie's dad didn't want him to go. He wasn't about to cough up the three thousand dollars so his son could go poach chicken. So I took matters into my own hands: I decided to host a fundraiser. I took over an Ethiopian place I'd been to a bunch of times and put on a forty-dollar tasting dinner: roasted duck salad with sweet potatoes; jam and hazelnut vinaigrette; crispy salmon with orange roasted fennel and purple spinach; and for dessert, warm chocolate cake with balsamic sorbet and candied pecans. I won't say I leveraged my boss status to get Aquavit staff to come, but I did *strongly* encourage attendance. The house was packed, and we got Paulie's money for him.

ON AUGUST 11, 1996, MY FATHER, LENNART SAMUELSSON, PASSED AWAY. He was at home in Göteborg; I was at work in New York. He'd been struggling with the aftermath of a stroke, but then he took a sudden turn and was gone. I couldn't leave the States to go to his funeral without jeopardizing my immigration status. My mother said she understood, my sisters said they understood, but honestly, it would take me years to say that I understood the choice I made. All I know is that I did what, by now, came naturally: I crammed my grief and fear into a little box and closed it up until I was ready to deal. There was no time, I told myself, to make a meal out of this misery. Nothing could get in the way of my cooking.

That night, I pulled out a copy of the letter my father had written, before he knew me, to the adoption agency:

April 3, 1972

Dear Maj-Britt!

Adoption Center in Stockholm, which helps us with the adoption of Fantaye and Kassahun, has asked us to write you and tell you about our family and our living situation. We do it here and with the help of some photographs. First, however, we want to thank you for the work that you perform and wish you success!

We are three people in the family. Father, Lennart, born on Smögen in Bohuslän in 1932, first studied to be a public school teacher. Then studied further for a master's degree. He has had employment as an elementary school teacher, teacher, lecturer, and is since 1969 a state geologist and director of the Geological Survey of Sweden, Göteborg Branch. During three months in 1971, I was a UNESCO expert at the Center for Applied Geology in Jeddah.

My work consists of the production of geological maps and my work for the next ten years will be in western Sweden. I also conduct lectures and classes in geology at the University of Göteborg. My income is between 5,000–6,000 kr a month [$1,041–1,250 USD].

Mom, Anne Marie, was born in Helsingborg in 1928. After practical school, she was employed as clerk and cashier until 1964. At that time we bought a house and she has since been a housewife.

In December 1965, we had a foster child, Anna, who was then fifteen months and now is seven and a half years. Her father is colored and mother Swedish. Both live in Sweden but live apart. We have good, although somewhat sporadic, relations with both. We wanted to adopt Anna, but the biological mother has hesitated and we have allowed things to be. The biological parents, however, both expressed their desire that Anna should grow up with us. Anna is a healthy and happy child and looks forward with great expectations to some smaller siblings! She has always found it easy to have good friends and playmates.

As a family, we are also a good dog (collie) and an equally nice cat, both very friendly toward children.

We live in a child-friendly residential area, Puketorp, of about three hundred families. There is a surrounding forest, where we hike in the summer and ski and saucer in winter. A couple of small lakes with crystal-clear waters are also in the woods, where we go skating and swimming. Puketorp is in Partille municipality, one mile east of Göteborg.

Our site is about seven hundred square meters and a mostly flat lawn with a playhouse and sandbox, so children tend to gather with us and tumble about properly, jumping and playing with balls and croquet.

The house consists of three rooms, hall, kitchen, bathroom + basement with 2 rooms, hall, combination toilet-shower room, laundry room, boiler room. We plan to build a new house next year, on forest land ten min. down the road from us.

Anna's paternal grandmother has houses on Smögen, so we usually go to the archipelago and the sea when we wish to change from the forest.

Her maternal grandmother and grandfather live in the same residential area that we do, just five minutes away, and they are very good with small children and are retired, so they have plenty of time and also help us if we need babysitting or care of animals when we cannot take them with us.

I do not know if this data is sufficient, if not, please let me hear from you and we will respond again.

Our dearest greetings

Our dearest greetings. That letter marked the beginning of our life together—my father and I—and it did not seem right, nor possible, that the journey was over before I had become chef of my own restaurant, before I had proven to him that I could do it. My father and I were meant to taste the world together. I wanted to take him to Jackson Heights in Queens so he could see why they called the neighborhood Curry Heights. I wanted him to try real fried chicken in Harlem. I wanted to chow down on po'boys with him in New Orleans. I imagined us eating hot dogs and beer at Yankee Stadium and conch fritters in Florida. My father was sixty-four when he died. Maybe that was why I took the news with what must have seemed like cold resolve: The numbers simply did not add up. I thought, I hoped, that we had as much time ahead of us as we did behind us. It seemed unfathomable to me that we did not.

When *Mormor* died, it had been easy to feel connected to her at work. Any kitchen could invoke the spirit of Helga; the smell of chicken roasting, the smell of fresh herbs, the sound of onions sizzling in the pan could conjure up my grandmother and make her seem close. My father, though, had been an academic, a bit of a taskmaster, a conservative Swedish man who had nonetheless crossed continents to find a son and love him. My relationship with my father was more complicated and the sweetest parts of it—fishing at the summer house in Smögen—felt outside of my reach. My father's death left me rudderless; I'd guided myself by him for as long as I could remember. He was the one who taught me how to read a map, bait a hook, make a fire, fix a bike, pitch a tent. He taught me, by example, that some principles, no matter how clichéd they sound, really do mean something. Hard work *is* its own reward. Integrity *is* priceless. Art *does* feed the soul.

I went to work at Aquavit the morning after he died, and told nobody about what had happened. I had responsibilities to the restaurant, to Håkan, to my staff and my customers. This is the way restaurants work. No matter what happens in the course of a day—death, birth, celebration, love, ruin—you show up for your next shift. For some people this becomes a burden, but that constancy over the years has kept me grounded. And it was Lennart who taught me how.

I talked to my mother every couple of days, worried she would fall apart without Lennart in her life. But she did not; she turned out to be a lot stronger than I'd given her credit for. She kept on, so I kept on. For six months after my father died, I didn't stop working. If anything, to avoid dealing, I picked up the pace. I was working fourteen, fifteen hours a day. I was numb. By then, I'd changed apartments. I still lived in Hell's Kitchen, but Magnus had moved in with his boyfriend—his brother-in-law, technically—and I'd moved in with Mes. One night I came home from work. It was late, but Mes was still up. We sat on our couch, watching MTV. We were talking about nothing in particular and, suddenly, I just lost it. I cried, for the first time since my father's death and for the first time since I was a child. Mes sat with me, listening as I tried to repeat every single wise word, funny story, and lesson in manhood that my father had shared with me. When I finally went to bed, it was almost dawn.

NO MATTER WHO YOU ARE, whether you've got a small town Italian restaurant or you're an Iron Chef, you want to create a signature dish—one you create or execute in a way that becomes forever associated with you. All chefs put our own twist on the food we serve, but a signature dish requires more than merely customizing. I considered many of the changes I'd implemented at Aquavit to be mere tweaks, whether it was changing the size of the meatballs, pulling back on the smoking of the salmon, or updating a mustard sauce by adding the nutty accent of espresso. The truth is, most chefs will never come up with a signature dish because it takes luck and time and the ability to look at things in a fresh, new way.

One approach to a signature dish is taking something famous like coq au vin, and making it so well that everyone knows it's yours. The other approach is to go out and create something entirely new. That's the exciting route, especially for young chefs. For me, the path to my first signature dish was through foie gras.

I didn't grow up with foie gras; I grew up with my grandmother's liver pâté, which was rustic and grainy, but good. The first foie gras I saw was at Belle Avenue, but even that came out of a can. It wasn't until Switzerland and France that I began working with real foie, and in both places, the ultimate expression of that core ingredient was in terrines that took days to prepare. When I came to America, chefs approached foie differently. They took American-produced foie gras from upstate New York—the idea of it being not only domestic but also local floored me—put it in a pan and seared it quickly, serving it on brioche toast with fig jam, say, or a slice of mango. I loved this taste; it seemed cleaner and it really explained the difference between French cooking (traditional) and American (flamboyant).

The only problem was that everyone was doing it, and I didn't want to be like everyone else.

So I decided to focus on texture and temperature. My first idea was to make warm foie gras blinis. These little pancakes tasted good, but the overall effect was too chewy and dry, robbing the foie gras of the velvety texture that was one of its greatest assets. What would happen, I wondered, if I took that blini batter and steamed it in the oven like a pudding? That gave me back the velvet, but the texture struck me as too uniform. I tried one version after another after another. Along the way, in one of our post-lunch conversations, Nils and I debated what the end goal should be, and we hit upon the model of an extremely popular dessert at the time, the molten chocolate cake. These were incredibly rich little cakes that had a crusty exterior and a runny liquid center. You didn't need much of one to satisfy you; in fact, too much would leave you stupefied.

With the molten cake model in mind, I turned to individual ramekins, lightened my batter by cutting back on the egg, and switched from steaming to high-heat baking in order to set the crust. This delivered the contrasting textures I wanted. I felt I was getting closer, but I didn't like having the taste of flour in the mix, so I replaced that with almond flour. I also found the standard four-ounce ramekins a little too big, so I hunted and hunted until I found a source for cups half that size. In France, I saw the customer often left us holding his sides, almost like, Oh my God, I'm never going to eat again. I wanted customers to leave Aquavit saying, Oh my God, I hope I can do that again tomorrow. You have to be careful with this when you're presenting yourself as a luxurious restaurant. It's a fine line between leaving them feeling good and appearing stingy.

As I developed my foie gras dish, I played with the seasonings. I adjusted amounts of butter—although it's fair to say there is always plenty of butter involved—shallots, white pepper, cloves, and cardamom. Foie gras works well with a good wine, so I reduced some port, steeped tarragon in it, and then added that reduction into the batter. Then I added in a little garam masala, one of my favorite spice blends at the time, to give it a hint of heat.

Finally, I made a test batch. Nils was there to try a first bite when I pulled the tray of ramekins out of the oven, and when we put those first spoonfuls in our mouths, we looked at each other and didn't have to say anything. We just smiled. I had it at last: foie gras ganache.

Over the years, I've served different versions of this dish, infusing it with sea urchin or corn, serving it straight from the hot oven alongside tuna or cool cubes of salted watermelon. I've cooked it all over the world with everything from orange marmalade to truffle ice cream. What stays constant is the texture, the temperature, and the quality of the ingredients. Once I got it right, meaning that it hit all the marks I cared about, I knew I had my first signature dish. I've served my ganache to kings and starlets and three-star chefs and people who simply love food. Everywhere I go, the dish is a hit.

My success in creating signature dishes wasn't just about what I was doing; it was that what I was doing found an audience of people who were curious about the flavors I was chasing. They were willing to chase them, too. As chefs, we definitely are in the memory business: We are creating a memory with ingredients. I wanted my customers to leave my restaurant satisfied but also curious about what made their experience so great. I wanted them to turn to each other during the cab ride home and ask, "What *was* that?"

Another signature dish started with a trip to Boston. I was driving along the Massachusetts coast on the old scenic highway, and every five minutes I passed a seafood shack promising the best lobster roll in the state. I'd never had one, so I pulled over and had lunch. For months afterward, the memory of it stayed with me. I'd loved the straightforwardness of it: Take some fresh lobster and mayo, put it on a soft, buttered roll, and boom. That's it. In Sweden, lobster is called "black gold," but at Belle Avenue, we drowned it in the cream-laden French sauces of Newburg and Thermidor.

I wanted to celebrate the richness of the lobster, not obliterate it. Even the American seaside version struck me as a bit heavy-handed when it came to the mayonnaise used to bind it. I wanted a creamy texture, but not all that oil. At the same time, I didn't want to just plop a pile of naked lobster onto a plate and let it fend for itself. How could I introduce the experience of discovery? I'm a big believer in the negligee, that nearly invisible screen standing between you and the object of your desire. I wanted to create the sense of before and after. With the lobster, I had to figure out what that screen could be. Since I was always looking for ways, at Aquavit, to filter food through Sweden, I turned to the idea of pickling, a flavor counterpoint to the richness and sweetness of the seafood.

As I had with the ganache, I went through a trial-and-error process until I hit it: lobster rolled in a skin of thinly sliced pickled Japanese plums, a homemade mayo on the side, and a topping of diced bacon and glistening red caviar. This, along with the ganache, became a fixture on the Aquavit menu. I think if they were ever taken off, there'd be a riot, at least among the regulars.

TWENTY-ONE BY THE CONTENT OF MY COOKING

So much of what drew me to New York was the chance to blend in, to *not* stand out for once because of the color of my skin. In my personal life, I found a chosen family. On the subway and streets, I found my deepest, truest community. I was still playing soccer on the weekends with other Swedish expats. We called our team Blatte United because we were a multicultural tribe of guys who had all grown up as outsiders, in one way or another: our patois of Swedish, English, and soccer slang felt as good on my tongue as a cold beer at the end of a long, hot shift.

Yet, professionally, I struggled to overcome the constant subject of race. I didn't want it to go away. Color is not just what I see in the mirror, it's how I cook and how I live. But inevitably when people bring race into the professional arena, it's never as rich, complicated, or tasty as I would like. I was never *the chef at Aquavit*. I was *the black Swedish guy from Aquavit*. What does that mean?

In 2000, three years after I became an American citizen, I'd come a little closer to accepting my inevitable role as "the black chef" or "the black Swedish chef" mostly because I was confident that with enough success and exposure, I'd eventually get people to look past the easy racial stuff and address the cultural complexity of my cooking. One huge step in that direction came my way in 2000, when I was invited by the Lanesborough hotel in London to guest chef for a promotion they did each year celebrating the world's top up-and-coming chefs. I was asked to represent America. This felt like a big moment for me.

I'd landed in New York, but I'd always had my sights on London. Although the term *British cuisine* can still raise an eyebrow in some circles, by the time I had started my career, the London restaurant scene was exploding and the influences of immigrant populations were making themselves known in the flavors. You could walk across the city and taste Chinese fish with black bean sauce, an amazing array of Indian curries, Caribbean rice and peas, or a yummy *suya*, a Nigerian meat kebab coated with peanuts and chili pepper. London was a city where cooking and culture had come together in powerful ways. For months beforehand, I fielded calls from British media. A couple of the reporters asked me to name some British chefs who had inspired me. I mentioned the Roux brothers, Albert and Michel, and I named Marco Pierre White, not as much for his food as for how—by virtue of becoming an apron-wearing rock-star bad boy—he had broken the mold of whom a chef could be, which was something I could relate to.

I got to London to find the Lanesborough dining room packed each night, a general excitement shared by everyone involved, and incredibly posh digs from which I could step out each morning into Hyde Park and take a good long run around Buckingham Palace.

On my second day, I was cooking when a phone call came into the kitchen. The executive chef answered and, with a puzzled look, handed me the receiver. Trouble at Aquavit, I figured. I put the phone up to my ear, expecting to hear Håkan's familiar *"Hej, Marcus."*

Instead, there was screaming.

"How the fuck can you come to my fucking city and think you are going to be able to cook without even fucking referring to me?"

This went on for what seemed like five minutes; I was too stunned to hang up.

"I'm going to make sure you have a fucking miserable time here. This is my city, you hear? Good luck, you fucking black bastard."

And then he hung up.

I had cooked with Gordon Ramsay once, a couple of years earlier, when we did a promotion with Charlie Trotter in Chicago. There were a handful of chefs there, including Daniel Boulud and Ferran Adrià, and Gordon was rude and obnoxious to all of them. As a group we were interviewed by the Chicago newspaper; Gordon interrupted everyone who tried to answer a question, craving the limelight. I was almost embarrassed for him. So when I was giving interviews in the lead-up to the Lanesborough event, and was asked who inspired me, I thought the best way to handle it was to say nothing about him at all. Nothing good, nothing bad. I guess he was offended at being left out.

To be honest, though, only one phrase in his juvenile tirade unsettled me: when he called me a black bastard. Actually, I didn't give a fuck about the bastard part. But the black part pissed me off.

Restaurant kitchens will always have an element of playground justice to them. Big guys will pick on little guys, and new kids will be teased for whatever makes them stick out from the rest. If there's a weak spot, somebody will find it. Up to a point, that kind of bullying is built into the hierarchy of the kitchen; as an underling, you deal with it or find a different job. But what I finally realized in London was that I wasn't an underling anymore. I didn't have to take that kind of bullshit. There was no action I needed to take; I didn't need to talk things through with Gordon Ramsay and come to a *kumbaya* moment. In the years since, I haven't felt a need to make myself available when a mutual friend brought Gordon into my restaurant, or go out of my way to be his friend. I have better things to do.

The sad part is, there are so few black chefs out there whom I could have called about Gordon Ramsay that would have understood the situation. Who would I have called? In New York City, I could think of one person: Patrick Clark, the second-generation chef from the Bronx who, if he hadn't been felled by a heart problem at forty-two, would probably be running a number of restaurants right now. In the few years I knew him, Patrick taught me a lot about how to navigate our profession as a black man.

In our earliest interactions, it always seemed like he was determined to ignore me. I remember Håkan taking me to a James Beard House event shortly after we'd gotten our three-star review, and when Patrick and I crossed paths, he looked right through me. By then, I'd learned some of the subtleties of black American communication, and one was to give a slight nod to any black person you encountered, especially if blacks were underrepresented in the room. Just a simple head nod was enough; it was a way of saying, "I see you, even if we're almost invisible here." But Patrick looked right through me. I was thrown off by this, especially since he was well known for mentoring aspiring black chefs. Patrick was also generous toward charitable causes, and many of those had a specific agenda to help people of color: He cooked for a scholarship fund for African American chefs; he cooked for Meals on Wheels; and he served as a mentor for the Careers through Culinary Arts Program (C-CAP), a program in public high schools that rigorously prepared mostly minority students for positions in the culinary field.

Patrick ignored me for the same reason Bobby Flay turned down my request for a favor: I was too new on the scene. It wasn't yet clear whether I belonged. A year later, when Patrick decided I was in it for the long run, he embraced me, calling me up to join him at events, getting me hooked into C-CAP (where I now sit on the board of directors), and bypassing the subtle nod for an energetic handshake or one of his signature bear hugs.

"Chef," he'd say, a big smile spreading out under the canopy of his mustache. "How's it going?"

Over time, I came to see that first snub as Patrick treating me the same way he would have treated a fledgling white chef. He was putting my experience before my color, which was a sign of respect.

Ironically, in many ways, the restaurant world has always stood out for its tolerance. We are one of the least homophobic professions you'll find, and you can't go into a New York kitchen without finding three or four languages spoken. We mix religions, ages, and political views. But blacks, and especially American blacks, are still shamefully underrepresented at the high end of the business. I do see some progress, though. More blacks are finding their way into the fine-dining world nowadays. Govind Armstrong, Marvin Woods, Roblé Ali, the Neelys, and Robert Gadsby all have mighty followings, and sommelier Brian Duncan and beer master Garrett Oliver are regular presences at the major food festivals and galas. But we're still few and far between, just the opposite of where we stand in the world of fast food restaurants . . . on both sides of the counter. And when Gordon Ramsey called me a "black bastard," it felt like he wanted to keep it that way.

I'M VERY MUCH AN IMMIGRANT when it comes to American racial history: I come from a European place, and don't have the sophistication about race and identity that my American-born friends have; you can only learn so much from MTV. But I have lived here for fifteen years and, over time, I've developed several theories as to why kitchens remain so white:

The Nest Egg Theory: Restaurants are a nickel-and-dime, low-margin business; I learned from Håkan early on that you can't stay afloat if you don't watch every penny. But to get into a restaurant on the ownership level requires money, big money, especially if you're trying to set up in a posh area where real estate prices can eat you alive. The fact is, blacks in America still don't have the financial resources whites have, and even the young black cats on Wall Street who *have* made it big usually aren't holding on to the kind of crazy wealth that goes back more than one generation. How likely are they to back an investment as risky as a restaurant?

The "I Didn't Iron Clothes So You Could Flip Burgers" Theory: Many of my middle- and upper-middle-class black friends have parents who had few professional options outside of the service industry, or who sent their kids to college by working as maids, porters, and janitors. The thought that their kid would take all those years of sweat equity and turn it back into the service industry is beyond inconceivable, so these parents have steered their kids as far away from that path as possible. A bit of good news on this front: My friend Richard Grausman, who founded C-CAP, sees that attitude starting to melt away, largely because of high-profile platforms like the Food Network, which has made being a successful chef more visible and respectable. He wouldn't go as far as to say the floodgates have opened in the years since the early nineties when he started C-CAP, but he does believe there's been a shift.

The Cost of Integration Theory: No thinking person would see the desegregation that came out of the civil rights movement as a bad thing, but when I talk to older black people, I realize that certain opportunities did disappear when black-owned businesses that served exclusively black communities began competing in the open marketplace. Pull out some old photos of Harlem and, everywhere you look, there are diners and soul food shacks, seafood restaurants and steakhouses. In the 1970s and 1980s, chains came into those black communities and it became very difficult for families to hold on to these small mom-and-pop restaurant businesses.

The Geographical Racism Theory: When I moved to Harlem in 2005, I noticed how many tour buses would come through my neighborhood, white faces peering out the windows, stopping only to duck into Sylvia's for an oversize plate of soul food. Beyond Sylvia's, Harlem is just not a destination for the people who go to Gramercy Tavern and Nobu and, as a result, the restaurant scene suffers. I never saw people catching a cab twenty blocks *uptown* for a nice dinner, and yet they'd think nothing of hopping down from the Upper West Side to the Village for a meal. (Look, when a lot of the Manhattan maps you can buy cut off at the top of Central Park—literally don't even bother to show Harlem—you know there's a disconnect.) I don't lay the entire problem at the feet of racism, but it would be naive to say it isn't a factor. How else did we come up with a vocabulary—not just in America but in French and Swiss kitchens—where *schwarze* and *nègre* are still synonyms for "peon"?

The Ethnic Food Theory: In the 1990s and 2000s, there were two restaurants in New York that took cuisines—Latin and Indian—that were for many years relegated to a lower-level "ethnic" status in American dining, and elevated them to the top. They have both now fallen victim to the economic downturn, but not before good, long runs that made their mark. With Patria, chef Douglas Rodriguez cemented the concept of a Nuevo Latino cuisine that didn't rely on cartoonish themes and melted cheese to draw people in. In Tabla, Floyd Cardoz did something similar with Indian food, taking it way beyond samosas and curry. I see a similar opportunity to preserve, protect, and enhance African American cooking. We have amazing regional diversity in American cuisine, and much of it is connected to the black community, whether it's Creole or Cajun, Memphis's dry-rub BBQ or North Carolina's vinegar-based sauce. As a nation, though, we don't embrace it. At least, not the way we should.

WHEN I FIRST STARTED TO GAIN some notice in the United States, I wasn't sure how to handle other people's desire to categorize me as a black chef. I was uncomfortable with it, resentful of having to discuss it, and worried it would define me. I turned down invitations to events or requests for interviews that seemed geared exclusively toward black audiences. But the more I traveled around the country, the more I came to see my race as an opportunity rather than a burden. Part of that came from meeting the few younger blacks who'd be in audiences at cooking demonstrations. They'd show up at a shopping mall demo or a cookbook signing, and I could tell they were rooting for me even if they'd never tasted my food. I felt the pride they had for me as a black person in a very white industry. I may never be a household name, but I will always remember how inspired I was by my earliest African American fans, how hopeful they made *me* feel about my own life's prospects.

Now that I have the power, however modest, to influence people's career decisions, I go to events and always feel that I am representing my race. Sometimes the pressure of being one of a few black faces in the industry is immense; every day, I tell myself, Don't screw up. I have done what I do for a long time so I am prepared and I know I won't be letting people down, food-wise. But at the same time, I also know I am on display, and that can be inhibiting. My actions have repercussions that go beyond me. When Barack Obama was running for president, I heard people complain that he wasn't being aggressive or tough enough in his stances. But I thoroughly understood the counterargument, which was that any sign of extreme assertiveness on his part would result in people accusing him of being an angry black man . . . and then his message would get totally lost. On my own, much more modest scale, I have had the same concern. My margin for error is much smaller.

After Nils Norén spent a decade with me as my right hand at Aquavit, he left to teach and became the French Culinary Institute's vice president of culinary and pastry arts; now he works for me again and is a key part of my team. Needless to say, when he calls, I show up. I was speaking to his students several years ago, explaining how I'd made a career of chasing flavors and how my travels around the world showed up in my food. The students were enthusiastic and engaged, and when it came time for questions, I called on a young black guy whose dreads were held in an enormous knitted cap striped with red, green, and black.

"What are some of the modern cooking trends in Africa?" he asked.

My mind was blank.

I had no answer. I locked my smile in place as I babbled through a meaningless observation or two—I'd, uh, been to Morocco several times and, umm, my memory of it was that even the high-end restaurants showcased only traditional recipes. I also knew about Ethiopia's chicken stew, *doro wat*, from going out to New York's Ethiopian spots with Mes, and that dish, too, struck me as homespun, as traditional as the meatballs and herring my Swedish grandmother would make. I fumbled around and talked about tradition . . . and tradition. I got away with my answers—at least the student didn't challenge me—but I felt as if I'd been slapped into awareness. I felt unsettled. Why *didn't* I know more about African food? Why was I so clueless about Ethiopian cuisine, when it was the country of my birth? How, in more than a decade of chasing flavors, could I have overlooked an entire continent so completely?

PART THREE **MAN**

TWENTY-TWO **BACK TO AFRICA**

RUTH REICHL, THEN THE EDITOR OF *Gourmet* MAGAZINE, CALLED ME AT work one afternoon.

"Marcus," she said, "I don't think you're going to be able to resist this."

The year was 1999 and a young journalist named Lolis Eric Elie had pitched a story idea to *Gourmet*: He wanted to do a feature on me, but he didn't want to rehash the same old stories about my Swedish upbringing and my arrival at Aquavit. He wanted to go with me to Ethiopia, to look at its food through my eyes, eyes that hadn't seen that country for thirty years.

Ruth was right. I couldn't resist this. I'd be gone for nearly a month, the longest I'd been away from the restaurant since becoming the executive chef.

"Of course you'll go," Håkan said when I told him I was debating over whether to be away for so long. "You have to."

We landed at Bole International Airport in the capital, Addis Ababa, the city where my mother had died, and I spent the next two weeks falling in love a hundred times a day. Ethiopia has faced terrible struggles and still does, but its ancient landscape and the warmth of the people were unbowed. My birth nation is sometimes called the land of "thirteen months of sunshine," and it was true: One crystalline day followed another. Decommissioned Russian taxicabs rattled down the city's main boulevards and battled not just other drivers but herds of goats and sheep and cows, the livestock completely unthreatened by our smoke-belching vehicles. The smell of freshly roasting coffee beans poured out from each little shop, even ones with paintings of computers or hairstyles in their windows. Reddish dust kicked up everywhere, and coated everything. The colorfully trimmed cotton scarves and shawls that covered every man and woman's shoulders were often used as masks, held in place by a hand.

In those two weeks, I saw my own face reflected a thousand times over, which not only gave me a sense of belonging unlike I'd had anywhere else in my life, but also a deep reminder of how fate had steered my life on such a different course. I'd see an eleven-year-old version of me with a cardboard tray of tissues and gum set up at an intersection. I'd see my own face dashing into coffee shops, my own hands using a branch to sweep the sidewalk in front of a butcher shop. I'd see an old and bent version of me, wearing a blanketlike *gabi* shawl in the cool of the early morning, his hand cupped and extended as he chanted his plea for money. *"Birr, birr, birr."*

One of my favorite discoveries was the Merkato, the largest open-air market on the African continent, so big that an entire lane is dedicated to butter merchants, an entire city block set aside for sellers of traditional clothing, woven white cotton with embellished hems. Donkeys were everywhere, standing in for pickup trucks, for dollies, for forklifts. I spent hours in the spice aisles, fingering nuggets of frankincense, buying packets of black cumin or deep orange *mitmita*, just so I could smell them later in the filtered air of my hotel room. Our guide translated, and showed great patience as I pointed at one bin after another after another, hungry to know the names of everything. I saw one chili powder blend everywhere and quickly came to recognize the Amharic characters that represented it.

"*Berbere*," explained the guide, whose name was Fiseha. *Bayr-ber-ay.* "We use it in everything."

In my room that night, I poured out some *berbere* onto a coffee saucer. The blend was finely ground, so I could only rely on nose and tongue, not sight, to parse out the herbs and spices that had gone into it. I wrote a list of the spices in my journal, and the next day I checked with Fiseha to see how I'd done. I'd guessed nine of the dozen ingredients. The base ingredients were obvious: chili pepper, black pepper, and salt. After that, I came up with a list I knew well from Swedish cooking—cardamom, ginger, nutmeg, cloves, cumin, and coriander. Fiseha helped me with the last handful. I don't know how I missed the allspice and the fenugreek, and what I could have sworn was thyme turned out to be *ajowan* seed, also known as bishop's weed, which layered in another fiery kick on top of the peppers.

"Sometimes there's garlic," Fiseha told me. "Also cinnamon."

How can I describe the result of this blend? It was both masculine and feminine, shouting for attention and whispering at me to come closer. In one sniff it was bright and crisp; in the next, earthy and slow. I couldn't wait to take it back to Aquavit's kitchen and start experimenting.

FROM TIME TO TIME, Lolis would ask if I recognized any smells or sights or sensations. If my sister Linda were with us, she might have answered differently, but as much as I would have liked to say yes, I recognized nothing. That first trip to Ethiopia was less a reunion than a whirlwind romance. I felt welcomed wherever I went, even when people realized I couldn't speak Amharic. I certainly dressed and acted like a *ferengi*, their word for "foreigner," but they often called out "Habesha" to me, claiming me as their own. I spent one afternoon in a teff terra, a small, poorly lit hut where a five-woman cooperative produced round after round of injera, the spongy bread that Ethiopians eat at every meal, using it as both plate and utensil. I watched as they pulverized the teff with a stone, then sifted it into powder. They mixed this with a sourdough starter and water, then set it aside for a couple of days. At the center of the hut was a broad metal griddle that looked a bit like a barstool, a wide drum for a top and set on long legs, but underneath was a small coal fire, which choked the air of the hut. These fires are everywhere, and in Addis, when I'd get up early to take a morning run, I'd see a blanket of coal smoke hovering above the city's homes, a signal that breakfast was being prepared.

As a chef, it's impossible to be in a place where serious cooking is going down and not want to try your hand at it. One morning, I watched a woman pour fermented injera batter onto the grill in a perfect, smooth spiral, starting at the outer edge of the hot surface, and I smiled and nodded at her until she handed over the dented can she used for a ladle. It looked so simple when she did it, but that's how deceptive expertise can be. My attempts were lumpy and misshapen, and her words of encouragement were delivered with the patient tone you take with a not-so-gifted child. Nothing wrong with being humbled now and then.

The first time I made *doro wat*, my teacher was a seventy-five-year-old woman named Abrihet. Mutual friends had set up my tutoring session, and we met at Habesha, the restaurant Abrihet cooked for that was right off Bole, Addis Ababa's main drag. In the Habesha kitchen, we started from the very beginning by killing a chicken, plucking it, and then gutting it just as I'd learned to do in France. We cut it into a dozen pieces, not the eight or ten I was accustomed to, and submerged those in lemon, water, and salt, a brine that may have evolved as much for food safety reasons as for flavoring. As the meat marinated, Abrihet plunked down a sack of red onions in front of me.

I felt like I'd gone right back to my *commis* days. While Abrihet washed the collards that would be an accompaniment, I chopped all the onions myself, pounds and pounds and pounds of them, finely, finely chopped. All I had was a bad knife and a horrible cutting board; I realized how spoiled I'd become, and even though I felt clumsy trying to navigate the divots and dull edge, I figured if Abrihet could do it with these tools, I could, too.

Abrihet looked slightly embarrassed and said something to our interpreter in Amharic.

"What?" I asked him. "What is she saying?" The interpreter looked a little reluctant. "Tell me," I prodded.

"She's embarrassed," he said. "She says it's not the Ethiopian way to have a man in the kitchen. But she says you are not from here, you are a *ferengi*, so it's OK."

We chopped up a little garlic and ginger and divided that, along with the onion and some butter, into two pots.

"She says this must cook for forty-five minutes," the interpreter explained. "With very little heat."

That gave us enough time to get a shot of Ethiopian coffee, espresso style. Nothing tastes better than Ethiopian coffee; almost everywhere you go, it is roasted right before it's brewed. In the United States, we think it's a big deal if you wait to grind the beans before you make coffee. Here, the benchmark for freshness is miles higher.

Our next step was to dry off the chicken parts and add them into the onion mixture in two batches. First the dark meat, which takes longer to cook, and then, twenty minutes later, the light meat. Thirty minutes after that, the stew liquid had turned a rich brown. Abrihet put on two more pots of water, one for the greens and one for boiling some eggs. When the greens were ready and the eggs were done and peeled, we ladled the stew onto the center of a big platter that had been blanketed with a round of injera. The collards and eggs were evenly divided around the perimeter.

We sat down to eat, and after the ritual washing of hands, we ripped off pieces of injera with our right hands and used them to scoop up mouthfuls of stew. Abrihet made a little packet of food and reached over to me, putting it into my mouth.

"This is *gursha*," the interpreter said. "This is a sign of hospitality. She will do this two more times and then, if you like, you should do the same to her." I could barely swallow before my next *gursha* came, and when it was my turn to reciprocate, I probably dropped half of the food out of the injera on my way to Abrihet's mouth. But she didn't mind, and I was too happy to mind. After all, I'd just learned a piece of my past. Like so many of the Ethiopian dishes I learned to make over the years, *doro wat* served a dual purpose of expanding my repertoire as a chef while, dish by dish, adding texture and layers to the African heritage I so longed to know.

WE STAYED AT THE SHERATON ADDIS, the most luxurious hotel in the country. It was not like Sheratons in the United States; this was a palace, so opulent it was almost uncomfortable, especially since the moment you left the hotel's heavily patrolled gates, you stepped into an open-sewered shantytown, patched-together sheets of tin and cardboard that housed huge, extended families, families that lived with no water and no electricity and nothing but tamped-down dirt for a floor. I had never considered myself more than middle class, but in Ethiopia, I was beyond advantaged. Anyone who goes to Africa and experiences this contrast will tell you that it is almost impossible to wrap your mind around it—the gulf is too great. To a certain extent, you have to just push this part of the experience to the side.

I was treated like a prodigal son everywhere I went, pampered and attended to and interviewed by local newspapers and magazines. I could see that our visit meant a lot to the Ethiopians we met, and so, to say thank-you, I felt like I should put on a dinner for our hosts, forty of Addis's movers and shakers and politicos. The hotel staff loved the idea. We set it for New Year's Eve—mine, not theirs, since they operate by a calendar that holds its New Year celebration in September—and the Sheraton gave me carte blanche to use its staff and resources. This was eye-opening. The support team of the kitchen was all Ethiopian, but the chefs were Europeans. Here I was in a black country—the only country in all of Africa that had never been colonized, mind you—and a bunch of white Germans were in charge of the kitchen crew? I knew enough about the hotel industry to know that this imported upper tier was not the first string. In the international hotel business, the A team goes to America, Asia, and Europe. The B team ends up in the Middle East. The C team gets Africa. I might have gotten more pissed off, but how could I, when everyone from Klaus, the executive chef, to Tesfahun, the man who ran errands for the lowest level of *commis*, welcomed me so warmly into their kitchen?

I spent most of the second week putting together my menu and inventorying the hotel pantry. Because most of the hotel guests were foreigners, virtually all of the hotel kitchen's ingredients were imported. When I suggested using some Ethiopian ingredients in our dinner, I got blank, slightly embarrassed looks. The Sheraton Addis Ababa, I was told, did not serve Ethiopian specialties. Borrowing porters from the hotel, we did several Merkato runs to stock up for the big night, which had somehow gone from forty to sixty.

"Or quite possibly seventy," the concierge said to me with a broad smile.

My second agenda for the dinner, beyond saying thank-you to the gracious people at the Sheraton, was to inspire the Ethiopian staff by showing them what one could do with traditional Ethiopian ingredients. I began to think of the meal as my homecoming dinner and decided I would also try to bring together pieces of all the cuisines I knew and loved.

My appetizer was smoked salmon crusted with *berbere*. I wasn't set up to replicate my uncle Torsten's smokehouse, so instead, I quick-cured the salmon, then put it in a makeshift smoking box along with green coffee beans, a little bit of water, and cinnamon. After fifteen minutes I took out the salmon and was satisfied, even proud of the smell—bright and clear like the ocean. I took *berbere* and rubbed it on top of the salmon and served it with *ayib*, the local cottage cheese, chopped dill, and wedges of dried injera that could be used as crackers. Out of all the dishes we served that night, this was the biggest hit. Not only because it was delicious but also because people saw for the first time what was possible with Ethiopian ingredients. The rest of the meal carried this theme through. I rubbed duck with *berbere* and served it with figs and foie gras and a honey wine called *tej*. For dessert, we did a hot chocolate cake with warm beets and finished it with coffee-flavored honey syrup. Everywhere we could, we honored Ethiopian ingredients, and we did it at a level no one had ever seen before. The Sheraton Addis had a lot of things to recommend it, but Habesha soul wasn't one of them.

When I got home, spilling over with stories about what a fantastic time I'd had, friends asked me if it had been hard to leave.

"Not at all," I said. "Because I know I'm going back."

I NEVER HAD THE DESIRE to go to Ethiopia when I was growing up. Linda did. She talked about going back someday, about visiting our village, about finding our relatives, if we had any left. Part of my ambivalence may have been a son trying to be gallant toward his mother; on some level, I suppose I thought it would hurt Anne Marie's feelings if I went looking for my birth family. I loved my Samuelsson parents. I had a great childhood. The *negerboll* and *blatte* moments were tiny pebbles on an otherwise smooth and happy road.

As a chef, I'd found a more comfortable way to reconnect to Africa: through its food. Before I went on that trip, I'd been casting about for ideas of what kind of cookbook I wanted to do next. I'd already published one in Sweden called *En Smakresa* (*A Journey of Tastes*), which was a tribute to all the amazing flavors and cultures I'd encountered while traveling on the cruise ships. I'd also just finished up the manuscript for the *Aquavit* cookbook, which was a tribute to the restaurant that had given me my first opportunity to lead a kitchen and had given me my first American home. *Aquavit* was written for Americans, and I made sure to put my recipes and ingredients into a broader cultural context, so readers would see where each dish's Swedish roots lay.

One idea that my editors suggested was a "Marcus Cooks at Home" book, but at the time I wasn't feeling it. For one thing, I never cooked at home. Chefs rarely do. I either grabbed food on the fly at work or ate at restaurants around town to keep up with what the competition was doing. If my meals weren't research for work, I picked up whatever street food was in reach, whether it was a slice of Ray's pizza or a gyro with extra *tzatziki* sauce from the guy with a cart near my favorite newsstand. I was a chef who lived and breathed food, but I had no home life. A cookbook that depicted me entertaining in my apartment would have been untrue and inauthentic. What I wanted to do was the book I longed to own but had never seen—a cookbook that could serve as a bridge between my home in Manhattan and my roots in Ethiopia.

I've always loved bookstores. They remind me of my father, Lennart, whose greatest pleasure was to sit in the living room at night with a book in his hands and a cup of tea by his side. Bookstores are a giant present waiting to be unwrapped, full of stories and discoveries and lives. For a chef, the best bookstore in New York is Kitchen Arts & Letters, on the Upper East Side. The entire store is dedicated to books about food and wine, and if you can't find something there, it doesn't exist.

When I came back from my trip to Ethiopia, I went straight there, only to find that Africa was almost nonexistent in this world. I could find an entire wall on Italy, with whole shelves devoted to each of its regions, and endless rows on France and Spain and Mexico. The Africa section was one Time-Life book from the 1950s and a handful of wonderful but tradition-focused books by the culinary historian Jessica B. Harris. Where was contemporary Africa? Where were the recipes?

As far as I could tell, it was invisible, so I figured if I didn't do something about that, no one would. At that moment, the scope of my next book project expanded, launching me into a seven-year effort to take the pulse of a continent through its food. I would eventually travel from Cairo to Johannesburg, collecting stories and recipes, learning new techniques and ingredients, and then filtering them through my own palate. The result was *The Soul of a New Cuisine*. I covered a lot of ground—thousands and thousands of miles—but I don't pretend to have said all there is to say.

I had multiple goals with *Soul*. One was to introduce Africans to each other's cuisines by compiling and delivering a comprehensive array of authentic recipes from all over the continent. In my travels, I noticed a separation from country to country when it came to food. I didn't see Nigerian families saying, "Hmm . . . today we are going to cook Mozambican." My book could be a way for fellow Africans to look at each other through their foods. I also wanted to show people in the United States that Africa offers an enormous breadth of cuisines that not only have a relationship to foods we already know—foie gras, okra, and jerk seasoning, to take just a few—but that can be made in American kitchens. Finally, I wanted to open up a dialogue between Africa and the contemporary fine-dining world. On this point I knew that the chefs would be curious—we are by nature an inquisitive bunch, and they would respond to new and interesting ingredients, just as they had to wasabi or salsa. This was trickier territory because as soon as you talked about Africa and food, many Americans only associated the continent with famine. I wanted to go beyond that stereotype, to recognize that every country has a middle class, every country has rituals and celebrations around food. Every country has a cuisine.

ON THE NIGHT OF SEPTEMBER 10, 2001, Nils and I were at the Observatory Hotel in Sydney, Australia, preparing for a promotion the next day. I'd gone to bed, but Nils was having a beer with the Observatory's chef, Jimmy, in the hotel bar. The TV was flickering away. "What movie is this?" Jimmy asked Nils.

It wasn't a movie. It was live footage. Two planes had slammed into the World Trade Center.

Nils woke me up with the news, and all we could do was watch the footage, over and over, feeling helpless and wondering how we were ever going to get home. I had done a demonstration down at the towers just a week before; I knew the cooks who died. We caught the next available plane, ten days later, and came home to find our world had changed. The city was in shock. Everything was uncertain.

Aquavit and my first casual restaurant, AQ Café, got hit hard, as did all restaurants in the city. I felt guilty for stressing out about that, given the magnitude of what other people had lost, but Håkan and I had a business to run, and we knew from the start that we were going to have to lay off a good chunk of the staff if we were going to survive. I'm OK with firing people when they fuck up, but canning them when they've done nothing wrong? That was painful.

The mood of the city was glum for months; the papers reported one bleak, heartbreaking story after another; very few people were in the mood for a night out. Tourists and business travelers disappeared. One day here, next day gone. In the kitchen at Aquavit, we started shrinking shifts to avoid a second round of layoffs, something I'm proud to say the staff supported. And that was the silver lining. The entire city may have been depressed, but I'd never seen such kindness and camaraderie, such goodwill in the air.

People in the restaurant world often share information with each other. They commiserate, bitch and moan, gossip. They'll recommend a new purveyor or warn against a sloppy plumber. They'll share crazy theories about why business is slow. But no one was about to say a negative word about the sudden downturn: We all knew we should be happy to be alive. Every day, Håkan and I sat down to scrutinize our game plan. What if we took two items off each menu? What if we featured pork belly and other less expensive cuts of meat? What if we skipped the morels? We looked at a giant spreadsheet of the projected costs for the next six months, and it wasn't pretty. One number stood out from all the rest, and Håkan tapped it with the tip of his pen. It was our rent.

"*Detta måste gå,*" he said. This has to go. Right then we decided to move, painful as it would be to leave the elegant townhouse that had been so closely associated with Aquavit's identity. I would have to give up my post as mayor of Fifty-fourth Street, but there was no room for sentimentality at this point. There was only room for surviving. Midtown may not have been as ravaged as downtown, but it was still a no man's land. An expensive no-man's-land.

By the summer of 2002, business finally began to pick up a bit, and we were cautiously looking forward to the fall season, which brings bigger crowds and a back-from-vacation revenue bump for restaurants. Things were looking up again. In addition to working on my Africa cookbook, I'd recently formed a consulting company with Håkan called Townhouse Restaurant Group to field the calls we'd both been getting. We made plans to open up Aquavits in Stockholm and Tokyo.

Then, on another bright and crisp September day, this time in 2002, one of our cooks accidentally knocked over a pot of clarified butter. It was in the morning, about nine, and Nils was coming in the door of the kitchen just as Toshi, the cook who'd knocked over the pot, and two other prep cooks were running out. Nils made a valiant effort to get the fire under control, and was just about to pull the lever for the room's fire suppression sprinklers when the firemen arrived.

We would have had to close down for a few days if the suppressant had been released. We would have done a massive cleanup, thrown away whatever bins and boxes got hit by the fire-retarding chemicals, but then we would have opened again good as new. Instead, before Nils could hit the switch, the firemen took their axes to the central exhaust hood. The custom-fabricated, weeks-to-replace, incredibly expensive exhaust hood. The exhaust hood we could not function without. We were shut down for a month. When we opened back up, the world went to hell again: President Bush launched a war in Iraq. It may sound selfish to focus on how a war affected business, but in the restaurant world things like this can make or break you. It's why I have to scratch my head when I hear people talking about "celebrity" chefs, as if they have it easy. Most people have no idea what a roller coaster the restaurant world can be, and I don't know one chef—celebrity or not—who doesn't have to get his hands dirty with the gritty realities of the business to stay afloat. I'm not talking about the manufactured theatrics you see on reality shows; I'm talking about the responsibility of dozens of livelihoods resting on your shoulders and the really fine line between profitability and disaster. We had September 11, then a war, then the fire, then another war . . . things were not good.

Then came a much-needed sign that the work we were doing *was* good—and what's more, that it mattered.

MY HEART WAS IN MY THROAT. Actually, it was in my ears, too, pounding so hard I could barely hear what Lidia Bastianich, the legendary chef and owner of Felidia, was saying. Lidia, as she's known to everyone including strangers, was announcing my category at the 2003 James Beard Foundation Awards in New York City. This shouldn't have fazed me. I'd competed in front of large crowds before. I was used to competition. But this was different. I was nervous. A few months earlier, *Time* magazine had referred to the Beard Awards as "the Oscars of the food world," and this year, I'd been nominated— along with four major players in New York—for the title of the city's Best Chef.

In the micro-world of New York restaurants, this was kind of a big deal.

I suppose my nervousness came from being caught off guard. I'd been so preoccupied with digging out of one hole after another that I hadn't stopped to think much about this moment. I'd had to rent a tux that afternoon—a stiff polyester number that moved like it had a mind of its own—and hustled to get there on time. But now I was in a room with my idols and my peers, and it finally dawned on me that I was being considered as one of them. In my category, Mario Batali had won the year before for Babbo, his lusty take on Italian food. The decade of winners before Batali was an all-star list that included Gray

Kunz (Lespinasse), Jean-Georges Vongerichten (JoJo), Eric Ripert (Le Bernadin), Charlie Palmer (Aureole), and Lidia, the night's host. The 2003 field was just as deep: Rocco DiSpirito (Union Pacific), Odette Fada (San Domenico), Alex Lee (Daniel), and David Pasternack (Esca).

I was surrounded by some of the most talented chefs in the world, but I couldn't help thinking of who *wasn't* in the room: my grandmother, Helga, the first person to show me the possibilities of food, and my father, Lennart. She'd been gone ten years and he'd been gone seven, but I missed them both every day. In every dish I created and every decision I made, I was living out the lessons they taught me. All I wanted was for them to be here, in this moment, with me.

I had spoken to my mother earlier that afternoon. She called from Göteborg because she'd heard from Anna that I was up for, as she put it, "some kind of award." Neither of us spoke of *Mormor* or *Pappa*.

"*Vad kommer du att ha på mig?*" she asked. What will you wear?

"*Oroa dig inte,*" I reassured her. Don't worry. "*Ingen bryr sig. Det handlar om mat.*" No one cares. It's all about the food.

"*Bara vara bekväm, okej?*" Just be comfortable, OK?

I was the farthest thing from comfortable.

Lydia opened the envelope and announced the winner.

"Marcus Samuelsson, Aquavit."

The winner's medallion was solid brass, hung on a wide yellow ribbon. When Lidia draped it around my neck, all I could think was: It's so damn heavy. And why shouldn't it be? Its namesake was the father of American gastronomy, the man who introduced middle- and upper-middle-class Americans to French cuisine in the 1950s, raising the standards and expectations around American fine dining. He was an extraordinary mentor for up-and-coming chefs, and he gave back to the community in a big way: Along with food critic Gael Greene, he started Citymeals-on-Wheels, a program that had come to provide millions of meals to New York's homebound elderly each year.

As I looked out at the audience and heard the applause, I felt a strong connection to the past, a sense of the roots that had given life to the food and flavors I create in my cooking. I was born in Ethiopia, raised in Sweden, trained in Europe, but now, like Beard, I was American.

To be honored this way among my peers was incredible, and would only expand opportunities for Håkan and me as we developed the restaurant concepts that were perpetually brewing in our heads. I saw Håkan in the audience. He flashed a grim smile. He was happy for me, but the dark cast over his face mirrored what we both knew was a bittersweet moment. Hours ago, we had shut down Aquavit Minneapolis, after four short years.

We had no choice. In the two years that followed the 2001 terrorist attacks on Manhattan's World Trade Center, restaurants across the country had been suffering. Teleconferences replaced conferences, and our Minnesota venture couldn't recover from the drop-off in business travel. Earlier that afternoon, we broke the news to our executive chef in Minneapolis, and in the coming week, we would make the decision public, laying off the loyal staff who helped it earn consistently fantastic reviews.

As crushing as this failure was—how the hell could a *Swedish* restaurant fail in the Swedish-American heartland?—we would move on. That was one thing I knew how to do.

TWENTY-THREE **THE MAN THAT I AM**

MAYA HAILE SHOWED UP, RELUCTANTLY, AT A HOUSEWARMING PARTY I threw for myself that March. She didn't want to come to a place she'd never been with people she didn't know, but a model booker she'd worked with kept pressuring her to come, promising that she'd have fun and meet some fellow Ethiopian expats. She started bombarding Maya with text messages about the party at eight p.m. "It's off the hook!" she wrote. "Tons of E's here! Sister, get over here now!" Maya finally showed up at 11:30, and dragged a roommate along for company.

I don't throw a lot of parties—between benefits and openings, I go to enough of them while I'm on the clock—but when I do, I throw *down*. I'd just moved that spring from a swanky but soulless place in the Time Warner Center at Columbus Circle to a swanky and soulful brownstone apartment in Harlem, and it felt like a lot more than just a real estate transaction. I was finally ready to make myself a home, something that had never occurred to me all those years I lived out of duffel bags. I invited everyone I knew, along with some I didn't; I had a live band, platters of everything from gravlax to sushi, and two tended bars set up, one on my new terrace and the other on the lower floor of my duplex. The night was unusually warm and the party was bumping, wall-to-wall with people. Then two tall girls came in, taller than anyone there, even Mes, who is a pretty tall guy. One was half-Asian, half-white, and the other was black. I swear the room went into a freeze frame for a minute; people actually stopped talking and eating just to stare. The black girl was gorgeous, with big round eyes and high, beautiful cheekbones, and didn't have a lick of makeup on. Definitely a model, I thought, although I hadn't seen her before. I would have remembered.

I am not a tall guy. Five-feet-nine on a good day. But cooking has always given me confidence, and if it's my food at the table, then I'm at least six-feet-seven. We were in my home, at my party, so I went right up to her.

"*Selam,*" she said. Holy shit, I thought. She's Habesha?

"Give me your number before I get drunk," I said. "And will you have breakfast with me tomorrow?"

"Maybe," she said, smiling, "if I'm up."

The next day, she met me for breakfast at the M & G Diner. I was sitting there with my boys, sure she wouldn't show, and then she walked in and I just knew. As Common rapped, "It doesn't take a whole day to recognize sunshine."

The M & G was on the corner of 125th and St. Nick. It's closed now, which breaks my heart. Because for me, Ethiopian born, Swedish raised, eating there was the culinary equivalent of seeing Marian Anderson sing at the Lincoln Memorial. M & G was the come correct / can't be denied / I've been done wrong but watch me make it right execution of an incredibly rich black American culinary history. It had a bright red and yellow logo and a neon sign that let three generations of neighbors know the Southern fried chicken was fresh, hot, and delicious. It could always be counted on for good people and better than good food.

It was at the M & G that I learned just how much Maya and I had in common. Maya, whose given name is Gate Haile, grew up in Ethiopia, the tenth of twelve children. Her family is a double minority in that they're from the small Gurage tribe and are Catholics in an overwhelmingly Habesha and Orthodox country. She grew up between Addis and the village of Gofrer in a family that was part of the country's tiny educated upper middle class, often called the Diaspora for how many of their ranks go abroad to study and live.

In order to give her the benefit of a European education, Maya was sent at the age of twelve to live with her oldest brother, Petrus, who was a priest in Holland. Like two of her sisters, Maya went to nursing school, but people asked her so often if she was a model that she decided to give it a try. She left school and snuck off to enter a beauty contest in Frankfurt, and when she won, she didn't tell anyone in the family. The first agency she went to see signed her, and when we met, she'd been living in New York for only a few months, doing runway work for couture collections.

Maya is ten years younger than I am, but in many ways she's been exposed to more. She speaks Amharic, Dutch, French, and English, and she's lived for long periods in Ethiopia, Europe, and the United States. Part of what I loved about her from the start was that she wasn't jaded about New York or the restaurant world. I'd take her to events, and the way she'd remember people was Daniel, "the nice French guy," or Eric, "the handsome guy with gray hair." And just as I was comfortable around women because I had sisters, she had a ton of brothers and took no prisoners when we'd go to play basketball with my buddies. If we went to a black tie event, she knew how to be gracious and meet people and, of course, how to pose for the cameras. Someone as tall and beautiful as she is could easily be intimidating to people, but Maya is so friendly and welcoming that people are instantly put at ease. In my world, where relationships matter, her people skills count for a lot. She understands that the restaurant business is really about two things: food and conversation.

Gradually I introduced Maya to the New York that I loved. We went to eat everywhere—she was open to everything from dim sum in Chinatown to late-night dinners at Nobu, but she liked Floyd Cardoz's Tabla best, probably because his Indian spices were closest to the ones she knew from home. For her part, Maya introduced me to Ethiopian culture in a way my *blatte* friends had never been able to. I may know more about African cooking in general, but Maya is a better Ethiopian cook than I am. She knows more about the food you eat on holidays and in certain regions and if you're from a particular tribe. She will explain how the couscous in Ethiopia is thicker, more like barley than semolina, and how to eat it for breakfast with honey drizzled on top. She crisps injera in the oven and breaks it into chips that we can use with dips, and taught me how to drink coffee with butter and salt instead of milk and sugar.

I lived most of my adult life avoiding real relationships, telling myself that they would get in the way of my cooking, or that my mother and my sisters in Sweden needed me to be the man in the family, or that I didn't have time for commitments. There was always an excuse, but the real reason was that I was not ready until I met Maya.

That housewarming party was that best damn party I ever threw. It changed my life forever.

OUR FATHER WAS ALIVE. Not Lennart, the one who loved and raised us, but Tsegie, the one who'd given me and Linda life. Linda discovered this. For years, she had been researching and retracing our Ethiopian roots. She was a diligent sleuth, and every year or so would turn up some significant new piece of the puzzle that was our past. One year, she got hold of our hospital intake forms from Addis, only to discover that we were not the ages we'd grown up thinking we were: I was a year younger and she a year older. It may sound silly, but my mind immediately flashed back to being in high school when I was axed from the soccer team for being too small. Knowing that I had actually been a year younger than my Viking classmates made me feel a little better, even all these years later. Pathetic, I know. But true.

Linda then managed to track down an uncle on our mother's side. He responded to a letter from Linda with stunning news. Our birth father, Tsegie, had not died in the war with Eritrea, as we'd always believed. He was alive and well and living in a twenty-five-hut village called Abragodana, about sixty miles south of Addis.

As it happened, I was due to make my second trip to Ethiopia in a few weeks. I was doing a piece for *Travel & Leisure* about Addis, and I went with the talented and fun writing team of the Lee brothers, Matt and Ted. I would take them to the Merkato, of course, and we would check out Addis's nightlife scene with a long-distance assist from Mes, whose uncle still lived in the city. But ever since I'd gotten the news of Tsegie, I could think of nothing else. I was going to meet my father. I was not the orphan I had spent thirty years believing I was. Imagine finding out that some fundamental truth about yourself, that you had long accepted, was not actually true. As if you'd grown up believing you were white, and then suddenly finding out you were black. I caught my reflection in mirrors, in the weeks before that second trip to Ethiopia, and marveled at the fact that I would soon be seeing some older version of my face—not figuratively, as I had on the first trip, imagining my older self in the faces of Habesha men on the trip, but literally, the way children do when they look into the face of a parent and see the family lines rendered in flesh and bone.

Mes's uncle Workasef served as our translator for the trip, and he agreed to come with me to Abragodana. We planned to leave the photographer and the Lee brothers behind—I didn't want the moment to turn into a circus—and hire a driver. Somehow, Workasef had gotten word to the village, and they would be expecting us. This in itself was nothing short of a miracle, since the village has no telephones, much less running water, gas, or electricity.

The drive—which took hours longer than it would have if we hadn't been traveling over pitted and dusty unpaved roads, stopping regularly for herds of cattle or donkeys carrying mountains of charcoal lashed to their backs—had to be reminiscent of the journey Linda and I made with our mother three decades before. Looking out the windows of our rattly van, passing through tiny villages and barren landscapes, I went over the details of my life story—at least, what I knew of it.

At birth, I was named Kassahun Tsegie. I was the third child of a farmer and his wife, and we lived in the Ethiopian highlands, in a small village outside of Addis Ababa, the country's capital. Most Ethiopians farmed or raised livestock; my father did both. He grew lentils and chilies and had cows. Their first child, a son, had died, and after him came Fantaye, my sister Linda, a girl with big round eyes and full brows like our father's. And after Fantaye, I came along. We belonged to the Amhara ethnic group, not as large as the Oromo, who dominated our area, but still one of the largest of the many, many ethnic groups that made up the country's population. I was born in 1971—not 1970 as I originally believed—when the country was in the midst of great turmoil. The Eritrean war of independence had been raging for ten years, and Emperor Haile Selassie's four-decade reign was gasping toward an end while potential successors jockeyed for position. Political strife aside, the country had been ravaged by malnutrition and a tuberculosis epidemic that had infected nearly eight hundred thousand people. If left untreated, more than half of the people who have active TB will die. In Amharic, TB is called *samba necarsa*, cancer of the lung.

By my first birthday, I had contracted TB. So had my sister. So had my mother, and her case was the worst of all. There was no medical help in our village, so the three of us set out, by foot, for Addis Ababa, where there were doctors and modern hospitals. My mother worked some unknown miracle to get us through the lines of sick people outside the hospital to get us the care we needed.

My mother died in that Addis hospital and there was no record of our birth father, just a rumor that he had died in the war. Fantaye and

I must have had less severe cases of TB, or maybe we found help—in the form of antibiotics—before our symptoms progressed too far to be put into check. We were taken in by the hospital, nursed out of crisis and back toward health. However long it took, we had beat tremendous odds. Months later, when we were well enough to be released, the hospital staff faced the question of what to do with us. One of the nurses, Ayem Alem—whose name meant "eye of the world"—stepped up.

"I'll take them home," she said. She took us to stay with her and her four daughters in a small house built on a postage-stamp plot of land issued by the government. "I'll find an adoption center to place them." True to her word, Ayem found a Swedish field hospital that administered adoption placements, and she convinced them to put us on their list. While she waited for us to find a home, she must have stretched to accommodate and feed two extra mouths. Maybe her daughters felt burdened by our presence when their mother was at work; maybe they liked us, fussing over us or delighting at my sister's easy laugh or my smile. My Swedish mother has kept Ayem's letters—which she continued sending to us over the years, long after we'd grown—and the way she tells us how her daughters haven't forgotten us, and that she hopes we remember our Amharic names, are all telling details of how deep Ayem's feelings were for my sister and me.

I mulled over these bits and pieces of my story as we passed through small towns and across long stretches of parched, barren land. Through the dust, I saw bright yellow and red signs for St. George beer everywhere. In towns that were having a market day, droves of people filled the road, indifferent to traffic. A man balancing a sewing machine on his head nearly walked into our front bumper, but a friend pulled him back just in time.

Did my mother, whose name was Ahnu, really make this trip alone? With two small, sick children? Perhaps my father went with her, or maybe he stayed with the farm while a brother or uncle accompanied us. I'll never know for sure. We probably went by foot, which would have taken days, and we would have traveled in the cool of the evening, and spent our days resting in whatever shade we could find. For food, we would have carried dried injera, and *quanta*, a beef jerky made from long strips of meat, seasoned with pepper powder and salt and left to dry for up to a week. We would have had to carry our own water. That we even made it to Addis astounds me, but of course it was no guarantee of salvation. Hospitals were so over-crowded that people slept in the streets for weeks just to get inside. Did Ahnu ever make it into the hospital? Did a doctor ever see or treat her? I don't know. What I do know is that she left the village with us and she died. And that she was twenty-eight years old.

Before I left New York, I'd gone to the bank. Anyone who has traveled extensively in Africa knows the drill. Cash is king, not credit cards, not traveler's checks. Just as important as the bank is the run I always make to the sporting goods store where I purchase two dozen brand-new soccer balls. These are the currency I will share with the kids that I meet.

On the plane from New York to Addis, I was so aware that for the first time in my adult life, I was traveling not as a chef, chasing flavors—but as an orphan, chasing history. And yet, I was also piggy-backing work on the trip—traveling with a team from *Travel & Leisure*. When I look back on it, I can see clearly that work was a buffer from all the question marks and possible disappointments that might await me in Ethiopia. If I did not get to meet my father, if he was in any way a disappointment, I could change course and focus solely on cooking and the food feature that we were creating for the magazine. But at the time, it wasn't anywhere near as clear, and I told myself that the day I was going to meet my birth father was merely a side trip, like the afternoon I had spent learning how to make injera with the old women in the hut.

Once our team arrived in Addis, we drove through the city to an old orphanage to meet my father and the woman who had brokered the deal. It was chaos to get there, as it is chaos to get anywhere in Addis. Goat pimps run across the street, herding skinny goats. You get dust in your eyes. A Mercedes speeds by. A hand is out and begging. At the same time, your eyes can't quite believe the beautiful embassies and villas that are home to the city's wealthy residents and the expat elite. And there are runners—both men and women, tearing down the sides of the street like it's the New York City Marathon. But it's not a marathon, it's just a day ending in *y* and Addis is pulsing with the rhythm of three million feet, many of them barefoot.

We were traveling in an old Toyota Land Rover. That's what all the expats drive, but even a Land Rover can't protect you from the waves of dust. An hour after we'd gotten into the car, we knocked on the door of the compound. There was a guard at the gates and he was dressed in old military gear from some long-ago war. It was a hundred degrees, but he had the full regalia: military pants, jacket, shawl, boots. It's the way every guard in the city lets his power and importance be known.

I walked in the door and the first person I met was Rahel, the woman who got us the information about my father. Rahel worked at the agency that handled Linda's and my adoption. But in a country with 75 percent unemployment, she took a great risk to let us know our father was alive. In fact, she and Linda had been in touch for years before we finally learned the truth. Rahel waited until three months before she retired to make this introduction.

There was an older man sitting next to her. Rahel gestured to him. "This is your father," she said.

My father. Not Lennart, fair skinned, Swedish, muscular, born of the sea, with a love of the land. This man had dark skin and gray, thick, long hair. Right away, I was impressed. To be eighty in a country where the majority of men are lucky to see forty is nothing short of a miracle. "He is a farmer and a priest," Rahel told me. I sat in silence as my birth father began to pray in these beautifully melodic chants. The whole thing was so overwhelming. I was holding it together, but then I started crying. Once the tears came, they never really stopped.

My FATHER JOINED our group, we got back into the Land Rover, and we headed toward his house. It was a two-hour ride. In that car ride, we had to get to know each other. We both knew that once we got to his house, his wife would be there, as would his other kids. The time in our car—it was our only real moment.

What to say?

I knew I didn't want the first thing I said to be, "Why did you give us up for adoption? Why did you let us think you were dead?" It couldn't be a blaming game. And that, in and of itself, was its own challenge. There was a part of me that wanted to jump out of the Land Rover and to run away from my father, the mystery, all of the questions for which I feared I would receive no real answers.

We passed the Haile Selassie palace. There was a brand-new tower. Always, always, there was the contrast between the luxe Mercedes-Benz sedans and the impoverished kids on the street. It is Harlem times twenty. I looked out of my window at the street vendors selling pictures of Usher and Tupac. The smell of *berbere* was everywhere. We zoomed past a Starbuckks with two *k*s. We zipped past a Mariott with one *r*. Men and women were eating out at a restaurant called Burger Double King. I stared out of the window to avoid staring at my father's face.

He started by asking me questions: "How's Anne Marie? How's Fantaye?"

He knew that my older sister Linda remembers more about Ethiopia than me. He remembered her more vividly as well. He said, "I have a very clear image of her."

I began to ask nervous, peripheral questions: "How was the harvest this year? Is it difficult to get water?"

I've talked to other Swedish Ethiopian kids who've met their parents. "It's just a money war," they told me. "They just want money from you." But I wanted to be open, I wanted to build a relationship. I wanted to sweep away the dust and swat away the flies and find something beautiful in my newfound family. I just didn't know how.

I was looking out of the window and after a while, there were no roads. The red clay caked my face and I coughed. I began to see more giraffes and fewer people. Kids were running toward us because they were so excited to see a car. Dried-up mud was everywhere. We were in the savannah of Africa and everyone was yearning for shade: Animals curled up under trees; families slept under the trees; everybody and everything were swatting flies.

I wondered, Is this the road my mother walked with us?

I wondered, When can I ask about my mother?

I couldn't wait to tell my sister Linda. When it comes to our life in Ethiopia, both before and in Sweden, Linda is my truth teller. I tell her things and I know that they are real. She tells me things and I know that I am hearing the truth.

I thought, Petrus, Linda's son, would go crazy if he was here. He is so much like his mother. He longs for Ethiopia, too.

My father talked about his firstborn son, my older brother, who died in infancy. He wept openly at the loss. I cannot gauge, or begin to imagine, what he has felt about losing Linda and me all those years ago.

Luckily, just when I was sure that the reunion was too much for me to handle emotionally, we arrived in my father's village. It looked like the same patch of dried-up mud that we had been scaling for hours, but my father knew where he was. He directed the driver to take a right.

I remembered being out in the ocean, in Smögen, with my uncles. They would say, "Stop the boat here," and we would find all these fish. As a child, I wondered how my uncles could see markers in the big blue sea. My father saw markers in the red clay, in exactly the same way.

We turned again on an even smaller dirt road and there were maybe sixty kids running toward us. All the kids in the neighborhood were jumping on the car. My father waved them away with a stick the whole time. We stopped the car and got out.

A woman ran up to me, wailing with joy. This, I would later find out, was Kasech, my father's second wife. She was closer to my age than his. She held my face in her hands and kissed both my cheeks again and again, then took me by the hand to lead me through the throng of spectators and into the yard. She walked me into their hut, gesturing for us to sit on the benches lining the wall while she and another woman performed the coffee ceremony. In Ethiopia, this is one of the greatest displays of hospitality: roasting, grinding, and then brewing fresh coffee for your guests. Burning frankincense is part of the ritual, as is a bed of grass strewn on the floor, a suggestion of luxury carpeting the parched earth. While you wait, you snack on popcorn, unsalted and cooked in front of you.

My father's home consisted of two clay houses—one with a roof, one without.

The one with no roof was where they went to the bathroom. There were two oxen walking around the compound. One skinny goat.

The house was all of forty square feet, with a small oven for making injera. The walls were decorated with beautiful clean pictures that Linda had sent—of Jesus, Petrus, me, my mother, Linda, even Zoe. There were eight people in the family and even without all of us visitors, there was no way everyone could fit inside at the same time; I saw the rolled-up mats in the corner and I knew that every night, some of the kids slept outside with the animals.

The clay compound shook me more than anything I had ever seen in Ethiopia because it wasn't just a place, it was my family home. I could have grown up here, in this shack, in this poverty—and how drastically different my life could have been. I want to believe that despite the challenges of war and famine and the way that even weather is an enemy, I would have made a happy life—the way my brothers and sisters have found their own glimmers of joy. But it is hard for me, as deeply connected as I feel to Ethiopia—the people, the history, and the culture—to see past the telethon-like images. I am distracted by the flies. There are flies everywhere. There are so many flies on the faces of the children, they don't even bother to swat them away. And in the end, it's the fly-covered faces of the little ones that have me beating back the tears. If only my love was a net that could keep the flies out. If only my love was a net full of food for all the hungry bellies. I understand why so many people have given up on Africa—no one wants to say we are leaving a continent of people behind to tough it out in a hundreds-of-years-old war of survival, but we are, and the reason is because the level of change it would take to make a difference, to heal past wounds and chart a new path is mammoth, gargantuan, almost unimaginable. But one of the things I have learned during the time I have spent in the United States is an old African American saying: Each one, teach one. I want to believe that I am here to teach one and, more, that there is one here who is meant to teach me. And if we each one teach one, we will make a difference. I cannot give up on my family, on this village, on this country, on this continent. So although I feel them coming—the pitying tears of a Westerner, I do not let them out. Instead I reach for my younger sister Ashou, who is five, but looks as if she is three. I pull her closer to me and I let her sit on my lap. I let the flies that cover her face also cover my face. And I do not swat them away.

I HAVE RETURNED TO ETHIOPIA at least once a year since, sometimes with Linda, sometimes with Maya, and sometimes on my own. I have met all eight of my siblings, four boys and four girls, whose ages were between three and twenty-two when I made that first trip. I feel deeply connected to them, deeply invested in helping them live better lives, and that has turned out to be one of the most complicated undertakings I've ever faced. We are family, and yet we are separated by not only an ocean. We are separated by language, culture, religion, and class. When I discovered that the ten of them lived on $200 a year—this, remember, is a country with a 75 percent unemployment rate—I began to wire money. It started with $150 a month, less than a car payment. The impact of that money has without question changed their lives. It has provided more food and better education. But from time to time—especially in those moments when it seems that they risk becoming "Western Union waiters," people who count on connections from the West to solve every problem and be their sole source of income—I'm not clear if it's all been for the best.

When I first met my father, none of my half sisters—Zebeney, Salam, Ashou, and Tigist—was in school. In rural Ethiopia, to educate girls who work so diligently on the farms and become wives so young is seen as a luxury. I had to bargain with my father for his daughters to go to school. I not only needed to cover their living expenses at the boarding school in Addis, I had to compensate my father for the loss of income that their labor represented.

"Fine," I told my father. I would pay him.

And still my father said no. Even if I sent extra money, the loss to his farm would be too great.

"You can send one," he said. "But not the oldest, as she is ready to be married soon."

Zebeney, at thirteen, and Salam, at eleven, were already being groomed to be wives. Their dowries would bring not only pride to my father, but financial comfort.

"I want Zebeney in school," I said, negotiating, the way Lennart had taught me to haggle with the fishmongers when I was a boy. But these were not fish, and my father was not a fisherman selling his wares. I struggled to keep the judgment out of my eyes and out of my voice. If I overstepped my boundaries and insulted his way of life, my father would shut the negotiation down, just to show me who was boss. I had to remember that he loved my sisters and, in his mind, training them to be hard workers on the farm was a guarantee of future happiness. It was this strange, uncomfortable chess game. I felt like my sisters were the pieces on the board; how was I going to get at least one of these little girls all the way across the board so she could go to school?

Eventually, my father relented. Zebeney, the thirteen-year-old, was allowed to go to school.

I sensed an opening. "It's not good to send her off to Addis by herself," I said. "Salam should accompany her."

At this my father half smiled, pleased to see that despite a lifetime spent abroad, I still had some of that Habesha hustle inside of me.

"No, no," he said, shaking his head. "Salam must take on Zebeney's chores."

I knew it was a good idea to send the two oldest girls away to school together. They would need each other for support, I said, and eventually my father gave in.

The joy that my two oldest sisters felt at being given this rare opportunity was mirrored by the heartbreak in the two youngest girls. Tigist was not even five yet, and although she too worked on the farm and was up at dawn, she had only a vague sense of the opportunities she was missing. Ashou, at seven, was preternaturally sharp, and when I saw the look on her face when she learned she was staying home, the way the rejection hung above her like a cloud, it was all I could do to blink back the tears. How many orphaned children had that look when Linda and I were adopted and flown away to a fantastical land where warm water ran in the bathtub and cold water ran in the kitchen and a treasure chest doled out food every time you opened it?

I held Ashou close and whispered to her, "Don't worry, it will be your turn soon." The look on her face was disbelieving. Not only was she being left behind, but despite the extra income, Zebeney and Salam's departure meant that her life was about to go from difficult to nearly impossible. Her days would begin at four a.m. when she walked miles to get water from the village well, and would not end until well after dark, when the last dish was cleaned and everything was put away. She was seven years old and her shifts were longer than those of any of my restaurant staff.

IT TOOK ME ANOTHER TWO YEARS to get Ashou into school and another year after that to get my father to part with Tigist, the youngest. Tigist is now the happiest of all of my sisters. She has been in school since she was seven years old and, with every passing day, farm life feels more like a distant memory. Ashou, who is now going into sixth grade, is also thriving. She is the one who never quite believed me when I told her she'd get out, too, and her skepticism, as well as the years she spent on the farm after the oldest two left, has given her a sophistication beyond her years. She is the one who reminds me most of myself. Ashou is the one who is always going to match one shot of luck with two shots of hard work.

The additional financial responsibility of my sisters is nothing compared to the way that the revelation of my father has complicated my own emotional life. In the absence of real communication, it is hard to know what to believe. Did my father abandon my mother? Did he abandon us? He told Maya on one visit that he came for us within weeks of our mother's death, but was told it was too late, even though we were still in the country, staying with Ayem. If that's true, was it just a miscommunication or did the person he spoke with decide that Linda and I would be better off where we were? In his grief, my father has said, he went off to live in the northern mountains, hermitlike, for ten years. When he came back down, he had a religious epiphany and became a priest.

Was that what really happened?

What seems clear is that my father is a man of great strength and endurance. He has lived twice as long as the life expectancy for men of his generation, he has come back from losses that would ruin others, and he has a spark of leadership that illuminates any room he enters. There's a brightness to him, a power that comes from having lost everything and survived. And while I will always think of Lennart as my father and Anne Marie as my mother, Tsegie gave me something I never thought I'd have—a living family tree in Ethiopia, and another place to call home.

TWENTY-FOUR **MAKING IT RIGHT**

MEETING MY FATHER, AND KNOWING THAT I HAD BEEN LOVED BY HIM despite his decades-long absence, gave me the courage to meet my daughter. Not that I didn't want to meet her before, it was just that it had to be on my terms. Chefs, after all, are well-known control freaks. And so I wanted to make sure that my first meeting with my daughter went off with the precision of a four-star, seven-course meal. I felt like I had to perfect *myself* before meeting her, so that she could find no fault; that's the chef's mentality. But after traveling to Ethiopia, to a village that did not exist on any map, and sitting with my father in his dirt-floored hut, something changed: I realized that meeting my daughter was not at all like orchestrating the perfect restaurant meal.

All I needed to do was give Zoe what my father had given me: my own flawed self, without excuses or promises.

My mother, Anne Marie, is baffled by my career—more specifically, what I have given to my career and what I have allowed it to take from me. "How do you have the energy, Macke?" she asks. "How do you do it?" Not being there, she finds it hard to imagine. Just as she rushed, without doubt or hesitation, into motherhood—adopting first Anna, then Linda and me—she never for a second doubted her capacity to love and care for Zoe, her first grandchild.

Almost from the moment Zoe was born, my mother wrote to her in German, a language she'd always loved, and once Zoe was old enough, she began to write back. The summer that Zoe was seven, my mother invited her to visit Smögen, where she spent two weeks with her cousins. My mother never asked for my permission, of course; she merely informed me once the plan was set. I told her I was too busy setting up Aquavit Minneapolis to come along, that work was just too crazy. I always had an excuse. My mother knew it wasn't a question of having too much work that kept me away. I was still not ready to be a father to Zoe.

My mother was also the one who, from the beginning, took charge of Zoe's financial future. I established a bank account and funded it, but my mother watched it, invested it, and sent a check to Brigitta, Zoe's mom, every month. I felt good that Zoe wanted for nothing, money-wise, but that was about as far as it went. The sad fact is, for the first fourteen years of Zoe's life, I never went to Austria, never sent a postcard or a gift, never picked up the phone and had a conversation with her, never made the slightest effort.

How to explain this and not sound like a jerk? Think of it this way—my absence in Zoe's life was a train I boarded the moment Brigitta told me she was pregnant, that she was keeping the baby, and that I was free to go. So I went. That train was powered by the steam of my own ambition: I hopped on and I didn't know where it was headed; I just knew that I couldn't step off. If I had ended up for good in Switzerland at a resort like Victoria Jungfrau or in France at a place like Georges Blanc, I truly believe I would have made my way into her life sooner. Things would have been different. But that train didn't stop there. It kept going, and I followed it around the world, driven by my ambitions. I was young—twenty when I first boarded—and, if I'm going to be honest, incredibly self-absorbed. Along the way, two of the people I loved most in life—my grandmother, Helga, and my father, Lennart—died, and I wasn't there for either. There was no therapy. There was no working it out. There was just me riding the train and thinking, When this thing stops, when life calms down, when I get there—wherever *there* is—I will deal with it. All of it. The past—whom I left, whom I loved, what I lost—and the future, the future being Zoe.

Thank goodness my mother's moral compass was so perfectly calibrated. She didn't just send checks to Zoe, she loved her and let her know that she was a *Samuelsson*. And the relationship my mother had built and nourished for so long kept the lines open long enough for me to come around.

In June 2005, I arranged a trip to Austria. I was ready. No more excuses. No more hiding in shame. Zoe was now fourteen and as a teenager, she could either embrace me with open arms or kick me to the curb. All those years ago, I had made my choice: run. Now it was her turn. I'd present myself, let her set the rules for our relationship, and live with the consequences.

First, I flew to Sweden to meet my mother, who would join me on my trip. There was no way I could have made the journey to Austria without her. Meeting her in Göteborg, knowing the journey I was about to take, I'd never needed her strength so much before. Because anything that Zoe and Brigitta did or said would be legitimate. How would I cope if I was forced to spend the night in a windowless hotel room after being rejected by Zoe, crying my eyes out? It would be what I deserved, of course, but how would I deal? There was only one woman in the world who would support me, who might even shed a tear for me—and that's my mother. In that moment, when she could have snapped me in half with her judgments of my failures, she chose to treat me with tenderness. "You did what you could, Marcus," she said, as we boarded the plane for Graz. "You were just a kid yourself."

Josef, Brigitta's brother, picked us up at the airport and drove the forty-five minutes from Graz to Zoe's small town in the beautiful, pastoral Steiermark region of the country. Josef was welcoming and laid-back, just far enough removed to make us feel at ease. He was much more than an uncle to Zoe; he was the father figure in her life. Although he worked in the city and Zoe lived in the country, he came home almost every weekend, for fourteen years, to be with her. I could tell that he adored her.

It surprised me how jealous I felt. Jealous of what they obviously had, and what I did not. But I hadn't come all this way to be jealous. I came to be humble, to try to begin a relationship that, I hoped, would be filled with friendship and love the rest of our lives.

But my intention couldn't quite overcome my heart or my training. It's a little known fact that most chefs are mathematicians. We are constantly calculating: how many pounds of meat, how many orders, how many cups of water, what's the baking temperature, for how many minutes. If you've been a chef for as long as I have, you can't help but have thousands of formulas in your head. So it didn't take me long to start doing the math. Josef, tall, handsome, protective, easygoing, was the guy who had been here unfailingly for fourteen years . . . which is 168 months . . . which is 5,110 days. That's a wall I could never scale, because no matter what I did going forward, Josef would always have done more. He would always have *been there*.

I was counting in my head—measuring time, calculating my failures—when I first saw Zoe, and saw the affection in her eyes. She didn't know me, but she knew me. I was her father and there was no one else who could do the job that I came here, after all these years, to do. She didn't have to say a word to let me know that she was glad that I was here and that, in this moment, she was not counting a thing except the time it would take for me to embrace her.

So I did. I put aside the shame, and hugged my daughter for the first time.

As a gesture of gratitude—not to mention a deep desire to be back in my comfort zone—I immediately offered to cook for Zoe and her family. I asked Zoe to walk me into the village so we could shop together for groceries. The region where she lives is known for its apples, so I decided to make a potato apple soup for lunch. For dessert, I bought a bar of bittersweet chocolate and a small tin of sea salt.

Peeling two pounds of potatoes kept my hands busy and my nerves in check while Zoe and I worked through the awkwardness and got to know each other a little bit. "Zoe, you're the one who knows where everything is," I said. "So if you show me, we'll do the meal together." My German isn't very good, but it was strong enough to fill in the gaps of Zoe's almost perfect English. Sautéing the onions and the sliced apples was so familiar that it helped take the edge off. I had, in some small way, taken my first step toward being a father that Zoe could know and, hopefully, one day, love. It was a very basic soup, but as I poured the ingredients into the pan—apple cider, milk, nutmeg—I felt as if I were trying out for Escoffier himself: That is how much winning the trust of this girl meant to me. I ladled the soup into a bowl, topping it with chives, and took a breath.

With flour, eggs, and butter, I made a batter that I let rest while Zoe, her family, and my mother ate the soup. I ate mine standing, quickly and without fuss, as if I were on duty at a restaurant with dinner service just about to begin.

After she was done eating, Zoe helped me make chocolate blinis, two-inch pancakes that I topped with melted butter and a sprinkling of the sea salt. Zoe laughed when she saw me with the salt. Salt? On dessert?

"Just wait," I said.

After she took her first bite, she stopped for a minute, a look of deep concentration passing across her face. Then she broke into a huge smile.

"*Gut!*" she said. "*Das ist gut!*"

At Aquavit, we served a version of the same little, luxurious chocolate pancakes I made with Zoe as one of our desserts. They are not actual blinis, which are made of buckwheat, a flour that can make some people (including me) violently ill; these have just a touch of cake flour and almond flour in them. They get much of their richness from the egg whites we fold into the batter . . . as well as the stick of butter that goes into them, the clarified butter they're fried in, and the melted butter we drizzle on top. I didn't want to go crazy and create Death by Chocolate here, so I focused on other aspects: quality of ingredients—the freshest butter, a high-quality chocolate like Callebaut or Valrhona; getting the right crispiness by using both a fry pan and the oven; and complexity of flavor, sprinkling the pancakes with melted butter and just a few grains of *fleur de sel*, a pink sea salt from off the coast of Brittany. This contrast between salty and sweet hits the tongue at the same time, and the result, as Zoe said, is *gut*.

When we were together that first day, it was funny: I could see hints of how we were similar. Zoe has confidence and I have confidence. Her room was messy like my room is messy. She had so much of me in her. She liked spicy food; she liked food, even though she never cooked the way I did when I was a kid. It was eerie to stand there and see her move through the kitchen like my grandma Helga—not trained, just a natural. We even laughed in the same way. Everybody noticed it. It was a lot like meeting my brothers and sisters in Ethiopia. We didn't grow up together, but we had these little commonalities that let us both know that we were not strangers—we were connected.

Each night in Austria, I cooked a meal that I hoped would bring me a little closer to winning Zoe over. I was reaching out the only way I knew how. I cooked her the dishes of my childhood: Helga's roast chicken; my mom's spaghetti and peas, to which I now add pancetta; and my grandmother's fish balls, which I now make with an Indian-style curry. Every day, I went out in search of ingredients I wasn't sure I would find: red curry paste, lemongrass stalks, coconut milk—but thanks to the globalization of our food culture, even in a little town near Graz, I could find everything I was looking for. I'm not a gifted pastry chef, but it became clear to me that my daughter had a sweet tooth, so I made sure to give myself plenty of time to compose simple, delicious desserts like red berry cobbler, made with biscuits and a rich, complex filling: sour cherries, raspberries, strawberries, a splash of red wine, and confectioner's sugar, boiled to bubbly goodness.

A few days into my visit, I was feeling exhausted and overwhelmed by the emotion of it all. It helped to have my mother there as a buffer, especially because her German is so good, and she's such a kind, open person; she put everyone at ease. But the whole deal: It was a lot to take in. One afternoon when I was feeling the need for some air, I put on my sneakers and said, "I'm going out for a run." Brigitta surprised me and said, "Wait two minutes, and I'll come with you." I think both of us needed to make some peace. For almost fifteen years, we'd never talked—at least not in a real way. We chatted on the phone a few times when something important came up with Zoe and a decision needed to be made, but that was maybe once a year. Not a lot.

It was late August and already feeling like fall, and the sun was low in the sky. People were out picking apples. Brigitta and I ran and ran, talking about Zoe, and I felt so lucky that this woman never judged me, never punished me for not being there. There were never any shouting matches between us, no turning Zoe against me. My mother helped, for sure, but her efforts would have been useless if Brigitta hadn't been so willing to keep the lines open.

There was so much ground to cover. Brigitta was married now and had two kids in addition to Zoe, and she brushed away my apologies, said it wasn't necessary for me to ask for forgiveness. Her strength was incredible. I saw right away the ways in which motherhood had been a gift for her. Just like my mother had not cared whether Linda, Anna, and I had been black—all she cared about was being a mother— similarly, Brigitta had not been tortured by the circumstances of Zoe's birth. What mattered to her was the love she had funneled into her child. I was in awe and told her so: "Congratulations," I told her as we finished our run, not that she needed to hear it from me. "You promised you would raise Zoe to the best of your capabilities, and you did it. Thank you."

LAST SUMMER, Zoe and her uncle Josef came to visit me in New York. I took her to Rockaway Beach, Central Park, Chinatown, the Museum of Modern Art. She's a teenage girl, so she wanted to go shopping, so I sent her off with a Metrocard and a subway map and she explored the East Village and Soho. She hung out with me at the restaurant and I tried to show her that as a chef, my world is the back of the house: It's hot and noisy, I'm on my feet for hours on end, it's not glamorous. I also took her to a fancy party at one of the city's most glorious spaces: the New York Public Library. Zoe was thrilled to meet Kanye West, but I was thrilled that she got a glimpse of the people who make New York what it is: the fashion people, the artists, the gay community, the gay and fabulous community. To cap it off, Liza Minnelli performed.

It was good that we had a night to remember, because the next morning, the moment I'd been dreading—and which I knew was inevitable—arrived. Zoe broke down. She got it all off her chest. She let me have it for all the years I'd been absent, all the disappointment she felt, all the feelings of betrayal and loss. "You didn't want me," she said. "Is it true you didn't want me?"

"No," I kept telling her. "No, no, no. That couldn't be further from the truth. If what you're asking me is whether I was young and scared, then yes, that's true. If you're asking me if I am sorry for the way I acted, I am."

"Why didn't you ever call? Why couldn't you come see me? You knew where I was." She was sobbing.

"I *wanted* to," I said. "Really. But it was so hard to figure out how."

"Whatever," she said, dismissively.

It's amazing how universal the term *whatever* is. All around the world, teenagers toss it around like Frisbees. But Zoe's "whatever" had a little more bite. Because I owe her so much, there is a certain percentage of the time we spend together where I am, in one way or another, apologizing and she is, in one way or another, giving me hell. But that's the funny thing about the years I spent building my career as a chef. A lot of people have cut me to the core with their insults, and I know why. There's a part of me that hopes it's great therapy for Zoe to tell me how she feels, to let me have it. In my head, I'm thinking, Go for it, Zoe. Ask me anything. Call me anything. Say anything. Because while she's still figuring me out, I know, finally, who I am. I'm a father and I'm a chef, and the one thing I can take is the heat.

TWENTY-FIVE **MERKATO**

IN FEBRUARY 2008, I OPENED A NEW RESTAURANT IN NEW YORK CITY called Merkato 55. It was a pan-African restaurant and it opened to much fanfare. We got tons of coverage from the press: I was on everything from the *Today* show to *20/20* to the monitors in New York taxicabs. John Legend performed at our opening, and from day one, we were doing 150 covers a night. I had picked what I thought was a perfect spot, too: the Meatpacking District, a former warehouse sector along the northern end of the West Village, and the space was roomy and beautiful. I'd had my eye on the two-story building for over a year; I loved how it was in a low-skyline neighborhood of cobblestone streets, how it was slightly off the beaten path but also full of vitality. The area's former reputation as a place that trafficked in sides of beef during the day and transvestite hookers at night didn't bother me one bit. That was ancient history by the time we signed our lease, and the neighborhood was becoming known as the place to hang out. There was the venerable Florent bistro, the new Standard hotel, a new restaurant from Jean-Georges, and the soon-to-be-opened High Line, a stunning pedestrian parkway retrofitted onto a stretch of elevated train tracks that run up the west side a block from the Hudson River. Photography studios and cool boutiques had opened up here and there, which gave another dose of chic to the landscape.

I walked away from Merkato 55 six months later, the biggest failure of my professional life. Plenty of chefs I admire have failed. Alfred Portale couldn't make One Fifth Avenue work. Thomas Keller's Rakel didn't last. The list goes on. But while I'm sure they were passionate and committed to those restaurants, I don't know if they were as deeply and personally identified with those restaurants as I was with Merkato 55.

Merkato was a part of my life story.

It's a good thing I don't drink much or do drugs; this would have been a perfect time for that to spin out of control. I've never felt so low, or so humiliated. I'd never in my life had trouble sleeping at night; suddenly, I was waking up at three a.m. with my mind racing, trying to untie the knots of what had started out as a dream, only to become a nightmare.

Here was the dream: I would merge my passions, skills, and heritage with a business opportunity that had been sitting untapped for far too long. I actually began to conceive of an upscale African restaurant while I was working on a cookbook, *The Soul of a New Cuisine*. Sure, the book was a way for me to open up a dialogue with Americans about the flavors of Africa, but to get even more people past the stereotype of Africa as "the needy brother," and instead to see its bounty and its flavor, I knew they would need a more direct experience. They would need to taste.

One of my biggest hurdles was financing. Investors want a good return on their money, and they tend to feel more comfortable putting their money into a familiar formula. But I didn't think Manhattan needed another great Italian restaurant or another French bistro. At least not one run by me. I set up a lot of meetings. I laid out my vision a hundred times. No, I'd say, not a soul food restaurant. Not a Moroccan restaurant. An *African* restaurant. London has Momo, I'd explain, and Paris has the Impala Lounge. Each spot offers a way of seeing Africa through modern, sophisticated eyes. We could do the same thing in New York, only better.

People would ask me: "Is it in bad taste to have an African restaurant when so many people are starving there?" And every time, no matter how many times I heard it, the question was like a punch in the gut. I got versions of it on a weekly basis.

If I'm feeling charitable, I guess I can sort of understand where it comes from; if you live in the United States, the images of Africa that come across TV screens and newspaper headlines sometimes seem to be all about war, corruption, and impoverishment. Everyone's seen the pictures of small, malnourished children with flies walking across their faces, crowding around Red Cross sacks of rice. All of that is true. I know there is great need, and I know it because I visit orphanages every time I go to Ethiopia. I've come face to face with the images that make comfortable Americans turn away. So I understand why my pitch wasn't a gimme. But what I also knew was that this view of Africa as only deprivation was a distorted view. It was a lie. There are middle-class Africans. There are sophisticated restaurants in cities from Johannesburg to Cairo. Even among the poorer people, there are rich traditions of celebrating with food. I wanted to bring some of that to American audiences, to show there's not just one version of the African food experience. I wanted to capture African cool.

If I'd been interested only in delivering authentic, traditional dishes, I would have left that to the existing African restaurants, the ones that are cordoned off into ethnic enclaves, down a few flights of steps from the street, serving to expat cabdrivers and budget-conscious but adventurous college students. But what I wanted was to show the many ways in which American and West Indian food links back to Africa, how strong the flavor connection is between Senegal and North Carolina, how the cuisine of Mozambique resembles the foods of Portugal.

Where better than New York to try it?

After nearly two years of pitching and countless dead-end meetings, I finally found an investor who understood my vision. Probably not a coincidence that he was African American, a banker who had made it big and was ready to try something new.

"Are you sure?" I asked him for the twentieth time, just before our lawyers were about to draw up papers. "Restaurants are tough. We don't know how this will turn out."

"Marcus," he said, "it would be my honor to be part of this project."

Two days later, he died of a heart attack.

As always in the restaurant business, the mourning did not stop the making of the meal at hand. There was personal grief—this was a man I had tremendous respect and affection for—but this was also a major setback for the project. Things had moved far enough along, however, that I'd developed a relationship with the landlord of the building I wanted, and when I mentioned one day that I was still looking for a backer, he suggested I talk to a guy named Ramses, a Haitian American club promoter he knew who had a bunch of investors lined up, but no project to attach to. I knew Ramses and his brother Maxime from my occasional dips into the nightclub scene.

"We should do something together," he'd always say, which I figured he said to people as often as he said hello.

Ramses and I met. He was a very sweet guy. I hadn't even gotten halfway through my spiel when he was nodding his head and saying that he wanted in, that my concept was exactly what he and his group had in mind.

"If you want to do this," I said, "you have to let Townhouse Group run the project. I'm talking about building a restaurant, not a club; if it even comes close to a club I won't do it."

"No, no," he assured me. "I want to do this."

We worked out a deal and signed the papers. I'd have a tiny ownership stake, less than 5 percent, but they would hire Townhouse, the management company I owned with Håkan, to design and run the restaurant for a fee. Part of running it meant that I would put in the staff, spearhead the marketing, and use whatever brand power my name had built up to attract people. Ramses and Maxime's crew would be silent investors. I didn't know then that there is no such thing as a silent investor.

At first, the partnership ran smoothly. We all loved the name we'd brainstormed: Merkato 55, a tribute to my favorite spot in Addis combined with the street address of our site. Ramses found a great Dutch architect, Menno Schmitz, to do the space. Menno was a young guy who had never been to Africa, but I liked that about him; he was starting with a clean slate. I also liked that he wasn't a regular on the New York restaurant design circuit—the last thing I wanted was to look like we'd teamed up with half a dozen other restaurants to bulk order our fixtures and paint. With capacity for 150, we were 50 seats smaller than Aquavit, but the open-plan duplex made the space feel vast. We turned the first floor into a pub, with the bar flowing into a seating area. You could sit anywhere and see the rest of the room, which fit with the people-watching that is such a part of African street life. The second floor, accessed by a double-wide spiral staircase, was more of a proper dining room, with leather booths and folding privacy screens to break up the space.

Inspiration for the decor came primarily from two sources. The first was early 1970s Africa, a time of great style and hope. Many recently decolonized countries were excited about self-rule, and that sense of a burgeoning autonomy could be found everywhere, including pop music. You can see it in the work of photographers like the great Malick Sidibé, or in one of my favorite movies of all time, the documentary *When We Were Kings*, which is about the 1974 Ali–Foreman fight that took place in Zaire. The fight was billed as the "Rumble in the Jungle," and all of the background footage shows a liveliness and cool that couldn't be more appealing to me. In the restaurant, we tried to translate the modernity of that era with colors and textures and patterns. We hung giant silkscreens of African faces on wall panels. We used large woven baskets as pendant lamps over the bar, and in stairwells and alcoves we hung photographs taken over the course of my travels. The one thing I would not allow was African masks. That was too much of a cliché for me.

The end result, I thought, was magical. But I also know you can't succeed on the space alone. To communicate the sense of a vibrant, sophisticated Africa, I had to be very precise in my food. I knew I should aim for fun—not fine—dining. In fun dining, flavor—not concept—is king. You're providing more comfort than challenge, so you have to make it easy for the customer to understand what he's eating, and to know how to eat it. There's precision in that, too, as weird as it sounds. Aquavit is a more cerebral dining experience, where part of the meal's pleasure may come from wondering how the hell we put those flavors together. With Merkato, I wanted full flavor, accessibility, and a range of appealing dishes, so you could take a picky nephew there and find something he'd like. Some dishes I made in a fairly straightforward, old-school way. *Doro wat*, the chicken stew that comes from my own Amhara tribe, was made the same way I'd been taught on Bole Road, but we upped the quality of the ingredients and used only chicken legs in order to guarantee the most flavorful, juicy meat. We didn't mess with the recipe for traditional *piri piri*, a tangy hot sauce that's used in Mozambique and other countries as a dip or marinade: Why fiddle with perfection? We put it on grilled shrimp, leaving the shells and heads on. That dish was an instant success.

Maybe my next African restaurant would be a fine-dining experience, with fewer seats and a more specifically matched wine list. But Merkato would be a starting point. Merkato would open the door.

I SHOULD HAVE KNOWN something was up when our investors had trouble making it to our regularly scheduled meetings. At the time, I just brushed it off as the price of working with club guys—they ran by a different clock. I also felt like they were meeting their basic commitments; when the project ran over budget, they always found the money we needed; they always came through. Besides, I couldn't dwell on the worries too long. I needed to focus on the seemingly endless work that still needed to be done and also the overflowing plate in front of me and Håkan. In less than twelve months, we were scheduled to open eight new restaurants, including Aquavits in Stockholm and Tokyo.

After three months of delays, Merkato finally opened. The house was packed, and the feedback from the public seemed positive. It was especially gratifying to see how much people of color enjoyed Merkato. Without hanging out a sign that said "Welcome to the Diversity Club," we were just that, and the cross-section of patrons was one of the broadest I'd ever encountered.

Our greatest hurdle turned out to be the press. Established critics seemed almost uncomfortable with the food, as if they were unsure what to make of the flavors we were working with. Any chef has that one terrible review that he can quote to you word by word, years after the fact—negative reviews are part of the game—but the reviews for Merkato stung to the core. People didn't like the flavors, they didn't like the space. Everyone says not to take things like this personally, but how could I not when I knew that ultimately most of us *taste* things personally, with a palate that is framed by our own—often limited—experience. For example, we were criticized for our play on Ghana's chicken-and-peanut soup, but the objections had no basis in the history of the dish. It felt a little like trying to tell a joke to someone who doesn't have the same cultural reference points as you do: It's just not going to sound funny to him.

I know this sounds like sour grapes. The fact is, I have to take responsibility for some of the chaos and inconsistency that surrounded Merkato's opening, and its ultimate failure. I should have been able to communicate the concept clearly, and to make it work. The thing about starting a new restaurant, though, is that it takes time to settle in and find your groove. We weren't going to get things right out of the box; no one can. We needed time to develop and refine our dishes, to respond to how they were received, to correct mistakes. It took *years* for me to develop Aquavit's foie gras ganache; after three months at Merkato, I was only just beginning to identify a few dishes that might be headed for signature status. Our black bass topped with chermoula had potential, as did our rack of lamb with mango couscous and our chickpea dumplings. But, really, everything was still evolving.

While we struggled with getting the menu right, trouble started piling up with my investors. I wanted to cut back on reservations, to slow down the pace so we could tighten up the front and back of the house. Our waiters needed time to develop expertise about the food so they could present it effectively, and our kitchen needed time to fall into a steadier rhythm. When you're slammed every night, you can't do either, but my investors had a big nut to cover, and they didn't want to turn anyone away. We were packed every night from six to midnight and waiters were ordered to turn over tables quickly to accommodate the crowd, which meant the service was never where it needed to be.

In hindsight, I know you can't be naive in making partnerships. That's bullshit. You can't plead the victim. You can't be a fool. You can't turn fish into fowl and you can't expect club promoters to understand how to run a restaurant. Still, we might have powered through and smoothed out the initial bumps—I certainly had the will to do that—until I got a phone call from my PR company.

"Marcus," my rep said. "What's this I read about Merkato putting in a nightclub?"

"What are you talking about?" I said.

"I read about it online. It says you're putting in a club called Bijoux."

"That's bullshit," I said. I had a contract. This was all spelled out in the contract. No nightclubs.

More people called to tell me they'd heard we were building a club in the basement, in a space that we'd been planning to use as a lounge for corporate parties.

I confronted one of the investors.

"Yeah," he said, matter of fact. "We're opening a club."

Not only was this a problem in terms of my contract, it violated the provisions of our liquor license. Håkan and I talked it over—the conversation didn't take long—and even though we faced losing real money in consulting fees, the decision was clear. I wasn't about to get on the wrong side of New York's liquor control board. I had too many responsibilities to Håkan, to Aquavit, and to my family, both in Sweden and in Ethiopia, to break the law, even just by looking the other way.

I picked up the phone. "We talked about this," I said when Ramses answered. "This isn't right. I'm out."

"As of when?" he asked.

"As of right now."

I suppose I could have made a big stink over leaving; I could have taken my story to the media and come out smelling like a rose. But my heart was broken, and I didn't see anything positive coming from the shit-slinging contest that would inevitably result. So I watched from the sidelines over the next six months as Merkato went down and became a sad joke. It was like watching a loved one die. There was nothing to be done. I just had to take it, to learn from what had happened and move on. And once again, I drew strength from knowing that I had triumphed over much tougher odds when I was a child. I would find a way to write my love letter to Africa another time, under different circumstances.

TWENTY-SIX FOR BETTER AND FOREVER

After three years of dating, I asked Maya to marry me, and she said yes—an outcome, believe me, that I never took for granted. Maya and I laugh together and support each other; I don't think I've met anyone, aside from my mother, with a more solid sense of fairness or a steadier moral core. We both have one foot in Ethiopia and one foot out, and we both love America. But what clinched it for me was seeing how welcoming Maya was to Zoe when Zoe finally came to New York for her first visit. I couldn't have made a life with a woman who wouldn't accept Zoe. For Maya, that wasn't even a question.

Maya has grown to love our annual Samuelsson family vacations in Smögen, where the best thing the island has to offer is that nothing is going on. Ever. And it counts for something that Maya walked into my old room—actually, the room my mother refashioned for me in the townhouse she moved to after my father died—and did not turn and run the other direction when she saw that it had been set up as a Marcus time capsule, circa 1984, complete with my original posters of Michael Jackson, ABBA, and Bob Marley pinned to the walls.

Once we decided to marry, we had to figure out how to bring our far-flung friends and family together for a proper celebration. We solved it two ways. First, we had an informal party in Smögen during the summer of 2008. Zoe flew in from Austria, friends drove up from Göteborg, and we invited almost everyone on the island just by telling a few people to pass the word. I happily left most of the organizing to Anna and my mother; beyond curing a huge salmon, I sat back and enjoyed the show.

Then we had the real wedding right after Christmas, in Addis. Maya wanted to be married there, and I wanted her to be happy. I felt conflicted about the money we'd be spending to make it happen. I'm not a big spender as a rule. At home in New York, I take the subway almost every day and when I fly, even for business, I won't buy anything but a coach seat, even on international flights. But those are American standards, not even close to the measurement of wealth that you'd apply in Ethiopia. The bridesmaids' dresses we picked, for example, equaled my Ethiopian family's annual budget. The one-day limo rental matched the private-school tuition I pay for three of my sisters. After a point, I had to stop myself every time I'd start to translate what *could* be bought for what we were paying. I was spending my money in Ethiopia, I told myself. That was worth something.

We planned a huge celebration. We had to, if only for the friends and family who were flying in from more than six countries. Mats was coming with his wife and two kids and his father, Rune. Mes was coming from New York; his mother and his uncle Workasef would throw their own party for us in Addis during the wedding week. There would be a church wedding, with Maya's brother as the presiding priest, and a reception at the Hilton. There would also be another, less formal reception in Maya's village, where her mother would cook for a week to prepare enough food not only for the two hundred invited guests, but for another few hundred people from the village who would decide to drop in and say hi. There would be more than one ceremonial slaughtering and one beautiful coffee ceremony after another. Hanging at the end of buffet lines were entire sides of raw beef that came with their own butchers—a kind of carpaccio that was extremely popular, at least among the Habesha.

All in all, we would have eleven flat tires, not enough hot water for showers, seven live bands, three choirs, nine hundred guests, and a magnificent set of memories to take home when it was done.

When I am stressed and nothing seems to be coming together the way I want it to, I pull out images of this day when all of the far-flung pieces of my life joined together in a symphony of story and music, laughter and good wishes. I took my Swedish mother, Anne Marie, to Abragodana and she met my birth father, Tsegie. She sat in a straight-backed wooden chair that had been set out in Tsegie's yard, with him on one side and Kasech, my stepmother, on the other, and each of the Ethiopians holding one of my mother's hands. Anne Marie presented Tsegie with a pair of reading glasses—she had heard that lately he had trouble seeing—and he cried briefly, then put the glasses on, pulled out a weathered bible from under his robe, and started to read in the ancient language of Ge'ez.

One of my Ethiopian sisters, the sixteen-year-old Salam, translated for me as I tried to use the occasion to rouse my father into allowing Ashou, another one of my sisters, to leave the farm and go to school. After much back and forth, my father finally agreed and the look on my sister's face was the best wedding present I could have ever received. Her smile was an explosion of surprise and happiness that I will play over and over again in my mind for as long as I live.

Although I longed to sit and ask Tsegie questions, I did not bring up the other woman, my birth mother. I did not ask how my father met my mother, Ahnu, or what Ahnu looked like, or how she laughed. I did not ask him what it felt like to lose Ahnu, Linda, and me in one fell swoop, or if, having lost Ahnu, he couldn't bear to bring us home. I did not ask him what he did in the months after, or how often he wondered about us, out alone in the world. Those are all questions I'm not sure I'll ever be able to ask him.

My Swedish mother observed all the goings-on in my father's village with the wide-eyed wonder of a European visiting the continent for the very first time. She hugged and kissed all of our sisters and brothers, as they are extensions of Linda and me and as such, she had love to spare for them, too. Taking in the poverty, she said to me afterward, "Macke, is that truly where you grew up?" No, it was a different village, I told her, but exactly the same.

My sister Linda was with us, too. It was her diligence that brought me to our father, and during the wedding she served as a bridge between our two families. She was the one who convinced my father's family not to slaughter a cow in honor of Anne Marie. They were uncomfortable with what was surely perceived as an extreme lack of graciousness, but it had been a hard year, and this was their only cow, so they heeded her request.

The day before the wedding, we all went out to lunch and ate *pasta saltata*, a national favorite, one of the legacies of Italy's repeated and failed attempts at colonizing Ethiopia. The dish is a kind of bolognese, but liberally spiced with *berbere*. My little sisters drank too many Mirindas, the orange soda they always want but never get to have, and I was too distracted and happy to stop them. We stopped in the nearby town of Meki on our way back to Abragodana, and Linda surprised me again with her latest discovery, two male cousins from our mother's side, both significantly better off than our father's side. One was a farmer and one owned a small restaurant, so we invited them to the reception at the Hilton. When they came, they put me in a chair and hoisted it over their heads and onto the dance floor, and as I bounced above the crowd, held up by my own family, and with Maya and Mes and Mats laughing and clapping along, I felt more grounded in this country, and in this world, than I ever had before.

NOT LONG AGO, I HAD JUST FINISHED EATING DINNER AT A HOTEL RES-
taurant in New York City when I got word that someone in the
kitchen wanted to see me. The guy who came out, Tyrone, was a
graduate of one of the mentoring programs I'm involved with. When
I met him a few years before, Tyrone had a GED, a chip on his shoulder, and the kind of home life that made *Oliver Twist* look like a fairy
tale. Now a *sous-chef*, Tyrone looked sharp and professional in his
kitchen whites. There was an ease in his smile and a confidence in his
walk. This being a prominent hotel restaurant, I knew Tyrone was
making $75,000 a year, easy. Tyrone was thriving, and I felt good
about that. But the thing is, the kitchens of America's finest restau-

rants aren't full of guys like Tyrone. A hundred years ago, black men and women had to fight to get out of the kitchen. These days, we have to fight to get *in*.

When I met Michael Garrett in 2000, I was the executive chef at Aquavit and he was a line cook with two restaurants on his résumé: Houlihan's and Olive Garden. It took serious balls to walk into a restaurant like Aquavit and ask for a job with those kinds of chops; nine out of ten chefs wouldn't have let Michael past the coat-check girl. But I'm not most other chefs. My stance is clear: I will bring in some of those kids. The way I look at it is, if I don't, they would never get a chance. Once they work with me, they're in. I'm a gate opener or a gate closer, depending on how they do. So Michael was one of those guys. He would never, in a million years, get the job at Aquavit.

I met him and said, "Let's give him a job."

Sometimes I think my success makes others forget that it isn't easy for a black person to make it as a chef in America. Our ancestors, who built the culinary foundation of this country but were only referred to as "the help," would be shocked to learn that there are more black men and women who are partners at law firms than black men and women who are executive chefs at the top restaurants in this country. When I arrived in New York nearly twenty years ago, you could count on one hand the prominent chefs who looked like me. It's almost two decades later now and you can still count us on one hand.

OK, two hands if you count the chefs who cook only on TV.

The business of being a chef, whether your goal is to run the kitchen of a top restaurant in New York or to open your own establishment anywhere from Atlanta to Anchorage, is still an old boys' club. Making it is a combination of hard work, luck, mentorship, and opportunity. And while I have met hundreds of young black chefs who aren't afraid of hard work, for far too many of us, the luck, the mentorship, and the opportunity are hard to come by.

The problem with somebody like my friend Michael from the Olive Garden isn't what he can or can't cook, it's what he has and hasn't tasted. When I hired him at Aquavit, he'd never tasted *yuzu*, he'd never tasted sushi, he'd never tasted real saffron. He could execute the dishes we were doing, but if you don't know how these things should taste, what we're trying to go for, then the learning curve is beyond steep. But what Michael had, what made the difference, is that he was humble as shit. Humble, humble, humble, humble, humble.

When Michael came on, he wasn't ready for Aquavit. So I started him at Riingo, a more casual place that Håkan and I had opened . . . and he never went away. He just kept getting better and better, bouncing higher and higher, full of energy. Every time there was an extra shift or an opportunity to work a special event, he was there. His work ethic was amazing.

One thing I believe with all my soul: Don't try to guess somebody's ceiling. I'm never going to be the one to tell that girl she can't get a record deal, or that guy he's never going to write a best-seller. I would never be the one telling what you can or can't do. Same deal in food. Who was I to tell Michael he didn't have what it takes to succeed? I brought him along, never knowing where his limit was. I figured that when he couldn't keep up anymore, it would show. Next thing I knew, guys started to fall off left and right and all of a sudden Michael was *sous-chef* at Aquavit. Which was a *huge* step up. A guy who'd cooked at Houlihan's and Olive Garden—who'd never even been to Canada, let alone Europe—was the one teaching the Swedish guys to make Swedish food.

I told Michael that in order to take that next step, to become an executive chef, he needed to dine. He needed to explore. When I came to New York, all of my money had gone into learning about food and flavors. But back in the day, I was all about figuring things out: What's so hot about Vong? I'd save my money, go to Vong, and then I'd be broke again. But I knew I needed to have that experience to become a better chef. You might just taste three or four appetizers. You're sitting there to deconstruct how the hell this lemongrass tastes so good with this piece of fish. You're not drinking wine because you can't afford it. You're not eating, you're not belonging. You're *tasting*. You're there to study, learn, get it, and own it.

Today, Michael is the executive chef at my Harlem restaurant, Red Rooster, and what's more, he's my right hand. He's incredibly curious and creative. These days, I'm the one asking *him* stuff: "Michael, let's find out how to do this," and he will go off and research and find out. "OK, Marcus, this is what will happen if we cook this *sous-vide*, and this is what will happen if we cook it this way. These are our options. You tell me left or right." Taking somebody from a very humble background, and watching him become fluent in the language of food—French terms, Italian terms, Japanese terms—that makes me happy to do what I do. It's not just that I believe in food that is global. I believe there's a door that opens from inside any great kitchen, a door that opens out and gives us the world.

I PROBABLY SHOULD HAVE ENDED my partnership with Håkan when we moved out of the old Rockefeller townhouse and into the new space on East Fifty-fifth Street in 2004. I was young, hungry, and ready to rewrite the rules on my own terms. Even then, it was clear to me that my mission was to bring guys like Michael in and to change the game on the plate and in my hiring practices. Håkan was older than I was, and his main concern often seemed to be, How can I protect my retirement? Those are two completely different approaches to life. It doesn't mean that one is right and one is wrong. He was in his fifties and I was in my thirties. We were bound to clash.

I never had my guard up as a chef. When I debuted at Aquavit, I was twenty-four. So for me, doing the cooking and being known as a chef were the same. Håkan, at the end of the day, was the one who brought me along, gave me the PR, and showed me how it was done. In the beginning, he was the one that wanted to push me and my story. As long as I told a story about myself in the context of his restaurant, he loved it. I didn't know the first thing about PR. Håkan was the one who gave me all of these tools.

Then came the most shocking twist. In 2008, as I tried to assert some independence, Håkan and his lawyers argued that the only reason the name Marcus Samuelsson had value was because of its association with Aquavit. So if I wanted to leave Aquavit, or do any work outside of the partnership associated with my name, he would be entitled to a percentage of the money. This was tough to swallow. Yes, Håkan had trained me in the world of restaurants. Yes, he had afforded me the kind of opportunities most young chefs would kill for. Yes, he had treated me very well. But I had also brought something to the table. I had been tireless in my pursuit of excellence and I had expressed gratitude in word and deed. The idea that he could own a piece of anything I did that was associated with my name forevermore was ludicrous.

I consulted a series of lawyers, and they all confirmed that he had a case. Unless I provided him with a hefty financial settlement that would take the place of future earnings, I would be like an indentured servant trying to work off a debt that would never be repaid. There was apparently no way around it: Not only was I going to have to buy my way out of this partnership with Aquavit—buy my freedom, as it were—I was going to have to buy back my own *name*. And the more press I did, the more expensive my name got.

I was so used to thinking of Håkan as a big brother, a mentor, the guy who gave me my break. But I was starting to realize that ours was a friendship that thrived only under very particular circumstances. Some things were going great. Aquavit Stockholm was going gangbusters, but Aquavit Tokyo was tough. I was in Tokyo when the market crashed and I saw the dramatic effect it had on the restaurant; it was clear that it simply wasn't going to survive. Our midtown New York restaurant had been hit hard, as well. The Merkato deal imploded. Our little empire was under siege, and we were getting ready to go at each other for whatever was left.

The invitation to compete in Bravo's *Top Chef Masters* was what ultimately forced me to make a decision about getting out of Townhouse for good, and buying back my name. If I stayed with Håkan and did the show, all the exposure of being on TV would probably make my name exponentially more expensive. Sarah, my PR rep, called me and said to bite the bullet and buy out Håkan. My agent said the same thing, and yet I was not convinced. I'm an orphan from Ethiopia. In the most improbable of ways, I was adopted by a caring Swedish couple and given a nice middle-class Swedish life. I worked my way up from the bottom of so-so kitchens in Gburg to the bottom of some of Europe's greatest kitchens to the top of Aquavit. It was not at all easy for me to write that check to Håkan and to get nothing back in return but my name.

I began to consider going back to my Ethiopian birth name, Kassahun Tsegie. Who *was* Marcus Samuelsson after all? That was just a name that was given to me by Swedish parents. I was fond of it, but it was a name, nothing more. Maybe for the sake of my pride and my bank account, I needed to give myself another name so I could be free.

In the end, I emptied my bank account to Håkan and I bought the rights back to "Marcus Samuelsson" because it's the name that people know and it's a name people remember. And because it's part of my story.

In return, I got a stack of paperwork that proves something most Americans never have to think twice about: I am the sole owner of my name. I never once thought that when I came to New York with three hundred dollars in my pocket I'd have to fork over my entire life's savings for my name. When I was first interning at Aquavit and my citizenship status was far from clear, if somebody would have offered me a green card and a new name, I would have gladly taken it. But what I know now that I didn't know then is that our names are our stories. We sew our experiences together to make a life and our names are both the needle and thread. "Marcus Samuelsson" is more than the name of a chef who has done X, Y, and Z. It's a name that reflects my life: where I started, each stop along my journey, and the man that I've become.

FOR MONTHS AFTERWARD, I would look at my diminished bank account—the life savings that I had brought proudly into my marriage—and wonder if I had not made a terrible mistake. Was Aquavit the pinnacle of my success? Could I make it without Håkan's help? Without the perch of that storied restaurant and my well-salaried position there, who was I?

After I left Aquavit I was a chef without a kitchen to cook in and feeling more rootless than I had in a long time. I spent a lot of time thinking and dreaming. I had a vision for the next restaurant I wanted to open—Red Rooster, a new incarnation of a legendary Harlem hotspot—but after the Håkan transaction I didn't have anywhere near the money it takes to make it happen. My experience with Merkato had taught me to be careful whom I did business with, so I made myself be patient until the right partners came along.

During this time, my mother worried a lot about me and Maya. She was older, in her seventies, and even if she was young in her mind, her body was aging: She's got a bad back and bad knees and it hurt me just to think about it. I called her every Sunday and I tried to allay her concerns.

She asked, "So where are you cooking now?"

I told her, "I cook more than ever, Mom. I do a lot of events and demos."

She asked, "When is Red Rooster opening?"

"Soon," I lied.

We had the same conversation over and over again. Each time, it was like she forgot. I didn't want to keep explaining. It was the same with Zoe and also my father in Ethiopia. This industry and my place in it were hard enough for them to understand. I tried to convey that I was not really unemployed, that I would have a restaurant again; everything was going to be OK.

For more than a year, the Rooster lived only in my imagination. I kept myself busy with corporate gigs and charity work, but there was more empty time in my day than I'd ever had in my adult life and, not knowing how to fill it, I spent it exploring my neighborhood. From the time I first arrived in New York, I knew of Harlem's reputation as the mecca of black America. I had seen the photographs of Harlem in its glory days—stylish men in bespoke suits, women so well dressed that they'd put the models in *Vogue* to shame. I knew that Harlem was music: from the Apollo to the jazz clubs that were incubators for new renditions of blues, improvisation, and swing. I knew that Harlemites loved to dance, to pray, and to eat. I made my way to the churches and the clubs, the restaurants and the old-school saloons.

But for the first time, I began to notice how *beautiful* Harlem was, how magnificent its architecture. During the neighborhood's first boom at the end of the nineteenth century, some of New York's greatest architects flocked to Harlem and did some of their most inspired work. Architect Francis Kimball did a row of townhouses in Harlem on West 122nd Street. James Renwick, who designed St. Patrick's Cathedral, did the All Saints Roman Catholic Church in Harlem. Beaux arts titans McKim, Mead & White, responsible for such New York landmarks as the old Penn Station and the Morgan Library, designed the 139th Street portion of the area known since the 1920s as Strivers Row, "the most aristocratic portion of Harlem," as Wallace Thurman wrote in 1928. In those early days, when I was dreaming about Red Rooster and walking the neighborhood, I would end my day with a stroll down Strivers Row, marveling at its pristine brownstones. It was Strivers Row more than anything that made me feel I could open a fine-dining establishment north of 125th Street. Yes, it was true that decades of drugs and poverty had decimated a lot of what was once glorious about Harlem, but one need only walk down Strivers Row to be reminded that there are jewels in the crown of Harlem that never dimmed.

I FIRST MET THELMA GOLDEN, director and curator of the Studio Museum in Harlem, when she was a young hotshot at the Whitney Museum and I was just a legend in my own mind at Aquavit. I hadn't yet earned three stars, but I was swinging for the fences every night. The Studio Museum houses a trove of great artists, from Romare Bearden and Loïs Mailou Jones to present-day greats like Kara Walker and

Glenn Ligon. Thelma's journey to the top of her field had a lot in common with mine. We both left very established, very elegant, east-side institutions for Harlem—a move that takes a certain kind of maverick sensibility and willingness, sometimes, to be content shouting as a voice in the wilderness.

Thelma was invaluable to me logistically and professionally, in a step-by-step "this is how business is done in Harlem" way. But more than that, she helped me frame the bigger picture in my head. How many of us were either too young or too far away to have experienced New York in the late 1970s and early 1980s, but longed to be part of that incredibly creative time in the city? How many times had my friends and I wondered what it would have been like to hang with Jean-Michel Basquiat and Keith Haring, to dance with Madonna at Danceteria, to see Bad Brains and the Ramones at CBGB?

What Thelma helped me see was that Harlem was not just black USA in a snow globe; it was one of the last bastions of New York City as creative people long for it to be. Harlem is not a playground for rich bankers and consultants. It's got students of all colors. It's got old people who keep history and tell tall tales. It's got musicians and artists and I swear I know a guy who is the next incarnation of Prince. (He's completely unknown, but to quote another renegade musician, he's a bad mamajama.) It's got foreigners and fifth-generation families. It's got million-dollar brownstones and sprawling housing projects. Like any place with edge, it has its dark side, too. Soho has stores, Harlem has street life. People are selling stuff on every street corner. (This is, for me, the Africa in Harlem.) And the ones who are lucky enough to own real brick-and-mortar stores aren't just standing behind a counter, waiting for you to stroll in—they stand at the doorway in order to badger and cajole you into shopping. Harlem may not be high-tech, but it's an *interactive experience*. People speak to each other on the street in Harlem. They'll tell you when they like what you're wearing and when they disagree with the slogan on your t-shirt. Men compliment pretty women and the women either respond in kind or tell them to keep on stepping. All you have to do is stand outside on a summer day in Harlem to get a sense of what it means to hear people sing the Amen Chorus.

Speaking of which, there are still church ladies and bow-tied Muslims in Harlem selling bean pies. On any given Sunday, you can see whole clans rolling deep and looking spiffy on their way to a gospel brunch that is their reward for surviving yet another backbreaking week and a longer-than-necessary sermon by a minister whose greatest sin is that he loves to hear himself talk. The south side of Central Park is all horse-drawn carriages and bygone-era hotels turned into luxury apartment buildings, but the north side of Central Park sits squarely at the feet of Harlem. Our Central Park is different. Why? More color on the skin and in the clothes. More passion in the loving and the fighting. More impromptu renditions of the Isley Brothers' "Between the Sheets" than you've ever heard in your life. When I lived uptown and cooked downtown, I knew—and yet didn't *know*— how much living was being packed into the 3.8 square miles that I now call home.

Just as Thelma transformed the Studio Museum into an institution that preserves the legacy of African American artists while promoting new voices in art from around the world, I dreamed of creating a similar space for food. I wanted Red Rooster to guard the history of black cooks in America while starting new conversations in food. During the long, doubt-filled, crazy-making months between my exit from Aquavit and the opening of the Rooster, I had little more than a logo to show for my dream. But in my head, I used that time to immerse myself in the history of Harlem. And I meant to apply all that learning in the most ambitious way possible. Harlem, I knew, deserved nothing less.

AT SIX P.M. on a late summer Monday in Harlem, I walked the streets between the Studio Museum and my apartment like a politician working his district on Election Day. Everybody knew me, even if I didn't know them, and there's not a soul between 118th Street and 145th who felt the least bit shy about stopping me on the street and giving me a piece of their mind.

If I make only one contribution in this city, I hope it's to help change the footprint of dining. I always thought that if I live in Harlem, I should own a restaurant in Harlem. I can own a restaurant in Tokyo, I can own a restaurant in Stockholm, I can own a place in Chicago, but I *should* own a place in Harlem. And that's where the journey of Red Rooster began.

When I decided to become a chef, my motivations were simple. I looked at my father, Lennart, and I wanted to be as good a man as he was. He provided his family with a comfortable home, he supported us all emotionally, and as a geologist he found a career that tapped into the deep passion he had for the land. If I was afraid of anything, it was of turning out to be less than that. I saw in my friends and my earliest coworkers the paths my life could take. I could be like the pizza guy at La Toscana, back in Gburg, a laborer who made a decent wage and went home on the bus every night to his apartment in the projects. I wanted something more.

The more I exposed myself to cooking, the more I realized that I wanted to chase flavors, that I will always get excited by tasting something new or taking something good and tweaking it until it becomes something great. The more you train your palate, the more sensitive you become. You instantly taste the difference between tap waters from one city to the next. You find inspiration for a dish in the licorice root you taste at a farmers' market or in the perfume of the chewing gum the kid on the subway seat next to you is chewing. Nothing is off-putting; everything is material to work with.

Food and flavors have become my first language. Not English, not Swedish, not Amharic. Whether I'm with the injera makers in their hut or a sushi chef in Tokyo, we speak a common language. We are all on the search for flavors. I've come to understand that this is an unending quest. I don't know what done looks like and I don't know what done tastes like. You can never sit back and relax: Audiences change, purveyors come and go, and economies fall apart. The only thing I know for sure is that I will always be in love with flavor-driven food.

At every major turning point in my adult life, there has come a point where I had to decide, Am I in or am I out? After Merkato crashed and burned, after things went to hell for me at Aquavit, after I proposed to the love of my life and then had to inform her that the "celebrity chef" she married no longer had any money in the bank or a kitchen to cook in, what I decided was that I was going to put all chips on food. Food's my only bag. It's my gig, my art, my life. Always has been, always will be. I'm always battling myself—the part of me that says I can and the part of me that says I can't. My greatest gift has been that the part of me that says "I can" is always, always just a little bit louder.

THE FIRST THING I DID AFTER BUYING BACK MY NAME WAS FLY OUT TO Los Angeles to compete in *Top Chef Masters*. I technically had no restaurant to call home, although I was in the planning phase on Red Rooster. Competing on *Top Chef* would, I figured, be a great way to build some buzz. That's really what it was, a way for me to raise interest (and financing) in what was then a tricky gambit—a high-end restaurant uptown. My business partners and I mocked up a logo, I had chef's whites made up, and I went off to Los Angeles to film the show.

When I landed in Los Angeles, I got a call from a friend named Sam Kass. I'd met Sam a few years ago and had since heard he'd landed a job as the assistant chef/food initiative coordinator at the

White House. Sam was calling to ask if I'd be interested in creating the menu for the Obamas' first state dinner. He told me he was speaking to a few other chefs, too, and that the state dinner was going to honor Prime Minister Manmohan Singh of India and his wife, Gursharan Kaur. Sam was asking if I'd make dishes that had a subtle Indian influence, and since the honored guests are both vegetarians, to make sure we could create a meal that would be very flavorful with no meat. The finalists would be chosen after evaluating each chef's menu. It was the kind of call chefs dream of receiving, and in many ways it was far more important to me than anything that was happening on TV.

Indian-inspired food was right up my alley, flavor-wise, but I knew I needed an amazing chef to help me. The first person that came to mind was a woman named Andrea Bergquist. She had cooked with Floyd Cardoz at Tabla, and had traveled through India. I tried to reach her and I learned she was traveling . . . in India. So it was just me and Michael Garrett for the first tasting. I had quickly learned that while it was easy to sit on the sofa and critique the contestants on shows like *Top Chef*, the actual process of adhering to that schedule and cooking for each challenge was far more difficult than it seemed. The competitive part of me came out while filming *Top Chef*, and I went from merely wanting the PR to build buzz for the Rooster to wanting to win. I was in LA, fighting not to be eliminated from the show, so I called Michael and asked him to do the shopping out in a Queens neighborhood called Little India.

When I told Michael what day Sam and his team would be arriving, he was dubious. "On a Sunday? Really?"

And I said, "Yeah, really."

Michael was stressing because Sunday is not the ideal day to go food shopping; the selection is far from perfect. The selection, in fact, is crap. You're never going to get the best fish or vegetables or fruit or even meat on a Sunday morning, hence the atrocity of prettified leftovers that many restaurants try to pass off as brunch.

A couple of days later, *The New York Times* reported that the field of possible chefs included Dan Barber from Blue Hill in New York, Charlie Palmer from Aureole, Michael Nischan from Dressing Room in Connecticut, and Patrick O'Connell from the Inn at Little Washington in Virginia. It was such a crazy, confusing time: In one arena, I was scrambling to compete against the top chefs in the nation. In another arena, on TV, I was getting my butt kicked in the challenges by Bravo's handpicked group of top chefs. And I didn't even have a restaurant. I was so, so focused. It wasn't about winning or losing, exactly. I knew that I'd get one big step closer to my dream—Red Rooster—if I could just stay in the game.

I sent Sam an e-mail. "This is the menu," I wrote. "Come to my house." We had to arrange a tasting dinner in order to stay in consideration for the state dinner, and I was going to hold it at my house. I didn't want to explain all the legal things that were still dragging on with Håkan and my leaving Aquavit. I didn't want to admit I didn't have a restaurant.

There was a break in the *Top Chef* filming, which was fortunate because my meeting with Sam was completely confidential. I couldn't go to the producers and say, "I'm up for the White House state dinner and I've got to get to New York for a tasting. Can you wait one day until I get back?" One of the things that would set the tone for my work with the White House was that my team and I knew nothing that had been discussed would ever end up in a blog or on Twitter. We didn't tell our parents. We didn't tell our best friends. I took a lot of pride in that.

When my plane landed in New York, I hopped a cab and went straight to Harlem. In the span of a few short hours, Michael and I prepared more than fourteen dishes for Sam to taste: eggplant salad, curry-rubbed chicken, tandoori-smoked salmon. None of these dishes would appear on the actual menu, but I wanted to show Sam we had range. Maya set a beautiful table and made these stunning, fragrant cinnamon-stick centerpieces, and we cleaned up as best we could. I looked around my apartment and it all felt slightly homegrown for a chef who was pitching himself to cook for the leader of the free world, but there it was. These big guys were coming in from Washington, DC, and to say the conditions were less than ideal was a wild understatement.

The goal of that first tasting was just to cook Sam Kass a delicious meal. I knew that when Andrea Bergquist returned from India, she would help us create a state dinner that was more than delicious: Her culinary gifts, along with my input and Michael's, would help us create a meal that was authentic and elegant and inspired.

When Sam called to tell me that our team had been chosen to cook the Obamas' first state dinner, I felt like a character in *The Matrix*: Time slowed and I could literally feel the air around me change. To say I was honored is to say nothing at all. How could it be that I had catapulted to all this incredible opportunity, when there are days where I still feel like I'm just an adopted kid, trying to find my place in the world? I trace my own footsteps and I still can't quite make sense of the leaps. First, I was a son, trying to make my father proud. If I have any mettle or maturity, it is because of Lennart Samuelsson and who he was, a man of curiosity and integrity. I did not excel in school and I failed at my attempt to be a soccer star. Because of the happenstance luck that I had a grandmother who was a talented home cook, and that she chose me as her helper, I grew into a chef. I made my way across three continents and in the process I won three James Beard awards. But when it all seemed so clear—Marcus Samuelsson, star chef—the relationship that was at the heart of that restaurant was destroyed and I found myself, at thirty-seven, never married but in the middle of a full-scale professional divorce. When Sam Kass and the White House team approached me, I was—professionally speaking—a car running on fumes, every cylinder of my being powered on hunger and hope. And then when Sam called to say that my team had been selected to cook the Obamas' first White House dinner, I was more than honored. I was excited about chasing new flavors with an Indian-inspired, vegetarian meal that would connect the dots between the roots of American culture and our American love of global cuisine. I was thrilled to meet the president who shared with me an East African heritage and, as Langston Hughes might phrase it, a childhood fueled on wonder and wandering. But mostly, I was happy because I knew that this state dinner and all the attention it would bring would shine a light on Harlem and the restaurant I hoped would be my new culinary home.

BACK IN LOS ANGELES, the last days of *Top Chef Masters* were turning into the weirdest three days in my life. Sam needed me for tastings, but I couldn't leave the set. So I had to ask Andrea, whom I had convinced to come aboard, and Jimmy Lappalainen, who cooked with me for many years, to go to DC without telling anyone and conduct a tasting without me. I knew exactly what I wanted to cook at this point, and we had gone over the dishes and ingredients so many times that I was confident they would do well. My team knows I trust their skills and technique. This was a huge test—and they nailed it.

I stood by the set of the show, texting Andrea about the state dinner.

No, no, the basmati rice is wrong.

It's good but not good enough for the prime minister of India.

We need to get okra into the menu, too.

Since the prime minister and his wife are vegetarians, we had a real challenge on our hands, the kind of food puzzle that I love: how can we pull together a menu that's seasonal, full of subtle Indian flavors, that would deliver and satisfy with no meat?

The first family actually lives in the White House, so I wondered how I would feel if I was hosting a grand evening inside this historical home. I really wanted everyone—especially the guests of honor—to feel welcomed and to have a good time. A bread course had never been served before at a White House state dinner, but I chose bread as the first course because I knew people would be coming from different parts of the country and from around the world. I thought it would be very symbolic to have everyone breaking bread together. So we served cornbread, chutneys, naan, and sambals.

This is what we settled on for the rest of the meal:

Potato and eggplant salad
White House garden arugula with onion seed vinaigrette
Wine: 2008 Sauvignon Blanc, Modus Operandi, Napa Valley, California

———

Red lentil soup with fresh cheese
Wine: 2006 "Ara" Riesling, Brooks, Willamette Valley, Oregon

———

Roasted potato dumplings with tomato chutney
Chickpeas and okra

or

Green curry prawns
Caramelized salsify with smoked collard greens and coconut-aged basmati
Wine: 2007 Grenache, Beckmen Vineyards, Santa Ynez, California

———

Pumpkin pie tart
Pear Tatin
Whipped cream and caramel sauce
Wine: Sparkling Chardonnay Brut, Thibaut-Janisson, Monticello,
Virginia

———

Petits fours and coffee
Cashew brittle
Pecan pralines
Passionfruit and vanilla gelées
Chocolate-dipped fruit

The stress of the show, combined with the stress of the state dinner, was intense. As if on cue, my back gave out. The pain was unreal,
but I couldn't give up. Being a chef is an incredibly physical job.
Standing for hours on end, the brutality of the kitchen heat, the burns,
the fires, the lifting—Mario Batali wears those Crocs everywhere not
because he's a fashion victim but because they give him some physical

relief. I'm strong because I'm a runner but my back is liable to give out on me at any given time. It doesn't happen often but when it does, when I'm on the floor and I can't move, I can hear my mother berating me when I came home from Belle Avenue after hours of lifting huge sacks of flour, potatoes, and trays and trays of meat. "Macke," my mother said. "Are they working you too hard?" And it's true: Everywhere I worked from Belle Avenue to Victoria Jungfrau to Georges Blanc to the cruise ships to Aquavit, they worked me too hard. And I was glad for it. It's what I signed up for. I manage to look young and strong in photos. But my back, the premature arthritis in my hands, the way my teeth are literally falling out—they tell the story of a lifetime of service. A chef's life *is* one of service, even in the age of *Top Chef* and Food Network stars. It doesn't matter if they send a fancy town car to pick you up, you can't sit on your butt in a comfy leather armchair and cook an incredible meal.

On a show like *Top Chef Masters*, the stuff they ask you to do is so grueling that you have to focus, otherwise you might as well pack up and go home. They don't really care about what chef comes from what acclaimed restaurant, or how many stars you've won. Filming *Top Chef Masters* was the kind of punishing eighteen-hour day that only someone who works like a chef can stand. During the shoot, there was no peace. One a.m. you're done. Two a.m. you're done. Then five hours later, seven a.m., you're back on the set. You know how on *Real Housewives* you see those grown women acting like monsters? Part of the monstrosity is the schedule: It will break you down.

What I loved about the whole experience is that we were all over the city. We were based in downtown LA, but our events could be anywhere. We cooked for people's weddings. We cooked for the creators of *The Simpsons*. We cooked in the parking lot at a Stanford-USC game. Tailgating. I didn't even know the word *tailgating*. I'd never been to a football game in my life. And all these fans had been there all night, sleeping in their vans, drinking beer for breakfast. It was like a cook-off. Each chef had a tent set up, and the fans came by each tent and tasted. But what the show really does is test your will. It knocks you off your pedestal. It's popular because it gets to the heart of things, what cooking is so much about: knowing what dish is appropriate, for this moment, in this location. And then doing it.

Still, you start to realize that you're not in control the way you are in the kitchen back home. What you thought you did well doesn't come across as three stars because you are not cooking in a restaurant. Maybe your food sat for twenty minutes because the judges were deliberating over someone else's dish. Maybe you were so tired, your back gave out, and you couldn't whip your cream properly. There are so many other outside factors. It knocks you down a peg. And the elimination process is very, very, very, very humbling.

I never worried that I was going to get sent home. I never looked at what the other people did. But I always felt that if I did *me*, I would give myself a chance of winning. My stuff was good, and as the rounds went by, I was still there. I stuck around, and worked hard. But I never won anything until the last three days. I was coming from behind the whole time. Sometimes I was on the losing side, but I managed to hang on.

I ended up winning this series of the show, and it meant so much to me because as cocky and arrogant as I sometimes seemed, I knew that it would help me open the Rooster. I had my partners by the time the show began to air and we were all surprised at how much press it got. I couldn't walk down a street in New York without seeing my face on a bus or a billboard. I sat on subway trains, the way I had a gazillion times before, only now I was sitting underneath an ad with my picture on it. It was amusing and slightly disconcerting to watch people scan from the ad to my face and back again. I'd shake my head no, "Nah, not me."

In Harlem, though, folks knew better. Once it started airing, I couldn't walk down the street without the hood letting me know how they felt.

"We're rooting for you, Marcus."

"When you going to open up that restaurant?"

"Show 'em what you're working with, Marcus."

"Where's the restaurant going to be?"

"You gonna have fried chicken on the menu? The original Red Rooster always had the best fried chicken."

"Yes," I would answer. "There will definitely be fried chicken."

"How about chitterlings? The original Rooster used to serve chitterlings and champagne . . ."

At the end of the show, I wish I could have been like one of those R & B stars at the Grammys thanking everybody from their record label to their boo, from Jacob the Jeweler to God, for hooking them up. Because Harlem truly blessed me during that competition. Like the B.o.B. song, they let me know that win or lose, they were my safety net. They were never ever going to let me fall.

AFTER WINNING THE COMPETITION, I celebrated by taking the red-eye from Los Angeles to Washington, DC. I checked into my hotel room, showered, and ran over to the White House. In an instant, I was in a different landscape, faced with a wholly different challenge. I had to laugh because for everything I just went through, it was nothing compared to what I was about to experience in the next twenty-four hours. It's the White House state dinner. I had to focus and be wholly in the moment. Every day is an important day in your life but some days are bigger than others. Winning a television competition, then flying out to cook at the White House, were two of the biggest days in my life and my career.

The big night had actually come. After endless meetings, phone calls, and tastings, I was going to feed 325 people within 45 minutes. I was exhausted but so excited to see everything we had worked on for several weeks coming together. I will be forever grateful to the very smart and talented White House executive chef Cristeta Comerford for welcoming all of us in her kitchen and helping us feel comfortable so we could do our job well.

The White House had twenty cooks and I brought in ten cooks of my own. I don't want to just change the race dynamics in a kitchen.

I want to change the gender dynamics in professional kitchens, too. So when I picked the cooks for the White House, I aimed for a fifty-fifty ratio: five women and five men. Not that the food would ultimately taste different, but the experience and how we can come together is important to me. I brought Swedes, I brought some African Americans, I brought some Jews—it was a mixed team. My wife, Maya, doesn't usually cook with me, but this was so special that I brought her as part of the team.

All along, I was thinking about my mom and what she always used to say to me in pressure situations: "Well, if you want to mess up, this is a good time to mess up!" You know, every time there was a major school test or a big soccer game, that was her way of saying, "Don't mess up. Don't stress out, but don't mess up." As service was getting underway, I walked through the White House with a smile on my face and my mother's voice in my head. I was going to feed 325 people, including the president of the United States, tonight. If I wanted to mess up, this was an *excellent* time to mess up.

Although most of the press after the dinner focused on the gate-crashers, it was a magnificent dinner. The Obamas seemed so happy. The prime minister, Dr. Singh, and his wife seemed to enjoy their food. Jennifer Hudson sang. A. R. Rahman, the composer who did the soundtrack for *Slumdog Millionaire*, performed. I didn't sit in the audience as a guest, with what my grandmother Helga would have called the "fine people." But I was there. And despite the fact that we were eating outside, in a tent, the service was flawless.

It was after eleven p.m. when the president and Mrs. Obama arrived to greet the staff. We knew they were exhausted, and didn't have much time, but they were so warm and gracious. Michael helped me cook the entire meal and was so excited and tired at the same time that when he met the president and the president asked him a question, he responded, "Yes, chef." Obama gave him a classic double take, and we all laughed. It was like a Southerner saying, "Yes, sir" or "Yes, ma'am." When you spend your whole life in a professional kitchen, when you're so tired you can't even see straight, you're bound to mumble, "Yes, chef."

JORDAN PRICE IS an eight-year-old girl who lives in my building in Harlem. She goes to PS 180, which is around the corner, a five-minute walk. I saw her in the hallway one day on my way to work, just after the White House dinner.

"I saw you on TV," she said.

"You don't have to see me on TV," I said. "Come to my house, bring some of your friends from school, and I'll cook the White House state dinner for you." And so I made for Jordan and her classmates the same dishes I cooked for the president and his guests: potato and eggplant salad, red lentil soup, green curry prawns, pumpkin pie tart.

Those boys and girls got the same experience as the president of the United States. And I cooked it in my apartment, not at the restaurant, so they could connect the dots: a chef who lives in Harlem in an apartment, with a kitchen no bigger than the kitchen my own parents cook in, went to the White House and cooked dinner for the president of the United States. These are the same lentils the president and Mrs. Obama ate, the same salad, the same tart. I did this in part so my young Harlem neighbors could taste how delicious good ingredients can be when they are assembled with care. It's all worth it if nine-year-old Amari—who looks like a brown-skinned Rapunzel with her long box braids and big, bright eyes—goes grocery shopping with her father and says, "Hey, Chef Marcus cooked red lentils for me. Let's get this." If Keyshawn, a football-loving third grader, asks his mother, "Pleeeaase, can we make Marcus's potato salad this weekend," then I will have done my job.

What I served was far less important than how I served it. One of the reasons that people enjoy coming to a great restaurant is that when an extraordinary meal is placed in front of them, they feel honored, respected, and even a little bit loved.

In 1948, Leah Chase decided to open a restaurant in the Lower Ninth of New Orleans. How much room did this country make for her, as a black female chef, at that time? She didn't care. She didn't ask to be lauded or ordained by the food community, she just went ahead and did it. As Leah always says, "The hood needs good food, too." And what happened was that her good food and her good intentions gave her restaurant a clout she never imagined it would ever have. Everyone who's ever run for office in Louisiana, or wanted to win a block of votes in Louisiana, knew that in order to get the votes, black votes, you had to go through Leah's restaurant. And because of that, blacks and whites began to sit at the table together and plan the future of the city together. Leah Chase created one of the first integrated restaurants in America.

I think about what I've been through to open Red Rooster and I know it is child's play compared to what Leah went through in the days of segregation. Leah gave me a vision of the kind of restaurant I wanted to open. In neighborhoods like Harlem and the Lower Ninth, people are loyal to a great restaurant. It would be my job to make the Rooster great. I knew it wouldn't happen on our first day, in our first month, even in our first year. But if I kept my heart in the right place and steeped myself in Harlem's history, then the people would come—and keep coming.

By the time I'd gone from buying my name to the White House state dinner, it was clear that I was going to be able to open another restaurant. But what exactly would this place be? One day, my business partner Andrew Chapman and I were just sitting and talking. I said, "I really want to build a place in Harlem. All this cooking and all the running around; I just want to change communities through food. What if we could get all the people I've been cooking for all these years, like the Charlie Roses, the Barbara Walterses, the business people, and the downtowners together with my Swedish crowd and some Harlem cats—all just eating in the same place?"

Andrew laughed and said, "That would be unreal." Then he said, "How are we going to make it happen?"

A couple of weeks later, we just went and chatted with Andrew's dad about it and said we wanted to open a little joint in Harlem. I saw the development on Frederick Douglass Boulevard and thought it should be there. Andrew's dad pulled out an old map of New York. He asked me to point out the Apollo and 125th. I pointed at 125th and said we should be here, close to the iconic streets and places, and Andrew's dad agreed.

Andrew and I have been friends for so many years, I can hardly remember us meeting. We connected because both of our mothers are Swedish, and there's a certain understanding between us because we have the same values. Although Andrew was raised in New York, he was steeped in the same Swedish culture I was: life, for us, is all about the simple pleasures: spending time with family and friends, eating outdoors at picnics, being physically active. When we decided to partner in the Samuelsson group, bringing Andrew's West Village restaurant, August, into the fold and opening Red Rooster in the process, we were united in our goal to create hospitality that reflects the values that are important to us.

We looked everywhere in Harlem for the next two months. Over by the West Side Highway, I felt too out of the conversation. It was definitely more affordable if we went all the way east, but a restaurant like this, which I wanted to be the first of its kind in Harlem, couldn't be off the beaten path. For weeks, Andrew and I texted each other constantly, tearing pages out of magazines, creating with words and pictures a virtual canvas of the place that we wanted to create.

A month went by and we did a presentation for Billy Hunter, the landlord of a building we loved right off 125th Street. My friend Derek and I are friends with his daughter-in-law, Meghan. We started pushing her relentlessly to get him to sign and all she would say is, "Let me work on it, let me work on it." Finally, in mid-April, we signed the lease. The place was big, more than we anticipated: two floors, and more than 10,000 square feet.

We figured we needed to raise about a million dollars. By the time we were finished with construction, it would cost us about three times as much. As we built out the space, every day, people came by and asked when we would open. The old ladies thought we were stupid for building a restaurant on the block next to Sylvia's, and all the young businesspeople in the neighborhood kept telling us to make sure we had takeout. Nobody could imagine a restaurant where people would sit and linger in the middle of all the drama that is 125th Street.

We built the bar in front to reflect the construction of churches, and used copper to echo the regal nineteenth-century history of Harlem. If we were going to build something for downtowners and Harlemites, we thought, it should be something everyone can be proud of. The bar had to be a horseshoe shape that practically screamed, "Just come on in!" At one end of that bar, we built out a little corner in the style of a street stand as a shout-out to the African street vendors on 116th. From the beginning, we filled the space with our personal treasures. There are recipes on the wall from Andrew's aunt Ginny and my grandmother Helga. Behind the bar, there's a gigantic bookshelf filled with things that meant something to me. I always wanted a shelf to tell my story to Harlem—the books tell my journey from my old Swiss cookbooks to *Amharic for Beginners*.

We did a preview of the restaurant downtown: We called it "Red Rooster at Soho House." It was supposed to be for 85 people but 150 showed up. It was good that there was a buzz, but not so good in the sense that we were just trying out dishes—almost like a friends-and-family dinner. But I forced myself to relax, to go with the flow. This was a new audience for me: they were younger, most of them had never been to Aquavit, they had no reference point for my Swedish-Ethiopian-uptown style of cooking. But it was a good test group. Did I wish that they had put their BlackBerries away during dinner? Yes. But they also loved the flavors and that, more than anything else, was what I cared about. We served a smoked salmon with grain mustard yogurt and bagel chips. Those were gone in seconds. The shrimp and grits were also a big hit. I thought we could have added sausage and some greens to the grits, but overall, it was delicious. And while I'm always trying to create something new and inventive, the bottom line is that the food has to taste good. The main course was a roasted chicken with sweet potato gratin, a wholly new dish for me: I cured the chicken in lemon and served it with an Ethiopian sauce. That went well, but I knew we could do better. For dessert, we served a Harlem favorite: red velvet cake, which we paired with a root beer float. All in all, a good day.

The Soho House preview stood out as a high point because there had been so many low points leading up to it. Building a new restaurant space in Manhattan is no joke. We were all in over our heads. I had never been so tested. We almost ran out of money but we never cut corners. I wouldn't change a thing about the experience—the panic, the stress, the core beliefs—but I also don't know if I'd ever want to live through it again.

As always, starting a new venture made me think about the people who helped shape my journey and my story. In the restaurant business, when you can't get a construction permit or a liquor license, you have to hire a fixer. For thousands of dollars, these people will work through invisible channels to get the jobs done. In New Orleans, they don't talk about the dead as ghosts, they talk about them as *your people*. When people in New Orleans talk about *your people* this is what they mean: an invisible tribe of fixers, loved ones who are working to help you on the other side. I have come so far from so little I do not doubt that my people are working double shifts. I know who they are: my father, Lennart. My grandmother, Helga. My Swiss friend, Mannfred. And then there is my mother. While it could well be that she's busy cooking up blessings for me, I do not see her as part of that spiritual counsel. She did her saint's work in life, not in death. She saved me with little more than the strength of her will and the pure might of her love. She's the ultimate fixer. She fixed me.

FOOD MEMORIES GIVE PEOPLE something to talk about—our food, our culture, our journey. The North Star here is Harlem. The restaurant had to be a place that honored and mirrored the mystique of the renaissance but showed the new Harlem—inclusive of both old and new. The menu had to tell the story of *all* of Harlem's residents—Latin, Southern, Caribbean, Jewish, Italian. When I cook, I see faces: When I make meatballs, I see my grandmother and her smile. When I make my flan with condensed milk and whipped chocolate, I try to honor all the young Latinas from Spanish Harlem for whom this is a signature dish. My take on dirty rice—shrimp with curry rice—is a tribute to all of the many multiracial Jamaican families who are a mix of black, Indian, and Chinese. I want to do them all justice.

I wanted the menu at Red Rooster to reflect all that Harlem has to offer, which meant it was designed with our neighbors in mind: For example, we serve our Jamaican beef patties with a Mexican-inspired *salsa verde*. Corn bread had been a fascination since we served it at the White House at the state dinner—there's just something comforting about it, something that says, "Come on in. Make yourself at home. Stay for a while." The Rooster corn bread comes with homemade honey butter, a nod to classic soul food, and an African spiced tomato jam. Instead of plain old mac and cheese, we served mac and greens: Collards are a soul food staple, but we make it luxurious with a mix of Gouda, cheddar, and Comté cheeses. There are some things on the menu that you'll taste, but not see: like *sofrito*, which I learned to make from the Puerto Rican cooks at Aquavit. A mixture of olive oil, garlic cloves, shallots, jalapeños, coriander, lemon, and cilantro, *sofrito* is like a shortcut to flavor. You just add it to the pan with everything from steaks to sautéed vegetables and it gives everything more kick.

Imperfection is exactly what I was looking for in the Rooster menu. I wanted the food to be done right, but to be more like a Polaroid picture than a high-def image on a flat-screen TV. I imagined plates that have a worn-out feel but food that tastes farmers' market fresh. I wanted the waiters to wear stylish tunics and clean jeans, something they were comfortable in. I wanted the music to be B-sides, not the hits. So much of what makes a restaurant are the things you don't notice, but only feel.

I knew that fried chicken would be an essential component of the Rooster menu, but it was one of the toughest dishes for me (a) to master, and (b) to reinvent. It's so hard to truly own a dish when you didn't grow up eating it. Chefs are trained, but inevitably our strength as flavor builders goes back to our childhoods and the tastes and combinations we learned as a kid. It's why I'm so comfortable with gravlax and meatballs and why, even in Harlem, you'll see those dishes on the menu. The tang, texture, and savory nature of those dishes are imprinted in my bones. I loved roasting chicken with my grandma, Helga, and coming back the next day for chicken soup and dumplings. But American fried chicken was different, and because so many people have made versions of the dish that are so good, it was almost too daunting to take that dish on.

It was a good thing that Michael Garrett, my executive chef, had fried chicken in his bones. That surely helped in my tutorial. I began with Michael's recipe—it's an excellent recipe. It's "you got that aunt who can really cook / it's family reunion time / get your grub on / yummy." Then I started to play around with the formula. Here's where I landed after an entire summer of my own private fried chicken master class: I marinate it in coconut milk, cure it in lemon, then I steam it—bone in. I fry it in day-old oil, then I serve it with greens, sweet potato fries, buttermilk dressing, and hot sauce. And then just to add a touch of myself to it: pickled watermelon rind.

The watermelon rind was an important touch for me because one thing that I've steadily grown into over the years is the idea of using the extras in the kitchen that traditionally get thrown away and converting them into food that's fantastic. My grandmother used to serve us fish liver. Then in the late eighties, when I began working in kitchens, fish livers were thrown away. Now monkfish liver is back—and it's an expensive delicacy. So I play around with the leftovers in the dishes we're testing for the restaurant. Wouldn't our customers love Ethiopian coffee–crusted duck with pickled watermelon rind? How about citrus-glazed broccoli stems? That's all luxury, but it comes from a waste-nothing mentality. I can't tell you how many broccoli stems the average restaurant just throws away. I want Red Rooster to waste nothing.

I walked by the Rooster every day as construction continued. How far were we behind? Would we open on time? Would we have enough money? The clock was ticking, rent was being paid on an empty space, the press was watching. Andrew and I talked about it; it's good to have pressure—it keeps you focused. During my walks, I looked at how Harlem has changed, even in the six years since I moved here. People were walking with Target bags now. It made me smile.

In the weeks before the restaurant opened I wondered at times if people would come. Harlem is eighteen minutes in a cab from mid-town, and Soho is twenty-two minutes. But those eighteen minutes are a very different ride. For our potential clientele on the Upper West Side and Upper East Side, it's just ten minutes in a taxi. But people keep asking me, "Is it safe? Will I be able to get a taxi home?" We were in all new territory. I had this feeling that the downtown crowd who know my work would come at least once, to check us out. But would they keep coming? In order for this restaurant to be successful, I needed them to keep coming.

Before the opening, I went home to visit my mother and, as I always do, I went out for a long run. I ran by my father's former office building; it's now a furniture store. I hear his voice so much in my head that it's hard to believe it's been a decade since he passed away. I ran by Mosesson, my old cooking school, and I remembered how much I loved everything I learned, how my dreams were so simple when I was just a naive, hungry kid. I ran by the Italian restaurant where I learned to make pasta and by Belle Avenue, where I first encountered the world of fine dining. When I thought about how much time had passed since I worked at those restaurants, how far I had traveled, it was as if I'd laced up my sneakers when I was fifteen and hadn't stopped running for twenty-five years. When I came home from my run, my mother loved me, as she does best, with her worry: "Marcus, take a break. Marcus, how are you getting paid?" I hugged her. "Don't worry, Mom," I said. "Don't worry." I went in the kitchen and started prepping a dinner of fish tacos, which I made with one of my favorite *sous-chefs*, my nephew Petrus.

On December 17, we opened. Two days later, there was a snowstorm. I tried to put a good spin on things for Maya before I left for work that day. "It's OK that we'll be empty," I said. "It'll be good. The staff can cook for each other, train more. We need that." But the restaurant was packed; people didn't want to leave. It was one of those snowstorms where snow is slapping you in every direction, but inside the Rooster it was all warmth, all love. I didn't get home that night until two in the morning. But I walked home, in the thick of the snow, with a huge smile on my face.

I knew then and there that we were going to make it.

Not that I let up. Two weeks after we opened, I was still going to bed every night around 1:30 a.m. and getting up at five. I'd been *living* at the restaurant and I wanted to make sure that everyone on my team knew that if I was being a demanding bastard, it was nothing less than I expected of myself. In Sweden, we do a lot of cross-country skiing. And when you ski, just in the woods, not in a resort, the first skier has to plow. That's how I think of myself—with the restaurant, with the Harlem dining scene. I'm the guy who has to plow. Sweden is a famously neutral country, but I'm not neutral. I have been a witness to the poor quality of groceries available in Harlem, the lack of healthy food options, the whitewash of New York's fine-dining scene—in the kitchen, among the staff, and among the guests. I'm activating myself to lead.

IN 1901, A BIG-BONED, BIG-HEARTED woman nicknamed Pig Foot Mary came to Harlem from Mississippi with five dollars in savings. She bought a baby carriage and a large boiling pan for three dollars and then spent her remaining two dollars on pig feet. Dressed in a gingham dress, Pig Foot Mary sold pig feet from that baby carriage on the corner of 135th Street and Lenox Avenue, just ten blocks north from where the Rooster sits today. Mary's only goal, she later said, was to make enough money to rent a room in an "old folks' home for respectable colored people." But her pig feet were so delectable that, two weeks in, retirement was the farthest thing from Mary's mind. A month after arriving, Mary married a man named John Dean, who owned a newsstand on the same block. She soon purchased an apartment building for the princely sum of $44,000, then sold it six years later for $72,000. By the time Mary retired, she had a net worth of over $375,000—all from selling pig feet out of a baby carriage. Not bad for a woman who couldn't read or write.

During the years of Prohibition, rent parties were a popular entertainment and, again, soul food played a central role. Admission was fifteen cents, but it was always worth it: Big pots of chitterlings and pig feet provided sustenance to those who had come to dance the night away. Corn liquor was made by the jug and sold in half-pint glasses called "shorties." And at the piano, boogie-woogie played until dawn. Rent parties were attended by anyone who wanted not to be alone on a Saturday night: domestics, Pullman porters, truck drivers, downtown white folks, and out-of-town black folks. As a typical rent party invitation read:

> There'll be brown-skinned Mamas. High-yellas too.
> And if you ain't got nothing to do.
> Come on up to Mary Lou's.
> There'll be plenty of pig feet and lots of gin.
> Just ring the bell and come on in.

Although the Cotton Club was the hottest club in Harlem, blacks weren't allowed in. Strivers Row resident W. C. Handy was famously barred from entering the club on an evening when his songs were the featured compositions. In an attempt to make nice, the Cotton Club owners distributed Christmas baskets to the community, but they were never able to shake the bad mojo of their segregationist policies. While today no restaurant in New York has the audacity to bar blacks, you only have to spend one evening barhopping at the finest dining establishments in the city to know that many of our best restaurants *feel* like they are whites-only. I was lucky that at Aquavit my presence attracted a naturally more diverse group of diners, but even still, my core audience there was moneyed and white. I wanted that tribe of Aquavit fans to follow me uptown, but I didn't want to create a twenty-first-century Cotton Club.

When I first sat down with the team, I knew that in some ways, we were doing more than creating a restaurant, we were creating a salon. We wanted and needed three types of diner to give the Rooster the flavor that we considered the yummiest: Harlemites, the men and women (regardless of color) who are our neighbors, whose very existence provides the culture and color that is Harlem; downtown diners who love restaurants and great food; and out-of-towners who have traveled from as far away as San Francisco, Sweden, and South Africa. It's easy to underestimate the out-of-towner because the chance of repeat business is so low. But the out-of-towner has gone through extraordinary measures to come to your restaurant and the experience they take back home with them is as precious as any souvenir. The out-of-towner will tell stories about your restaurant again and again, the way travelers used to show slide shows of their vacation. If they have a great time they will be your ambassador, telling anyone and everyone about your food wherever they go.

We are already making plans to expand. We have six hundred guests a day and two thousand requests a night. That means we're in the "polite no" business. We have to turn a lot of people down every day, but we want to encourage them to come back. So far, we're delivering. If we, as New Yorkers, stay collectively open-minded and eat in places and parts of the city we never thought about, then we expand what's possible. Maybe the next three-star restaurant will be in the Bronx.

When I close my eyes at night, I'm confident we are doing something larger than ourselves, that we can change the city in a positive way. I always felt that the Rooster had the potential to bring out the best in people, people from all cultures and ages, meeting one another and speaking to one another. There aren't many places in this city where there's a true intermingling of different perspectives and walks of life. What I love about my dining room is when I see a famous actor or musician seated next to the old-school Harlemites: church ladies in their pastel-colored suits and matching hats, senior citizen brothers in their Kangols and Panamas.

Whenever I felt unsure about what to do next at the restaurant, I thought about the original Rooster, a place that thrived when there were so many other places to go in Harlem. You stopped in for a drink at the Rooster, you went over to Jacques for dinner, and then on to the casinos for gambling and dancing. The politicians did business there. The laymen could come in and converse. People came dressed—to see and be seen. Now at the Rooster, we host special nights so people in the neighborhood will always feel like there's a place for them to hang their hat: Tuesdays are Latin nights and we have a salsa DJ and lots of dancing; Fridays are classic soul, Saturdays are rare grooves, and Sundays are gospel brunch with live jazz on Sunday nights. The Rooster is far from perfect, but we are lucky enough to be a part of creating a Harlem that's not some place in the wilderness beyond Central Park but just any other neighborhood to hang out in. It took a long time and a lot of money, but we did what we came to do—which was to start a new food conversation.

This week alone at the Rooster, we served Bono, Martha Stewart, President Clinton, Chris Rock, the Swedish prime minister, and Terry McMillan. The bold-faced names that came through the door were patrons that added to the high-low mix we aspire to create every night. I really struggled with the notion of how to provide five-star service with a front-of-the-room staff that wasn't experienced in fine dining. From the beginning, Andrew and I wanted to integrate not only the diners but the waitstaff, too. If you go to almost any high-end restaurant in Manhattan, you'll see very few black waiters. With tips as high as 20 percent and flexible schedules, waiting tables in New York is a legitimate way to make a very good living. I've met dozens of career waiters who serve at restaurants, pursue their art on the side, and make enough loot from waiting tables to be able to buy a weekend home in the country. Andrew and I wanted to create the same kind of opportunities for the people who lived in Harlem, the young black men and women who might not get a shot at a midtown or Soho restaurant. We wanted to be able to invest in our staff's success and see people in our organization and in our community succeed.

But that was easier said than done—especially for some of the black men. The women of color and the gay men of color really thrived in the early days of the Rooster. The straight black men came in with a chip on their shoulders the size of Lil Wayne's gold teeth and they stepped to me with all the impatience and fury of men who did not know how to deal with authority figures. One guy, Dwayne, was twenty-one, and he seemed to have so much potential. But he could never tie all the pieces together. I gave him warnings for not coming in with a pressed shirt, for being late, for wearing sneakers instead of shoes. Then finally I put him on probation. When it was clear that I was going to have to fire him, I tried one more time: "What's up, Dwayne? What do you need to make this job work for you?" Dwayne shrugged, saying, "It's too much. You can ask me to be on time *or* you can ask me to shave every day *or* you can ask me to iron my shirt *or* you can ask me not to wear sneakers. But you can't ask me for all of those things every damn day." The day that I fired Dwayne was like one of those old Bill Cosby comedy routines when the father is about to spank a kid and he says, "This is going to hurt me a lot more than it's going to hurt you."

"Each one, teach one" sounds so good. But what do you do when the one you're trying to teach doesn't want to learn? Before he cleared out for the day, Dwayne said to me, "You should've met me when I was fourteen. You met me now and it's too late." It's not just Dwayne; making both sides of the house reflect Harlem comes with challenges they rarely deal with downtown: Lopez, a young gay busboy, got jumped on the train—couldn't make it to work because of a homophobic beat-down. John, one of our busboys, had been out for a few days. He came by the restaurant on crutches with his head and spirits down. He wanted to ask for an extended leave of absence.

He said, "I got jumped. Six guys I went to school with waited until I cashed my check and they jumped me. They do it to all the guys who work."

I asked him if he went to the police.

He rolled his eyes. "The police don't come to the projects for stuff like that. What you going to do? I'm just trying to keep my head up."

I promised him that I'd hold his job, while I wondered if chefs like Daniel Boulud or Alice Waters ever had to deal with stuff like this.

They've cancelled the last of the television soap operas, but every day at work when the shift starts, it's like an episode of *All My Children*. Tammy, my lead runner, walked out. She said, "I feel like I'm being disrespected by some of my male coworkers." And I couldn't argue with her, she *was* being disrespected, I just wished she had stayed and helped me fight it out. The Muslim brother, Salaam, didn't want to take orders from a woman and he threw a racial slur at our white general manager, so he's out. We couldn't educate him so we had to fire him. We're packed every night, and to the outside world, Andrew and I are doing what we dreamed of doing. But sometimes, when I'm dealing with all the little things that go into making a restaurant work, it feels like Harlem is burning.

A GREAT RESTAURANT is more than a series of services. It is a collection of meals and memories. I met a man in the Rooster one Saturday afternoon who had worked as a personal bodyguard for Martin Luther King Jr. when he was on the historic Selma to Montgomery march. The man, now in his eighties, had never worked in security. He was a train porter who was simply big and fearless. He said that when he arrived in Montgomery safely, he took the soles off of his shoes. He owned only two pairs of shoes, but he never wanted to wear those shoes again. This man had dined at the original Red Rooster and wanted to come in and see what we had done with the place. He came for lunch with his wife. He also brought in the soles of his shoes and his address book from 1965 with Martin Luther King's phone number in it.

"Call Coretta," King had scribbled. "She'll invite you over for dinner."

The senior citizens are my favorite Rooster customers, mostly because so many of them remember the original restaurant. It's hardly a fair exchange: I give them a meal, they tell me stories that are priceless. They make me feel like a part of something.

We cannot honor them all by name, but I hope the old people can feel it and taste it: the love, the respect, the history, and the homage.

And once they've gotten a hit of it—our culinary laying on of the hands—I hope they loosen their ties, take off their church lady gloves, and settle in for a spell. For so long, these old black people have served. When they come to the Rooster, I hope they can enjoy being tended to. I hope they can give up on the giving for just one night and simply sit back, relax, and dine.

THERE'S A FARMERS' MARKET now in Harlem. It's in Mount Morris Park on 124th and Fifth Avenue. It's nothing like the one in Union Square. This market is tiny, just nine passionate stalls selling the freshest food this neighborhood has seen in decades—and even more revolutionarily, the vendors accept food stamps. Food is such a direct indicator of our luxuries or our poverty. I have a brother in Ethiopia who is a farmer and he plows the land with one skinny ox. The type of farming he does would be called "organic" here, but that is only because in Africa, organic is all they can afford. My brother has no cell phone, no electricity, but he sets his own schedule and his family eats, literally, farm to table. I'd like to connect the dots for people: If you put the meals that African farmers like my brother eat up against what most black people in urban areas eat today, you'll see pretty quickly that my brother is not the poorer one.

I've become friends with the peach man at Mount Morris Park. He gets up at two in the morning on Saturdays, fills his car, and drives all the way to Harlem. He's not black, but he understands the significance of the journey. He also sells the best peaches in town. As I walk home, eating one for breakfast, I feel lucky that I have the Rooster as a platform to share the delicious things that I find: Peach cobbler's going on the menu tonight. The Harlem farmers' market is open only one day a week from July to Thanksgiving. The Union Square market is year-round, three days a week, with dozens of stalls and fifty thousand visitors a day. We'll get there. It's my hope that the Rooster can eventually source most of our produce from the Harlem farmers' market. It's like Leah Chase said—the hood needs good, too.

When I think about my purpose as a black chef, the mission seems clear: to document, to preserve, to present, to capture, to inspire, and to aspire. I'm documenting Harlem's history at the Rooster, preserving the fine history of African American cuisine while presenting it through my own unique Swedish-Ethiopian lens. I want to capture the imagination of New York's dining communities, inspire a new generation of chefs and I aspire, always, to make food that makes a difference. When I look at Harlem institutions such as the Apollo and the Studio Museum and the Schomburg Center for Research in Black Culture, they have all done a great job of preserving and presenting black voices in music, art, and literature. In food, there are no equivalents. There are very few places where we can go and learn about the history of black food in America, and yet so much of what people think of as American food is inextricably linked to the African American experience: BBQ, Creole, Southern food, and Cajun. I learn how to be a keeper of culture from people like Jonelle Procope, Thelma Golden, Leah Chase, Jessica Harris, Marvin Woods, Brian Duncan, Garrett Oliver, and Edna Patrick.

Community is more than a buzzword in Harlem. This place and these people wouldn't have survived without the people who believed that building community was possible, necessary, vital—even during Harlem's darkest days. I don't know all of their names: the men and women who kept libraries open and instituted free breakfasts in the school; the professionals and paraprofessionals who refused to turn Harlem over to the drug dealers and the criminals; the people in church basements who gave food to the hungry. But I see them when I walk the neighborhood—the gray and the proud, the ones who never stopped wearing Afros and dashikis, the impeccably dressed older women who all look like they could be cousins or sisters of Lena Horne. There's a tribe of dapper, senior citizen Harlem men who look like they all have access to a secret stash of jazz musician threads: some are more Duke, some are more Davis; they all look extraordinary. I want to do my part to be part of the community, too.

But just because Harlem's got its own special community, that doesn't mean everyone agrees on everything. One day I was walking to work and a guy my age stopped me. He was walking his daughter to school; she couldn't have been much more than six years old. Her hair was combed into two giant Afro-puffs—and I thought, immediately, of Zoe and what I would give to be able to go back, know her at that age, and do something as simple as walk her to school.

"Are you that chef?" the guy asked.

I nodded.

He looked at me with narrowed eyes. "You're the reason my rent went up," he said. "White people are loving Harlem and now my rent is going up." Then he said something I would never forget: "You know what James Baldwin used to say? Urban renewal equals Negro removal."

And yet, later that same day, a young cook named Richard stopped me when I was on my way to buy some flowers for my wife. He said, "I've lived on 118th Street all my life. I never imagined there'd be a restaurant like the Rooster up here. Look out for me, chef. I'm coming in to apply for a job." Just like in the days of Langston Hughes, Harlem is a dizzying mixture of joy and pain: the weary blues, swing, and boogie all rolled into one. We are creating jobs, but I can't be blind to the fact that we are part of a changing landscape in Harlem.

Not too long ago, President Obama had his first Democratic Party fund-raising dinner in Harlem. It was an intimate dinner for fifty, with seats going at $30K a pop. I knew that part of the reason his team chose the Rooster is because of the multiracial crowds we've been attracting. It was exciting: The first time I cooked for him and Mrs. Obama was at the White House. Now they were coming to *my* house. I kept thinking about what I wanted to tell him. "I know it's been a tough year," I wanted to say. "Keep pushing." I wanted to let him know that I stood by him.

When it came time for me to greet him, we hugged—the way my black friends and I say hi on the street. We small-talked, but we small-talked fast. I knew how busy he was and didn't want to put the slightest crimp in his schedule. I said, "Say hi to the First Lady, the kids, and my friend Sam Kass." Then we cooked and served. We had exactly two hours: one hour for hors d'oeuvres and conversation, one hour for dinner. Nothing could go wrong. It was spring, so we started with a tomato melon gazpacho. Then we served our corn bread with the honey butter, followed by a lobster salad with asparagus, peas, and a hot biscuit. For the main course, there was a choice of smoked salmon, seared duck, or braised short ribs. Dessert was peach pudding, with the stone fruit we bought from the peach man, and a buttermilk sorbet. We also served chocolate cake and sweet potato doughnuts. After the meal, I thought about Helga. "This is cooking for fine folk," my grandmother would have said.

In 1939, when Harlem was still very much in vogue, Billy Strayhorn wrote the song that would become the signature tune of the Duke Ellington orchestra. Ellington had just hired the young composer and had written down directions on how to get to his Harlem home. The first line of directions read "Take the A train." Strayhorn composed a simple but elegant tune and the rest is history:

> *You must take the A Train*
> *To go to Sugar Hill way up in Harlem*
> *If you miss the A Train*
> *You'll find you've missed the quickest way to Harlem*
> *Hurry, get on, now, it's coming*
> *Listen to those rails a-thrumming (All Aboard!)*
> *Get on the A Train*
> *Soon you will be on Sugar Hill in Harlem*

I represent so many things to so many different people. In Ethiopia, I am *ferengi* or "white" because I am an American of means. In Sweden, I represent "new Sweden," which to them means an integrated Sweden. In America, I'm black or African American or an immigrant; it depends. For me, the labels aren't as important as the journey. I took the train from Göteborg to Switzerland, from Switzerland to Austria, and back home again. Along the way, I became a chef, a father, a husband, a mentor, and a friend. You can't take the A train to Addis Ababa but you can take it to Red Rooster, where I'll happily make you a plate of *doro wat* and serve you the finest selection of Ethiopian coffees and teas.

I don't live on Sugar Hill in Harlem, that legendary row of mansions that once belonged to Harlem's elite, men like Adam Clayton Powell Jr., W.E.B. DuBois, and of course Ellington himself. But I walk through Sugar Hill every day on my way to work and it is as sweet a commute as I've ever had. It may not be Martin Luther King's mountaintop yet, but it is as close to it as I have ever seen.

I spent so much of my life on the outside that I began to doubt that I would ever truly be in with any one people, any one place, any one tribe. But Harlem is big enough, diverse enough, scrappy enough, old enough, and new enough to encompass all that I am and all that I hope to be. After all that traveling, I am, at last, home.

ACKNOWLEDGMENTS

The real work of writing this book began when my friend Veronica Chambers agreed to help me tell my story. I first fell in love with her writing years ago, when I read her award-winning memoir, *Mama's Girl*. We have a lot in common, including the fact that we both have fractured and found families, and are both new Americans with a passion for black culture and Harlem history and good food. Now we also share the journey of making this book. It was my deep friendship with Veronica, as well as her incredible gift for storytelling, that helped me revisit and return to people and places and feelings that were sometimes difficult, and sometimes painful, to remember. Over and over again, Veronica made me realize that writing a memoir with omissions devalues my life experiences. It was necessary to explore everything. This is my story, but the fine touch on the words is all hers.

I have so much more to be thankful for, especially:

My two mothers, Ahnu, who sacrificed, and Anne Marie, who always supported my food journeys.

My father, Lennart, who made me the man that I am.

My wife, Maya: Thank you for listening and being there and making this journey loving, whole, and beautiful.

My Ethiopian family: Father, Ashou, Tiggi, Salam, Danny, Zebeney. *Mulugete worko. Ayailou.*

For Helga J. and Edwin J., who fed me a steady diet of love, tradition, and roast chicken.

For the leading ladies of my life: Anna, Vanessa, and Linda.

To RC and Andrew Chapman for believing in me and in Harlem. I love the guidance and support.

I want to thank my Rooster team:

Eden Fesehaye is as gracious as she is capable. Thank you, Eden—you are the glue and the glow.

Tracey, you are a fighter and I believe in you.

I could not do what I do without Erica, Nils, and Mike. Thank you to Andrea Bergquist: Your culinary gifts made this journey all the more delicious. To Jeremie and Akashia, the entire Rooster squad. Harlem is in the house!

My literary team:

Kim Witherspoon, I couldn't ask for a better champion for my books. Thank you for your vision and guidance.

Susan Kamil, this book is all about home. Thank you for making such a wonderful home for my life story. Andy Ward pushed me (and pushed me) and went over every page with the kind of attention and care that is rare in editors these days. Kaela Myers on his team provided invaluable, 24/7 support—thank you.

There's more:

Food Republic, we are on our way.

Thank you, Philip, Sarah, and Lucinda.

I am the product of all the cooks I learned and worked with.

Gburg—yes, we did.

To the good people of Harlem: Thanks for the love and support. The Renaissance is not complete; we've still got more to do.

I tip my hat to the Aquavit cooks 1995 to 2009. You know who you are.

Jimmy Lappalainen & Norda in the house.

My friends never "yes, chef" me and I love them for that: Mes, Mats, Teddy, Jonas, Andrew, Sven, William, Brian, and the Blatte Crew.

Big blessings and big thanks for those who paved the way:

Maya Angelou. Harry Belafonte. Leah Chase. David Dinkins. I am because you all walked before.

Thelma Golden is both my dear friend and a never-ending source of passion, creativity, and intelligence. You are the architect of the new Harlem Renaissance and I'm so glad to be uptown with you.

And, finally, my deepest appreciation to Michelle and Barack Obama. Thanks for the inspiration, and the opportunity to serve.

—Marcus Samuelsson, December 2011

ABOUT THE AUTHOR

A James Beard Award–winning chef and the author of several cookbooks, Marcus Samuelsson is the owner and executive chef at Red Rooster Harlem in New York City. In 1995, he became the youngest chef ever to receive a three-star rating from *The New York Times* for his work at Aquavit. In 2003, the James Beard Foundation named him Best Chef: New York City. In 2009, he was chosen to be a guest chef at the White House under the Obama administration, where he planned and executed the administration's first state dinner for the first family, Prime Minister Manmohan Singh of India, and four hundred guests. He was also the winner of Bravo's *Top Chef Masters* in 2010.

Marcus currently lives in Harlem with his wife, Maya. For more information, visit his website at MarcusSamuelsson .com.